I AM SPOCK

I AM SPOCK

by

Leonard Nimoy

BOOKS

NEW YORK   BOSTON

To Stoots,

For the love
and laughter.

Photo on page ii © 1995 Paramount Pictures.
Photo on page iii © Jeffery Newbury
Photos from *Never Forget* provided by Turner Pictures Worldwide
and Turner Network Television.
Photos from *Three Men and a Baby* and *The Good Mother*
courtesy of Touchstone Pictures.
The letters of Isaac Asimov courtesy of the Isaac Asimov estate.

Hachette Books
Hachette Book Group
1290 Avenue of the Americas
New York, NY 10104
www.HachetteBookGroup.com

Printed in the United States of America

RRD-C

Originally published in hardcover by Hyperion
First Hachette Books trade edition: May 2015

10 9 8 7 6

Hachette Books is a division of Hachette Book Group, Inc.
The Hachette Books name and logo are trademarks of Hachette Book Group, Inc.

The publisher is not responsible for websites (or their content)
that are not owned by the publisher.

Nimoy, Leonard,
   I am Spock / by Leonard Nimoy. — 1st ed.
      p. cm.
   ISBN 0-7868-6182-7
      1. Nimoy, Leonard. 2. Actors—United States—Biography. 3. Star Trek
(Television program) 4. Star Trek Films. I. Title.
PN2287.N55A3   1995
791.45"028"092—dc20
   [B]   95-24504
                                                                          CIP

ISBN 978-0-316-38837-5 (pbk.)

DESIGN BY ROBERT BULL DESIGN

ACKNOWLEDGMENTS

Thanks to Jason Sloane, Russell Galen, and Brian DeFiore for opening the door;

To Larry McCallister and Harry Lang, for providing images;

To Cyndi Mladinov, for managing my schedule, reading my writing, and controlling the madness;

And to Jeanne (J.M.) Dillard, for her extraordinary talent, tact, and taste.

CONTENTS

NUMBER ONE SURAK PLAZA, SHIKAHR, VULCAN 43 ERIDANI STARSYSTEM

11 Tasmeen 156,093 V.O.D.*
Stardate 496123.3

Mr. Leonard Nimoy
$^c/_o$ Hyperion Publishers
New York NY 10011
Earth
Sol Starsystem

Dear Mr. Nimoy:

I write this note in response to yours, which asks: "Would you consider writing a foreword to my new book?"

This book, you inform me, contains the saga of your experiences in your various capacities as actor, writer, director, and producer of *Star Trek* stories. It is to be called *I Am Spock.*

I must admit to some degree of confusion. By all accounts, I am in full possession of my memory—and I distinctly recall the title of your previous book on the above subject. It was, in fact, entitled *I Am* Not *Spock,* which seemed both logical and accurate—since, indeed, you are *not* Spock, and I have always believed and shall continue to believe that *I* am. To indulge in a human colloquialism: Have you lost your small glass gaming spheres?

I herewith take the liberty of reminding you of a dialog between us in the aforementioned publication:

NIMOY: Spock . . . this competition between us is silly.
SPOCK: I am not aware that one exists.
NIMOY: Well, it does. And it's silly. Don't forget that I'm real, and you're
    only a fictitious character.
SPOCK: Are you sure?

—*I Am Not Spock*

Yours for literary accuracy,
Spock

galaxynet: hyperspock@vsa.edu

*Vulcan Old Date

I AM SPOCK

ONE

HUMAN
VERSUS
VULCAN

or

Of Luck

and

Probability

LET'S OPEN THIS BOOK with a couple of shattering confessions right up front:
1. *I talk to myself; and*
2. *I hear voices in my head.*

Or rather, I sometimes talk to an *aspect* of myself, and I often hear one *specific* voice replying in my head—a very calm, very rational voice, one I suspect many of you are familiar with. And if you were to listen in on the silent conversation taking place in my head at this very moment, you might hear the following exchange:

NIMOY: Spock, do you have any idea how lucky we are to have each other?

SPOCK: *I do not believe in "luck." I believe every event is statistically predictable.*

NIMOY: Really? So—at the moment I was born, what were the chances that I would grow up, go to Hollywood, meet Gene Roddenberry, and become famous as a green-blooded, pointy-eared alien from outer space?

SPOCK: *At the moment of your birth? Approximately 789,324,476.76 to 1.*

NIMOY: Aha! You see? It was luck, after all! The odds were against it!

SPOCK: *Hardly. Because with each passing moment of your life, one event precipitated another, which made each subsequent occurrence more probable. For example, by moving from Boston to Los Angeles and working hard to perfect your craft, you increased your chances of a successful acting career by a substantial margin, from*

> *1,726,534.2 to 1, to 351,233.82 to 1—just as, by attending Starfleet Academy, I increased my chances of serving aboard the Enterprise. As your own Miguel de Cervantes said, "Diligence is the mother of good fortune."*

NIMOY: Yes, but even once I got to Hollywood, what were the chances I'd play a space alien—from the planet Vulcan?

SPOCK: *(small sigh) Approximately 3,400,679,929.936 to 1 . . .*

NIMOY: I rest my case!

As I write these words about fortune and statistics, I'm sitting on a plane bound for Florida, with pen in hand and yellow legal pad balanced on one knee. And I can't help thinking that I'm one lucky guy. You see, I'm on my way to speak at a *Star Trek* convention, where I will be greeted with an incredible outpouring of affection and warmth.

And earlier this morning at the airport when I stepped from the car, the sidewalk baggage handler recognized me at once and gave me a broad smile. "Good morning, Mr. Nimoy. Have a good trip."

I shook his outreached hand and thanked him, then found my way to the shuttle, which would take me to my gate. Once again, I was welcomed cordially. "I'm afraid I can't beam you up," the driver said with a grin, "but I'm happy to drive you."

When at last we arrived at the gate, the smiling attendant greeted me with, "The flight crew's been coming out to ask me whether you've checked in yet."

And here I sit in my seat, comfortable and well taken care of, knowing that more pleasant receptions await me in Florida.

Why all the good will and warm feelings from total strangers?

Well, a great deal of it comes because of my relationship with a certain extraterrestrial—a supposedly *unfeeling* character who claims he can't return the enormous groundswell of public love directed at him. Even those few hardy souls who have never seen a single *Star Trek* episode somehow know all about that guy with the pointed ears.

Should I be jealous of him?

•

5

I joked about that, in a book I wrote in the mid-seventies called *I Am Not Spock*. I described my conversation with a group of actors, and how, as I was leaving, one of the actresses said, "Leonard, we love you." I was very warmed and thanked her, but at the time, wanted to add: "I'll tell him when I see him." As I said in the book:

. . . standing silently behind my shoulder is a very jealous, ever-present Vulcan!!

SPOCK: *Tell her I accept her compliment, emotional though it may be.*

NIMOY: What compliment?

SPOCK: *She said they love me.*

NIMOY: That is not what she said. She specifically said, "Leonard, we love you." And I know there's nothing wrong with your hearing!

SPOCK: *If you're so certain of her intent, why are you becoming agitated?*

NIMOY: That's ridiculous. Every time I'm paid a compliment, you grab it away. You grab it up for yourself!

SPOCK: *Would she have paid you that compliment if not for me?*

NIMOY: No . . .

SPOCK: *Then how can you claim it for your own?*

I enjoyed writing the book and creating the dialogs between myself and Spock. I wanted to answer a lot of often-asked questions and also explore the relationship between an actor and the character he breathed life into—especially since that character seemed to take on an existence of his own.

But I made an enormous mistake in choosing the title for the book. I've made a lot of mistakes in my lifetime, but this one was a biggie and right out there in public. Perhaps it wasn't quite as bad as Roseanne Arnold singing the "Star-Spangled Banner" off-key, grabbing her crotch, and spitting in a stadium full of baseball fans, but mine did start a firestorm that lasted several years and caused a lot of hard feelings. In fact, it almost prevented me from having a directing career—but I'll deal with that later.

When I wrote that book and handed it in to the publisher, we discussed the title, and agreed that Spock should be mentioned. We tossed around ideas like "Spock and I" and "My Life with Spock," but they seemed insipid. I wanted a title with some bite.

So I recalled an incident mentioned in the book, when a woman pointed me out to her young son and said, "That's Mr. Spock." The little boy had stared at me blankly, without recognition because I wasn't in costume as the Vulcan. I had used that event—and the fact that I was often asked to sign autographs as "Spock" rather than myself—as cornerstones for a chapter entitled "I Am Not Spock," where I had fun with a philosophical discussion about whether or not an actor "was" the character he played. It began:

> I am not Spock.
> Then why does my head turn in response to a stranger on the street who calls out that name? Why do I feel a twinge when someone says, "What happened to your ears?" I am not Spock.
> Then why do I feel a wonderful warmth when I hear or read a compliment aimed at the Vulcan?
> *Spock for President* reads the bumper sticker on the car in front of me. I'm filled with pride and I smile. I'm not Spock.
> But if I'm not, who is? And if I'm not Spock, then who am I?

Now, in discussing title possibilities with the publisher, I thought *I Am Not Spock* might work. Certainly, it would attract the attention of potential readers and arouse their curiosity. But the publisher was worried and explained, "It's a negative title, and negative titles don't sell well."

Clever guy that I am, I shot back with, "What about *Gone With the Wind?*"

I won that argument. And I'm sorry now that I did, because I was completely wrong.

I Am Not Spock was published in 1975, at a time when the *Star Trek* phenomenon had just taken hold. Having had only marginal success on NBC, where we limped along for three years, the show took on new life in syndication. Local stations were able to schedule it at times that made it more accessible to their viewers and gradually the show and its audience found each other. By the mid-seventies, it was becoming a media event. Colleges avoided scheduling classes during *Star Trek* hours to avoid predictable absenteeism! Some professors took to using episodes in teaching their classes, and even today, entire courses on aspects of the *Star Trek* phenomenon are taught at many universities. Some television stations ran *Star Trek* marathons on the weekends, and in many cities the show was "stripped"—airing every evening at 6 or 7 P.M. Mothers jokingly complained that we were destroying the family dinner hour, since no one would eat when *Trek* was on!

Thousands and thousands of new devotees sat in front of their TV sets, memorizing each episode's dialog word-for-word. Soon, throughout the land came a heartfelt cry:

"Give us more *Star Trek!*"

And in the midst of this desperate demand, I won my little disagreement with the publisher and sent my book, my child, into the streets. And this child spoke with a naive, gentle voice, and said: "I am not Spock."

Clever, all right. My timing and choice of title couldn't have been worse. What came back was a deep, sad moan of public frustration followed by outbursts of anger, even hatred. I got some vicious mail, most of which said, "We made you and we can break you!" Unfortunately, press articles followed which served to fuel that anger. After all, it made good copy: "Actor rejects character who threatens to consume him."

For some years afterwards, the public assumption was that more *Star Trek* was not forthcoming because I had vowed never to play the Vulcan again because I hated Spock.

One of the reasons I'm writing this book is so I can forever put those ugly and unfounded rumors to rest. Here it is in print: I don't hate the Vulcan. In fact, I've always been downright fond of him, and as I mentioned in *I Am Not Spock*, if someone came up to me and said, "You can't be Leonard Nimoy anymore. But you can be anyone else you want," I wouldn't hesitate a beat with my answer. I'd want to be Spock. I like and respect and admire him.

And as for *Star Trek*, I'm enormously proud and pleased to have played a role (literally) in a television series that has become a cultural event. I talked earlier about feeling a surge of pride when I saw a SPOCK FOR PRESIDENT bumper sticker; this morning, I felt the same emotion (sorry, Spock!) when I casually leafed through the *Los Angeles Times*. The front-page photo of the American astronaut

Norman Thagard and his cosmonaut buddies aboard the space station Mir was captioned: "The Next Generation." And flipping back to the Life & Style section, I found a review of a new Chrysler vehicle: "Boldly Going Where No Minivan Has Gone Before." *Star Trek*, it seems, has permeated our culture and is moving right along with us into the future. Log on to any major computer network, and you'll find the *Star Trek* section is one of the busiest, with messages from fans discussing all of the myriad forms of *Trek*, from the original series to the movies to the three spin-off shows. Some time ago, I saw a taped interview with the co-founder of Apple Computers, Steve Wozniak. As he sat talking in his office, I couldn't help noticing the large poster on his wall, of that green-blooded patron saint of computer scientists, Spock.

I'm thrilled to have played a part in such a phenomenon.

But yes, if you want to get technical, I am *not* Spock. I'm an actor named Leonard Nimoy who plays that character.

At the same time, a perfectly good argument could be made that I *am* Spock. After all, as an actor, I've used my own emotional (or *un*emotional) resources to help create the character. I brought parts of myself to the role; and frankly, over the years, a lot of the Vulcan's mannerisms and philosophy have rubbed off on *me*.

Is Spock simply a "mask" I wear, like the ancient Greeks wore in their amphitheater presentations—or is there more to it than that? Present-day performers no longer sport the large, stylized masks; modern acting demands realism. Does this mean we're looking directly into the heart and soul of the actor during the performance, or is there an invisible facade, a "mask," in place?

Perhaps the answer is both. I'm reminded of a scene in *Star Trek VI*, which Bill Shatner and I played in Spock's quarters. In a moment of self-examination, Spock asked Kirk, "Is it possible that we two, you and I, have grown so old and inflexible that we have outlived our usefulness?"

As the camera rolled, I suddenly felt all sense of "mask" slip away—as though it were Leonard Nimoy asking the question of Bill Shatner. (That, indeed, was the subtext. Spock's question had to do with our usefulness to the Federation; but as Nimoy to Shatner, the question dealt with our usefulness to *Star Trek*.)

In that moment, I felt a complete merger take place; the separation between myself and Spock disappeared. Not only did Spock speak to Kirk, but with one and the same voice, Nimoy spoke to Shatner. Spock and I had become one.

Now here's an interesting twist on an old story. Remember the story from *I Am Not Spock* about the mother with the little boy who didn't recognize me? A few days ago, I stepped into an elevator and there was a woman with her young son. (No, not the same pair from twenty years ago!) This little boy was around the same age as the first had been, though—around six or seven years old.

The woman's eyes widened almost immediately, and she gave her son a gentle nudge. I smiled, waiting patiently until she got his attention and pointed at me.

Well, he took a good hard look, but displayed not the faintest sign of recognition. I was sure I was destined for a replay of the event that created the title for the last book.

His mother finally gave up, smiled shyly at me, and asked, "Could I have your autograph for my husband, Mike? He's a big fan of yours."

I took the pen and paper she offered, signed my name (wondering all the while if I shouldn't just sign "Spock"), then winked at the little boy, who was still frowning, perplexed.

When the elevator reached my floor, I stepped off. And as the door was closing behind me, I heard the mother say, "That's Leonard Nimoy!"

I was pleasantly surprised, but at the same time, taken aback; I had honestly expected her to say, "That's Mr. Spock!"

And this time, I would have been completely comfortable with it. In fact, I almost wished she *had* called me Spock, because that might have made it easier for the boy.

And if, after the mother had identified me as Leonard Nimoy, the boy had asked me: "Are you Spock?" I would happily have responded:

"Yes, I am."

* * *

A LOT HAS HAPPENED TO ME—and Spock—since the publication of *I Am Not Spock* in 1975; that's another reason I wanted to share this book with you. Looking back on the past thirty years, I'm incredibly grateful for my involvement with the Vulcan. Because of him, I've had a number of wonderful opportunities. And I'd like to think that, just as his Vulcan logic has had a tempering effect on me, my emotional human personality has rubbed off on him a bit. I know we've both matured and mellowed a great deal over these three decades.

And if I could rewrite the quote from *I Am Not Spock* that began this chapter, I would say to him:

NIMOY: Spock, I hope you realize that I don't harbor any feelings of jealousy or competition toward you. After all, I *am* you. And you're me.

SPOCK: *I beg your pardon?*

NIMOY: You sprang from who I am. From parts of my own personality.

SPOCK: *(stiffly) I fail to see any obvious connection. You, after all, are an emotional human. And I —*

NIMOY: Yes, yes, I know. You're a Vulcan. *Half* Vulcan. But part of you is human. Let me put it another way. If I didn't exist, would you?

SPOCK: *(pause) Perhaps.*

NIMOY: If another actor had brought you to life. But then you wouldn't be exactly the same Vulcan you are today, would you?

SPOCK: *(reluctantly yielding) No. I suppose I would not.*

NIMOY: We're both very lucky, Spock. Lucky to have lived the lives we have, and lucky to have had each other. (bracing for the anticipated lecture on luck versus statistics)

SPOCK: *(softly) Yes, I suppose we are . . .*

T W O

CONCEPTION AND GESTATION

SPOCK: *As my parents were of different species, my conception occurred only because of the intervention of Vulcan scientists. Much of my gestation was spent outside my mother's womb, in a heated, specially designed environment.*

NIMOY: The environment was heated, all right—by the camera lights on *The Lucy Show* set.

SPOCK: *I beg your pardon?*

ALMOST THIRTY YEARS AGO, a group of visitors came to the *Star Trek* set while we were shooting the series. It was a common event, something we actors were used to. But that day, something uncommon happened. One of the guests, a dreamy-eyed young woman, came up to me during a break from filming and introduced herself, then revealed some information that took me completely aback.

"I represent a group of people in New Mexico who are in contact with an alien intelligence," she told me, very earnestly. "You may not be aware of the importance of the work you're doing. You have been chosen, in a metaphysical sense, to house the alien entity called Spock."

I don't remember exactly what I responded, but I was struck by the intensity of her belief. And as I suppressed my skepticism, I politely asked why these beings were so concerned about one particular Earthling's acting career, because she went on to explain that Spock's "purpose" was to positively prepare humanity for actual contact with alien life. After all, most science fiction at the time portrayed extraterrestrials negatively, as the stereotypical bug-eyed monsters bent on conquering Earth.

Sounds fantastic, doesn't it? Maybe I'm unwise to admit it. Just imagine the tabloid headlines:

ALIENS CAST ACTOR IN SCIENCE FICTION TV SERIES

I thanked her and went back to work. Spock had become a magnet for that sort of thing; I received numerous letters along the same vein back in the sixties. It was an era when people were experimenting with mind-expanding drugs and exploring mystical, metaphysical questions. Books like Erich Von Daniken's *Chariots of the Gods,* which hypothesized that Earth had been visited by extraterrestrials, were popular. Most of the time, the memory of that encounter with the young lady makes me smile in amusement. But every once in a while, I think: Who knows? Perhaps . . .

Well, okay, maybe I *don't* believe that I was chosen by aliens to be their earthly "ambassador" in Hollywood. But the truth is, unlike Spock, I'm an incorrigible romantic. I have a great penchant for nostalgia and irony and history, and can't help believing fate somehow had a hand in all this. When I think back about my first days in Hollywood—when I could barely scrape together six bucks a week to share a boarding-house room and earned maybe fourteen bucks a week scooping ice cream and jerking sodas—I feel a deep sense of amazement and satisfaction at the opportunities life has brought me. And many of them came because of my involvement with a particular Vulcan . . .

So if we accept the notion of kismet, destiny, fate—that I was always "meant" for the role of Spock—how did my past "prepare" me to become a proper channel, a vessel for this alien, this outsider who is at ease neither on his homeworld, nor on Earth?

When was the seed that became Spock planted?

To answer that question, I have to go back more than fifty years, to the Bowdin Theater in an ethnic neighborhood in the heart of Boston called the West End. Like a lot of other eight-year-old kids growing up in the late 1930s, I walked with my brother down to the movie house one Saturday afternoon and settled back in a cushy seat in the cool darkness to look up at the indigo ceiling with the twinkling little white lights that looked like stars. We usually went to the one o'clock Saturday show, and got there twenty minutes early so we could be first to pick out the best seats. Twenty-eight

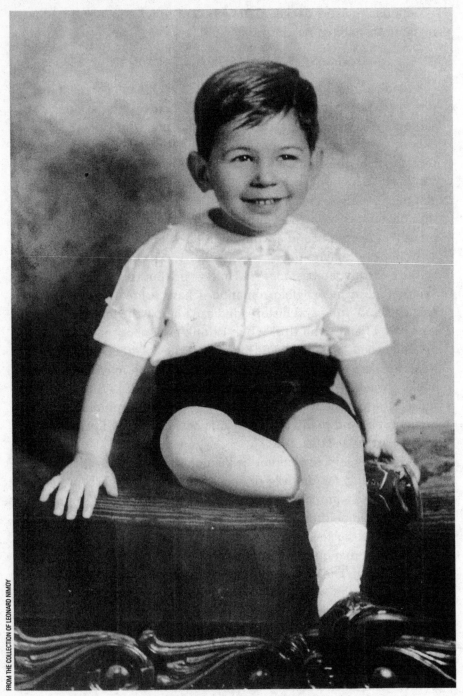

The budding actor at age 2½

cents entitled you to a double feature, cartoon, short-reel comedy, and the news.

I don't remember what else was playing that day, but the main attraction was *The Hunchback of Notre Dame*, featuring Maureen O'Hara as the gypsy Esmeralda and Charles Laughton as the title character, Quasimodo.

Poor Quasimodo's face and body were grotesquely deformed. A freak of nature, he lived a solitary and silent life in the towers of Notre Dame cathedral; the great bells, his only companions, had left him completely deaf. He was so ugly that when the movie began, I could scarcely stand to look at him: One eye hung much lower than the other, and the large hump on his back kept him permanently stooped over. I wanted to avert my gaze, but I couldn't— because as the story progressed, I saw that beneath his "different" exterior was a heart that yearned for love and acceptance.

So I watched, horrified, as poor Quasimodo was falsely accused of a crime and put on public display on a wooden pillory in the cathedral courtyard. The king's guards tied him down, flogged him with a cat-o'-nine-tails; he bore his punishment stoically, never crying out despite the pain. Then they left him to his humiliation while the pillory slowly turned, revealing his suffering to the huge throng that had gathered.

The crowd jeered at him, mocked him, laughed at him when he begged for water. No one took pity on him; no one saw the anguished soul beneath the twisted flesh. And when his thirst made him cry out again, someone soaked a rag in mud and slapped him across the face with it.

When that happened, I squirmed uncomfortably in my seat. I wanted to hide my eyes because, thanks to Laughton's marvelous performance, I identified deeply with Quasimodo's torment. The outward differences between us didn't matter.

And then a beautiful event unfolded on the flickering screen. Like the rest of the onlookers, the lovely Esmeralda was terrified and repulsed by the hideous creature on the platform. But her compassion overcame her fear, and she emerged from the hooting crowd to bring Quasimodo water from her own flask.

At first he would not take it. He turned his face—still dripping with mud—away, unworthy, and let the offered water flow over his face like tears. It was as though he could not admit his suffering to her, could not let her see beyond his stoic (and hideous) mask. But she persisted, and at last he drank.

When he looked up at her with shy, reverent gratitude as though she were literally an angel of mercy, the theater was utterly silent.

Later, when the torture had ended and Quasimodo staggered, weak and reeling, back to the cathedral, the hunchback gazed up at his caretaker and with a beatific smile, uttered the simple sentence that tore out my heart: "She gave me water."

I was grateful the theater was dark so that I could cry freely. The humanity trapped inside this seemingly inhuman creature profoundly touched me. And I'm sure I was not the only one moved to tears that day.

And at the movie's end, Esmeralda walked off happily with her handsome young beloved. Poor Quasimodo watched heartbroken from his high perch, then gestured at the cathedral's glowering gargoyles and sighed, "Why was I not made of stone like them?"

Who among us does not understand what it is to be an outsider, separate? Even at that tender age, I did. I was a Jewish kid living in a mostly Italian neighborhood. Many of my close friends were Italian, but I learned early on that I was somehow "different" from them. Our friendships stopped at the church door.

I carried Quasimodo's haunting image with me from the theater that day; the seed that would become Spock was planted. It was nurtured and watered quite by accident, when I landed my first acting job: the lead in *Hansel and Gretel*. There I was, an eight-year-old kid wandering down the hall one day at the Peabody Playhouse when an adult asked me, "Do you know this song?"

I nodded, and before I knew it, I was singing it onstage as the character Hansel.

I came to love acting, even though at first, I never sought it out. When I was growing up, all my friends were interested in sports. I was always last to be chosen for the team because I couldn't hit a ball. Turned out I was a lot better at acting than at sports. I was a shy kid, easily embarrassed, the last one you'd expect to see hamming it up onstage. But I found comfort in playing other characters because I was given what to say and do. I couldn't be blamed for my words or actions, I couldn't make a mistake. And the more I could cloak myself in the character, the more comfortable I became; I enjoyed wigs and heavy makeup. I felt protected behind the performer's mask.

After a while, I really began to enjoy acting, enough to actively seek out roles. At age seventeen, I was cast as Ralphie in the Clifford Odets play *Awake and Sing*. Ralphie was a teenager trying to free himself from the grip of a domineering mother; this role, of an alienated young man struggling to find his identity in the midst of a hostile and repressive environment, touched a responsive chord in me. I felt that I'd really begun to understand what acting was all about. Playing Ralphie was a turning point for me; the theater became my passion, my calling, my obsession. From that moment on, I was determined to become an actor.

Now, my parents were extremely diligent, responsible, practical people. I grew up during the Depression, which was a very tough time financially for most people. My parents had both escaped from Russia (my father by stealing across the Polish border at night, my mother by hiding in a haywagon) and they were grateful to be living in a country where they couldn't be killed in the street. At the same time, they were very fearful of becoming a financial burden. Hard work was for them a moral obligation.

Because of that, when I told them at age seventeen that I was going to study drama at the Pasadena Playhouse and become an actor, they were grief-stricken. After a lot of tears, useless pleading and arguments, they tried to dissuade me by refusing to give me the tuition, saying: "You'll have to do it without any help from us." Being stubborn, I saved some money by selling vacuum cleaners, bought a train ticket, and headed west to California.

By an interesting coincidence (or, if you prefer, by "alien design"), the character of Spock faced a similar reaction at a similar age, when he informed his parents of his decision to enter Starfleet—a career choice that brought his father's outspoken disapproval. Certainly, my own experience was something I could draw on as an actor to play scenes between Spock and his father, Sarek, in the *Star Trek* episode "Journey to Babel."

My first tremendous break in Hollywood came in 1951, when I was only twenty, and cast as the lead in a modest film called *Kid Monk Baroni*. The Monk was an Italian boy from New York's East

Side who became a boxer. The role was especially interesting because he had a disfigured face as a result of being a forceps baby. Hence the unkind nickname "the Monk," because he supposedly looked like an ape. The face made him an outsider, an alien in his own world.

The first day I arrived on the set, I didn't even know I had the part. I had auditioned over and over for the role, always finding myself in a waiting room with twelve or fifteen other guys who looked just like me. Finally, I did a real sales pitch to the producer

My big break: With Mona Knox in Kid Monk Baroni, *1952*

and he said, "Okay, let me think about it. I'll either hire you as the lead or for a bit role. Come back Monday morning." (This happened on a Friday night.) So I came back on Monday, went to the producer's office, and the secretary said, "Go over to rehearsal room C. The cast is there with the director."

Still not knowing my fate, I went to rehearsal room C, feeling very embarrassed and lost, and sat against the wall. Finally, the makeup man—a very talented artist by the name of Lee Greenway—came up to me and said, "Are you Leonard Nimoy? I'm looking for him."

He led me to the makeup chair and began to make molds of my face, so that foam rubber appliances could be made. At that point, I realized that I had been cast as the lead.

The day filming began on *Kid Monk*, I sat down in that same chair and watched as Lee affixed the finished appliances to my face. Awed, I watched the slow transformation in the mirror as my mouth, nose, forehead became no longer Leonard Nimoy's, but the Monk's. Even though I wasn't a thoroughly trained actor at the time, my emotions instinctively responded to this new face.

I looked like an outsider, a person who didn't belong. I could identify with the feelings evoked by being "different," could understand why the Kid had erected a protective shell of shyness and physical toughness to hide his true feelings. Yet like the Hunchback, he too had a heart that yearned for understanding and compassion.

(After *Kid Monk*'s release, my mother, who never mentioned the taboo topic of my career, wrote me a letter which included the cryptic line: "Well, we saw your movie." No praise, no criticism, not a single word about how my parents reacted to seeing their son on film. Frankly, I was crushed, and wrote back to my mother to tell her so. She finally confessed: "What can I say? You're our *son*: How could we possibly judge whether the movie was good or bad? All I know is, the minute you appeared up there on the big screen, your father and I began to cry, and we couldn't stop until it was over.")

The memory of those "alien" characters of the Hunchback and Kid Monk Baroni stayed with me, even though I went on to play many different types of roles for the next thirteen years. In fact, the role that led directly to my being cast as Spock wasn't that of the

•

alienated loner. Quite the opposite: It was that of a glib, fast-talking Hollywood type.

This was in 1964 on a fairly short-lived television show called *The Lieutenant*, in an episode entitled "In the Highest Tradition." I guest-starred as a flamboyant actor who wanted to make a movie on the Marine Corps base. The series lead—the lieutenant in question—was played by an actor named Gary Lockwood (a name that will surface again later). Anyway, I got the part after reading for the episode's director, Marc Daniels.

Marc was a wonderfully gentle, unflappable, greatly experienced workaday director who staged a lot of the *I Love Lucy* shows. He wore a hearing aid, and I always admired him for that, since I'd never seen anybody else in our competitive and frightened industry dare to display any sign of physical impairment. But Marc was very forthright and secure; he never played games, but simply came to work and did it professionally and well. It was the *I Love Lucy* connection through Desilu that would later lead Marc to direct several episodes of *Star Trek*.

But at the time, he knew me as an intense, dramatic performer, someone who played the angry young street tough. So when my agent, Alex Brewis, suggested me for *The Lieutenant* episode, Marc said, "Leonard Nimoy? He's all wrong! We need someone glib, loquacious, not a Kid Monk." But my agent persisted, and finally Marc agreed to see me. I did a quick reading of a couple of scenes, with energy and brightness and a little twinkle in the eyes. Marc didn't attempt to hide his surprise. "Hunh," he said. "I guess you *can* do this."

So I was hired for the part. Of course, no flamboyant Hollywood type would be complete without an assistant; mine happened to be played by a lovely young actress who went by the stage name Majel Barrett.

I had a good time on the set, enjoyed working with Gary Lockwood, collected my check, and thought nothing more about it—until my agent phoned a few weeks later. "Look," he said, "I just got a call from *The Lieutenant*'s producer. He really liked your work on the show, and he wants to talk to you about a role in a series pilot he's doing."

I was thrilled, of course. After guest starring on so many TV shows and always being the visitor whose name was written on the dressing-room door in chalk, the thought of a regular job and a regular income was very appealing. But I tried not to get too excited; I'd done enough auditions to know that I might not land the part. I also knew that most pilots never become series.

With that in mind, I went to see the producer, fully prepared to hard-sell myself again and do the best reading for him I could. He was a pleasant man, very tall and gangly and loose-limbed—sort of floppy, you could say, but not sloppy, and obviously very bright. Our meeting was pleasant and cordial. He gave me the complete Desilu studio tour—showed me the props, the scenic design shop— all the while explaining the series' concept and telling me how great it was going to be.

I kept waiting to do a reading. But as the producer kept going on about the series and about how interesting my character was going to be, I gradually realized that *he* was trying to sell *me* on the idea. And I thought to myself: "Don't blow it, Leonard. Keep your mouth shut, or you just might talk yourself out of a job."

So I tried very hard just to listen carefully and look interested while Gene—that was this producer's name, of course, Gene Roddenberry—told me all about this role I was to play, Spock, in a science fiction series called *Star Trek*. The character hadn't been completely fleshed out yet, but Gene was adamant about one thing: Spock had to be *obviously* extraterrestrial, in order to visually emphasize that this was the twenty-third century and these were interplanetary, not just international, crew members aboard a space ship. Spock would therefore be distinguished by a different skin color (probably red), a different hairstyle, and pointed ears.

He would also be different in terms of temperament. Spock was half-human and half-alien, raised in a world where emotional displays were in bad taste and firmly suppressed. This rational, "repressed" side would of course overshadow his emotional, human side. But despite his coolness, he would project a sense that there was danger lurking within him, a darker half that might take over at any moment.

I was at once intrigued and worried about playing the role. Intrigued because Gene described a very rich internal life for the character; worried, because the part might turn out to be a bad sci-fi

•

joke. Just how seriously could the viewing audience take a character with pointed ears and reddish skin? What was next, a pitchfork?

Yet Roddenberry had clearly taken the character *very* seriously, enough to give Spock an extremely interesting background. The essence of drama is conflict; and Spock, because of his divided nature, was pure walking, talking, breathing conflict.

So I gave the role serious consideration, and went to talk to an

The Creator: Gene Roddenberry

actor friend of mine, Vic Morrow, whose talent and judgment I respected. At the time, he had a leading role on the TV series *Combat*. Anyway, Vic and I went over the pros and cons of the situation. Finally he suggested, "Well, look—if you're *that* worried about Spock turning into a joke, you could insist on such heavy makeup that no one will ever recognize you."

It was a possibility I considered briefly, then dismissed; I wanted to do the role justice. So I took the job and voiced my concerns about Spock to Gene, who said, "I know you can make this character work." He was very firm about it, for which I'm now grateful.

But when preproduction on "The Cage" began, I began to think my anxiety was well founded. The first screen test with the ears was, to put it mildly, awful. Lee Greenway, who'd done the makeup for *Kid Monk*, had been hired to see whether he could come up with a pair of ears—with no budget and no time.

Now, normally, such appliances need to be made in a very painstaking fashion. First, a plaster cast must be made of the actor's anatomy in question (in this case, my ears). From that mold, they then create a "positive" cast of the ears, then build onto that with putty, sculpting the shape of the piece that's going to be added. *Then* they make a mold from that, and pour into it a particular kind of liquid latex and bake it. The resulting appliance will fit in a perfect, seamless way.

But the production heads had told Lee Greenway there wasn't any time or money for that, that he had to come up with a "down and dirty" version of the ears for this test. So he made an extremely crude version, piling papier-mâché and liquid latex onto my ears.

The result was embarrassing to both of us. I really *did* look like an "overgrown jackrabbit" or an "elf with a hyperactive thyroid." Ashamed, I made my way onto the set where *The Lucy Show* would be taped that night, and tried to appear dignified in the makeup before fifteen crewmen and rolling cameras. (It seemed somehow fitting that this took place on a comedy set.) I know that piece of film has to be floating around in a vault somewhere; I still swear that if I ever find it, I'll burn it!

So there I was, in street clothes under hot lights wearing those ludicrous ears. You might say it was the first public exposure of the extraterrestrial, Spock. I found myself taking mental notes, storing away memories that might prove useful in the role. I was like the poor hunchback on the pillory, subjected to a humiliating public display; I felt alien to the point of being ridiculous. I knew that once I left, the crew would exchange jokes about my appearance—and as I stood there on the empty, lighted set, I felt myself building defenses, attempting to elevate my thinking beyond any concern for the opinions of *mere humans*. Spock was beginning to come to life.

The camera test was enough to convince everyone that something else had to be done about the ears. A different makeup artist,

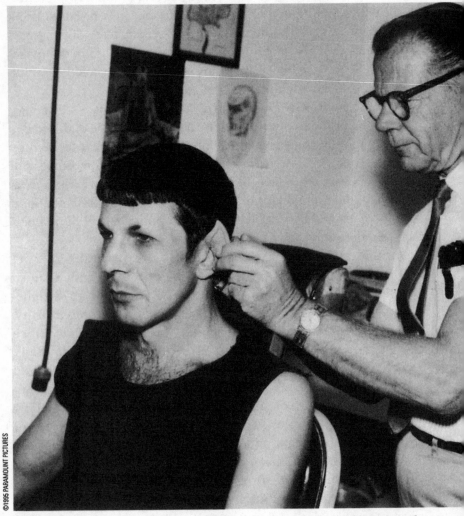

Make-up artist Fred Phillips at work, 6:30 A.M.: "Good morning, Leonard . . ."

•

Fred Phillips, set about trying to obtain a proper pair of ears made in the previously mentioned manner. But the effects house that was creating the ears wasn't right for the job; they were used to making big feet and hands for monster movies, more along the lines of *The Creature from the Black Lagoon* than the delicate appliance work Freddy wanted. They used a sort of rubber that just didn't look at all natural next to an actor's skin.

By that time, Spock's "look" was starting to gel. We had the proper skin tone—a yellowish-green, which looked far better on a black-

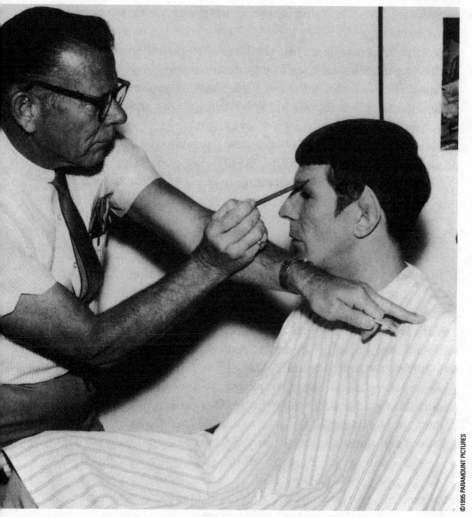

7:15 A.M.: ". . . and hello, Mister Spock!"

and-white TV screen than red, which simply turned Spock's face jet-black. The yak-hair (yes, *yak* hair) eyebrows were working, and even the haircut was working. (An interesting sidebar: I had suggested pointed sideburns as a specifically "Vulcan" look for Spock. Apparently Vulcans are galactic trendsetters, because you'll notice everybody in the Federation now sports those pointed sideburns.) But we still couldn't get those damned ears right.

Fred tried twice, three times, four, but each time, the ears that came back simply weren't acceptable. When he went and complained to studio heads, they told him, "Too bad—this is the company we've hired, and you've got to use them. We can't spend any more money."

But the final set of ears was the last straw; he pulled them off me, hurled them in the trash and said, "That does it!" He picked up the phone and called a friend of his, a specialist in appliance work over at MGM, and before I knew it, I was having a new plaster cast made and the whole procedure started over again.

Within thirty-six hours, I had a new pair of foam rubber ears that fit perfectly and looked natural. To this day, I am most grateful to Fred Phillips for saving the day and insisting on doing the job properly. Fred put his own job on the line; he could have been fired for spending the money without authorization. But had he not made that decision to spend the unauthorized six hundred dollars, the Spock character could have been a comic disaster from the start.

Instead, the Vulcan makeup served as inspiration. As with *Kid Monk*, when I saw my slow transformation in the makeup mirror from human to Vulcan, an inner transformation took place as well. Freddy noticed it, too; he always said that Leonard Nimoy reported for work at 6:30 A.M. . . . and Mr. Spock could always be counted on to arrive somewhere around 7:15!

At any rate, it soon became clear just how good a job Fred had done with the appliances. Shortly after Spock acquired a proper pair of ears, my agent came to visit the *Star Trek* set. I was in full Vulcan regalia when Alex came to see me. He was accompanied by a client, a lovely Irish actress named Maura McGivney. I believe Miss McGivney was the first person off the street to see me in my Spock costume, and her reaction was one of immediate, obvious interest.

"Oh," she breathed, lifting a hand to my—excuse me, to *Spock's*—

ears. "May I touch them? They're so *attractive* . . . "

I blushed a deep, decidedly un-Vulcan shade of red, and obliged. It was the first inkling I had of Spock's effect on women. Eventually, when the character's popularity soared, everyone was trying to figure out whether it was indeed the ears that were responsible. In fact, at the end of the first season when contract negotiation time came round, the main threat the studio used with me was, "Cooperate, or we'll put the ears on someone else!"

The ears were something of a blessing and a curse. They weren't really painful, just a little uncomfortable, and I couldn't lie down on my side while wearing them. The worst discomfort, I think, came in the first couple of seasons with all the jokes. I was branded as the Man with the Pointed Ears, and every article about me in the press was laden with ear puns. I can smile about them now, but at the time, I began to cringe at review headlines like EARS TO LEONARD NIMOY, THE EARS HAVE IT, and the million-times-repeated comment, "I didn't recognize you without your ears!"

But while I was becoming reconciled to them, the powers at NBC were doing the opposite. The network put out a promotional brochure about *Star Trek* that explained the series and the characters, and contained some production stills. This brochure was sent to stations and potential advertisers to help sell the forthcoming series. I looked at a copy, eager to see how the show and especially Spock were represented. He was there, all right, with the Vulcan haircut in place—but some very significant parts of him were missing.

The pointed ears were gone, and the upward-slanting eyebrows had been airbrushed out. Spock looked entirely human.

Needless to say, this filled me with concern. I called Gene and asked why NBC felt the need to do such a thing. "They're worried," he said. "They think Bible Belt viewers are going to find the character too 'satanic.'" This was my first inkling that the Vulcan's very existence might be in jeopardy—that Spock might die before he was ever really born.

But Gene said, "Don't worry. We're going to keep him just as he is." Once again, he was very adamant about Spock remaining obviously alien.

Shooting on the first *Star Trek* pilot finally began December 12, 1964. Should this be the official date of Spock's "birth"?

•

Nope. He was still gestating. For one thing, I didn't have a handle on the character yet. If you watch "The Cage," you'll see Spock emoting all over the place. He frowns, he smiles, and when the landing party is standing on the transporter platform, ready to beam down to Talos IV, and Number One and Yeoman Colt disappear, he leaps forward and shrieks, "The *women!*"

Even his intonation is different, and certain words are pronounced with a hint of a British accent. For example, Spock pronounces "answer" as "ahnswer." The reason for that was because

Gene thought Spock should be played as though he had learned English as a second language, perhaps by listening to tapes of classic British English. He gave me a record of W. Somerset Maugham reading his own work. However, I wasn't comfortable with the accent, and decided to let it go.

In "The Cage," I wasn't playing a Vulcan; I was playing a first officer. You know, where the captain says, "Full speed ahead," and his second-in-command briskly echoes, "FULL SPEED AHEAD!"

That was the character I portrayed against Jeffrey Hunter's Captain Pike.

©1995 PARAMOUNT PICTURES

"Full speed ahead!"

Jeff's most famous role was probably that of Jesus in *King of Kings*. He was a very soft-spoken, thoughtful, easygoing gentleman, and his character, Christopher Pike, was a brooding, introverted man who took his responsibilities as captain very seriously. In that way, Captain Pike and Mr. Spock were very alike as characters. So, for

that matter, was Number One, the cool, unemotional female commander (played by Majel Barrett). Spock was not yet distinguished
from the other crew members; I had not yet found his niche.

But I played the role, enjoyed the work, collected the check and
didn't worry much about what would happen with the pilot—
which, in fact, was not successful in selling the series. When Gene
called me a year later to do a second pilot, it was a total surprise. I
was thrilled, because it meant another two weeks' work.

I didn't learn until later that NBC told Gene to fire almost the

©1995 PARAMOUNT PICTURES

*A gestating Vulcan in "The Cage": Spock smiles with delight
while Captain Christopher Pike (Jeffrey Hunter) and Doctor Boyce
(John Hoyt) look on.*

entire cast—including me. The network execs were especially vocal about getting rid of two roles—the female second-in-command and the devilish-looking alien, Spock. "Drop the woman and the pointy-eared guy," they said. "TV viewers will never be able to accept such characters."

Gene agreed to let go of Majel and her part as Number One, but to his credit, he insisted that the Vulcan was absolutely essential to the show. The *Enterprise* had to have an alien crew member, or she wouldn't fly.

Gene was fond of telling the story this way: "NBC finally said that either the woman or the Martian—meaning Spock—had to go. So I kept the Vulcan and married the woman because, obviously, I couldn't have done it the other way around . . . "

So Spock survived intact, and absorbed much of Number One's cool, reserved demeanor. In fact, he became the only character to survive from the first pilot to the second, because Jeff Hunter was let go when his wife began to represent him and made what Gene considered excessive demands.

That left the role of captain empty. Gene's next choice to play the part was Jack Lord (who would later become known for his work on the series *Hawaii Five-O*). But negotiations with Lord fell through, so Gene contacted a young actor much respected for his work on the science fiction television series *Outer Limits* and *The Twilight Zone*: William Shatner.

Bill came to the show with a certain amount of cachet, a solid reputation, and a lot of expertise. He was always extremely hard-working, extremely well prepared, and totally professional, but at the same time, he brought with him a great deal of zest and passion about work, food, his Dobermans, his cars, his life . . . In

Checkmate: The first officer
and his captain (William Shatner)
in "Where No Man Has Gone Before"

other words, about *everything*. And he has a prankster's sense of humor. I think it's time the world knew the hidden, ugly truth about what *really* was happening on the *Star Trek* set: Bill Shatner is one of the worst punsters in the world, and it soon became his "five-year mission" to try to crack me up on the set.

In keeping with our theme of "destiny," it's interesting to note that, although we two are as different as salt and pepper, we're precisely four days apart in age. (Bill was born March 22, 1931; I was born March 26.) It's true that we were quite competitive with each other—but it was the competitiveness between two brothers who care a great deal about each other.

©1995 PARAMOUNT PICTURES

Bill's Captain Kirk was a swashbuckling Errol Flynn type of hero; he played the role with a great deal of energy and élan, and wasn't afraid to take chances. That élan has cost him at times; people have made fun of his exuberance because it made it easy to do a caricature of Kirk. His attack on a line of dialog, his unique way of paus-

Friends and fellow actors Sally Kellerman and Gary Lockwood suffering for their art in "Where No Man"

ing before blurting out the final word or phrase, were readily captured by imitators.

But that energy was vital for the show, and made it possible for me to finally find a niche for my role. I don't think the Spock character would have worked as well with Jeff Hunter, because Jeff's Captain Pike was introverted and soft-spoken, so that there was no contrast between the two.

I had actually worked with Bill before, very briefly in an episode of *The Man from U.N.C.L.E.* We only had one scene together; I was the wily Eastern bloc agent and Bill was a somewhat bumbling double agent. I had practically forgotten all about it until the other day, when I wanted to look at some "whip" pans for a show I'm currently producing. A whip pan is a type of camera pan used between shots, where the camera suddenly whips away from one scene, leaving everything a blur until it finally rests on something or someone in the following scene. I remembered that the technique had been used quite a bit on *The Man from U.N.C.L.E.*, so I sent an assistant out to buy three or four episodes. We were all very amused when one of the tapes she brought back was "The Strigas Affair"— which, unbeknownst to her, guest-starred William Shatner and Leonard Nimoy!

For the second pilot, "Where No Man Has Gone Before," Gene Roddenberry also hired some other notable actors to flesh out the *Enterprise* crew—Jimmy Doohan, George Takei, and veteran actor Paul Fix as the ship's doctor, Mark Piper. Sally Kellerman and Gary Lockwood guest-starred. Of course, I had worked with Gary when I was the guest star and he was the series regular on *The Lieutenant*, and I was happy to be working with him again. He had a solid professionalism that I admired.

I also knew Sally. Back in 1960, she and I had been involved in the formation of a small theatrical group called Company of Angels, which is extant today. A number of my acting students had banded together to form the company, and I joined in as a director; in fact, I'd directed Sally in a production of *Camino Real*, so it was a pleasure to see her again.

But I have to admit, the one thing that sticks in my mind about the second pilot wasn't so much my happiness at working with Gary and Sally, but rather, the anguish they both went through in

•

wearing the silvery opaque contact lenses the story required. You see, they had been zapped by a mysterious force which left them with incredible psychic powers—and also happened to make their eyes look very weird. In order to get the effect, Sally and Gary both had to wear hard contact lens (soft lenses hadn't been invented then). The lenses were enormously uncomfortable, and neither actor could see much of anything with them in. Some years later, when I got a pair of hard contact lenses myself, I really sympathized with them both during my miserable adjustment period!

Getting back to the development of the character Spock: He was definitely very close to being "born" by that time, but hadn't become a "real" Vulcan yet in "Where No Man." The first scene in that episode shows Captain Kirk having a friendly three-dimensional chess game with his second-in-command; Spock wears a gold tunic and a definite smirk as he tells Kirk, "I'll have you checkmated your next move."

When the captain makes reference to irritation, Spock cocks his head, still smirking, as he says: "Irritation? Ah, yes, one of your Earth emotions . . . "

He definitely shows more emotion than is Vulcanly proper, and still possesses a touch of the "first officer syndrome," bellowing out his reports with a lot more volume than necessary on such a compact bridge. And he makes a shockingly violent recommendation for one whose people are total pacifists—that Kirk kill Lockwood's character, Gary Mitchell, before Mitchell's psychic powers become too great.

But signs of the Vulcan are here, too: the calm, even intonation, the hands clasped primly behind the back, the clipped "affirmatives" and "negatives," the ever-ready dissertations on logic. Kirk's final line in the episode—after Spock confesses that he, too, felt for the now dead Mitchell—seems fitting: "There still may be hope for you, Mr. Spock."

Indeed there was. A Vulcan was about to be born.

THREE

BIRTH
OF
A VULCAN

SPOCK: *I was born in the year 2230 on the planet Vulcan, to Sarek of Vulcan and Amanda of Earth.*

NIMOY: Wrong again! You were born in the year 1966, on a Desilu sound-stage in Hollywood, California . . .

SPOCK: *I suggest you recheck your data.*

NIMOY: I don't have to, Spock. I was there.

I N *I AM NOT SPOCK*, I wrote about the births of my two children, Julie and Adam, and how I could pinpoint the precise time and place those wonderful miracles occurred. (Julie was born March 21, 1955, 9:30 P.M. EST in Atlanta, and Adam on August 9, 1956, 11:22 P.M. PST in Los Angeles.)

But coming up with a date, a precise moment, that Spock first sprang into being was far more difficult, even though I was in many ways more "present" for his birth than those of my children. To say he was "born" on Thursday, September 8, 1966 at 7:30 P.M. EST—the date *Star Trek* first aired—seemed at best arbitrary and artificial; besides, I knew he had already been with us for a few months by then.

However, I've had thirty years to think about it since then, and I realize now that there *was* a defining moment, a flash of revelation where I suddenly realized: "*Aha!* So *this* is who the Vulcan is . . . "

And it came during the shooting of the third *Star Trek* episode ever filmed, "The Corbomite Maneuver."

Let me backtrack a little and mention some of the transforma-tions that *Star Trek* underwent between the filming of "Where No Man" and "Corbomite." For one thing, after NBC executives saw the second pilot, they very quickly added it to their new fall schedule. *Star Trek* was finally a go—and I was thrilled at the prospect of regular work on a television series. After all, during the first season, I would be making $1,250 per episode, for a grand total of $37,500 that year—enough to keep my family comfortably supported without my having to worry about finding other jobs. But I had no inkling of the effect it would have on my life and my privacy; I was so naive, it never occurred to me that keeping my phone number listed in the directory would be a problem! But that's a whole other chapter . . .

After the second pilot, there was again some reshuffling of characters. Gene felt that Paul Fix's character, Doctor Mark Piper (who appeared only briefly in "Where No Man"), needed to be replaced by someone younger and feistier, who would have a closer friendship with the captain. He had a particular actor in mind who he felt would be perfect for the job (and he was right): DeForest Kelley.

©1995 PARAMOUNT PICTURES

De is a very calm, gentle soul, a true Southern gentleman; like McCoy, he was born in Atlanta. He was a seasoned veteran who'd been in Hollywood a long time—though he's as un-Hollywood as anyone can get, a sweet, humble man who's been married to his lovely wife, Carolyn, for more than forty years now. De was best known at the time for portraying the quintessential "bad guy" in Westerns. (In fact, he had such a

"Fascinating . . ." The Vulcan speaks in "The Corbomite Maneuver"

reputation for playing the gunslinging heavy that NBC refused to let Gene Roddenberry hire him as the *Star Trek* doctor for the first pilot, arguing that audiences would never be able to accept him as a "good guy." Try to picture, if you can, the lovable Dr. McCoy sneering as he cold-bloodedly shoots a dog! That's the kind of role De was known for.) He'd also worked with Gene on several projects; at the time *Star Trek* was just getting started, De was working in another television pilot for Gene called *Police Story*, playing a crabby but lovable criminologist.

De's Dr. McCoy became a very valuable addition, bringing a special chemistry to the show and further helping to define the characters of Kirk and Spock through the acid observations of that good-hearted curmudgeon, McCoy. McCoy and Spock evolved into verbal sparring partners—with the good doctor taking the human-ist stance and Spock the side of logic—but there was always a strong undercurrent of friendship and mutual respect.

©1995 PARAMOUNT PICTURES

From the very first moment he appeared in "Corbomite," De had that special twinkle in his eye; he knew from the start how to approach the character of Mc-Coy. Soon the writers would begin injecting humor into the scripts by taking advantage of McCoy's cantankerous emotionalism and Spock's ability to take any comment literally. Spock was the straight man—George

Burns, if you will, to Dr. McCoy's Gracie. The Kirk/Spock relationship might have been the Lone Ranger/Tonto, but Spock/McCoy was definitely Martin and Lewis, Gleason and Carney, or my favorite comedy team of all time, Abbott and Costello. Abbott was the cool straight man, and Costello the irrational "human," and most of the amusing exchanges between Spock and McCoy are variations of that wonderful routine, "Who's on First?" To liberally paraphrase:

COSTELLO: (frustrated) Now, wait a minute! When the first baseman gets his paycheck, who gets the money?

ABBOTT: (calmly) That's exactly right. "Who" gets the money.

The joke all rides on the fact that poor Costello simply *can't* understand that the first baseman's *name* is Who, and Abbott certainly isn't doing much to help clear up his confusion. Let's face it, it's not a very far stretch to rewrite this particular bit for the good doctor and his Vulcan friend.

McCOY: (frustrated) Now wait a minute, Spock! When the first baseman gets his paycheck, who gets the money?

SPOCK: It is only logical that he should do so, since he provided his services.

McCOY: Who did?

"Now, let me get this straight . . . who gets the money?"

SPOCK: Precisely, Doctor. "Who" did. "Who" receives the money.

McCOY: Are you trying to confuse me, you green-blooded son of a—!

SPOCK: Control yourself, Doctor.

Another newcomer to the *Enterprise* bridge in "Corbomite" was Nichelle Nichols. On the set, Nichelle was always very beautiful and very involved; and though she often was not given many lines in the script, she nevertheless was totally present and made an emotional investment in whatever was happening in the scene. Jimmy Doohan and George Takei had both joined the crew in the previous episode, and it was marvelous how perfectly each of them—Nichelle, Jimmy, George—filled their roles. (Of course, Scotty spent almost the entire episode on the bridge—which leaves one to wonder *who* was minding the engines.) Rewatching "The Corbomite Maneuver" recently, I was struck by the wonderful sense of camaraderie on the bridge between the characters, as the crew awaited possible death during a countdown. I feel honored to have worked with such a great group of professionals; the chemistry between the characters was there from the very start.

This was also the episode where Grace Lee Whitney made her first appearance as the captain's yeoman, Janice Rand. I got a kick out of watching her arrive perkily on the tension-filled bridge with coffee for everyone; and then there was the scene where she brings the captain a salad, insisting that he eat something. Of course, Grace Lee didn't finish out the first season, and the dialog in that episode seems to predict her character's demise. "I don't need a yeoman. I've already got a female to worry about," Kirk tells McCoy (meaning, of course, the *Enterprise*), and snaps at Rand to quit hovering over him.

(It might have been interesting if Rand had remained aboard the *Enterprise*; consider this excerpt from a Gene Roddenberry memo to the show's writers:

> About the only person on the ship who can joke with Mr. Spock at all is the captain's Yeoman, Janice Rand. Perhaps beneath her swinging exterior is a motherly instinct for lonely men—at any rate, Yeoman Janice can mention things few others would dare

to say to Spock's face. And in return, guessing logically at some of *her* secrets, Spock will give [if you'll excuse the expression] tat for tit. But if the conversation has him looking at her too intently or too long, she will feel the hypnotic quality and beg off—and Spock will look away. They have an unspoken agreement that the joke will only be carried so far.)

And this was the episode where Spock was "born." Perhaps it's somewhat arbitrary to choose "Corbomite," because the Vulcan is

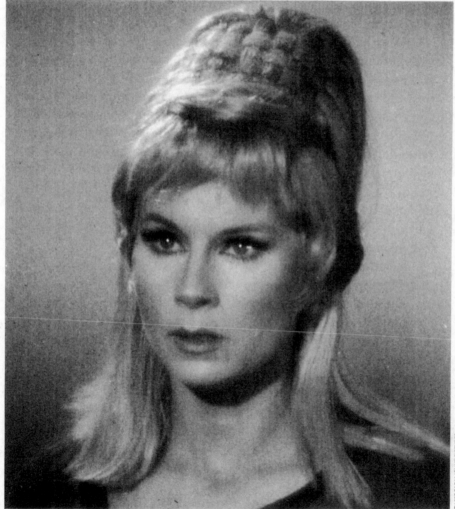

Grace Lee Whitney as Yeoman Janice Rand

still quite inconsistent in his demeanor; for example, in an early scene, a young crewman named Bailey raises his voice anxiously. The Vulcan accuses him of unnecessarily emoting (and when Bailey says it's a result of adrenaline, Spock dryly suggests he "have it removed.") Yet moments later, Spock does the very same thing!

Also, if you watch the episode, you'll notice that Spock wears blush on his cheeks, and that his skin is very shiny, suggesting that he's sweating because of the tension on the bridge. As time went on, Freddy Phillips eliminated all the pink stuff and used a flat greenish color. He also took great pains to keep me absolutely dry, once it was decided that Spock didn't sweat.

I guess I'd describe "Corbomite" as a crossover episode, where I was still learning to play the role. At some moments, I grasped it; at others, I didn't. There are still moments when Spock seems on the verge of breaking into a smile. Early in the first season, the character was overwrought, overdone—more emotional with slightly larger ears, bushier eyebrows, the jagged bangs. Over time, we refined Spock, toned him down, until at last he became the cool, elegant creature he is today.

But it was during the filming of this episode that I had a revelation of sorts that helped me realize exactly who the Vulcan was; and I owe the breakthrough to a wonderful director by the name of Joseph Sargent.

Joe was a veteran director, a professional who was extremely energetic. He had an uncanny sense of story, and of where the values and strengths lay in a particular script. I had met Joe long before *Star Trek* came along, when I was auditing on *The Man from U.N.C.L.E.* set in search of a directing job. Joe happened to direct several of the series' episodes, and I often followed him around. Early one morning, I made it into the office before him, and found some papers on his desk. They were notes on the opening few pages of a script he was going to be shooting that day. He'd done a very concise synopsis of the entire story—but what caught my eye was the line that came after his description of the teaser (the first brief scene, intended to "hook" the audience). "Our hero searches through the file drawers, finds the paper he's looking for, reacts," Joe had written. "Then the door slowly creaks open . . . and we're off!"

•

I got a big kick out of that little phrase, and have always kept it in mind when I direct, because it illustrates so perfectly Joe's élan and the joy he took in storytelling. I feel the director's job is to experience that joy and share it with the cast and ultimately, the audience. Joe Sargent, Marc Daniels, and Joe Pevney were three directors who possessed that infectious sense of exuberance about their work.

At any rate, I remember that Joe was directing a particular scene from "Corbomite" one day in late May 1966. It was one of the scenes on the bridge (in fact, ninety percent of the scenes in that episode take place on the bridge, making it one of our most economical shows), where the crew members were all reacting to an enormous glowing globe on the viewscreen. (Of course, we actors saw nothing but a blue screen.) We were all supposed to be concerned about this strange new threat, and my line consisted of that single fateful word, "Fascinating . . . "

I just didn't have a handle on how to say it. I was still somewhat in "first officer" mode, but it didn't seem appropriate to shout such a word out. Everyone was reacting in character—humanly, of course—but I couldn't figure out how the Vulcan would respond or how the word should come out.

Until, that is, Joe Sargent wisely said, "Look, don't act uptight about what you see on the screen. Instead, when you deliver your line, be cool and curious, a scientist."

The moment he said it, something inside me clicked; he had just illuminated what it was that made this character unique and different from all the others on the bridge. I composed myself, drew a breath, and calmly said, "Fascinating . . . "

What came out wasn't Leonard Nimoy's voice, but Spock's. And even though the Vulcan veneer would later slip from time to time (for example, when Spock smiles at Harry Mudd's glamorous entourage in "Mudd's Women"), I began to seriously understand where Spock was coming from. The Vulcan was truly among us.

I began to use more restraint in the character's movements, gestures, facial expressions. In *I Am Not Spock*, I mentioned one of my great sources of inspiration for this: Harry Belafonte. Back in the mid-1950s, my wife and I had gone to see Belafonte sing at Los Angeles's Greek Theatre.

•

For the first forty-five minutes of his performance, he scarcely moved a muscle—only stood perfectly still in front of a microphone, his shoulders hunched, his hands resting on his thighs. And then, after all that time, he suddenly made a move. He merely lifted his right arm slowly until it hovered parallel to the floor—but the impact of that one subtle motion on the audience was tremendous. Had he been dancing around the stage, the gesture would have been meaningless; as it was, it dazzled like a lightning bolt.

It was the memory of this concept that guided me in deciding on Spock's mannerisms during those early *Star Trek* episodes.

By this time, my days were beginning to blur together; working on a series is, to indulge in some Vulcan-like understatement, grueling. My routine was to rise at 5:30 A.M. weekday mornings so that I could be in the makeup chair for Freddie Phillips by no later than 6:30. I got into the habit of having my coffee in the car, and my bacon-and-egg sandwich with a thick slice of onion in the makeup chair. While Freddie applied the ears, I ate. He and I would have a nice, quiet conversation until 7—when Bill Shatner arrived, and all hell broke loose.

Bill at the time was into off-road motorcycling, and like all his other passions, he was completely obsessed with it for a while. He'd limp in on Monday morning like an arthritic old man, covered with bruises and scratches where he'd fallen off into the bushes—except for the face, of course, the only part of him he took care of. He'd rag me about the smell of my breakfast (including a few choice philosophical observations about the effects of the onion on my breath), and I'd tease him about being the macho daredevil biker who couldn't seem to stay out of the shrubbery.

As I said earlier, Bill is an incorrigible punster, and we two would tell each other jokes and carry on like kids, laughing and yelling and generally making life difficult for the poor makeup people, who were desperately trying to get us to sit still so they could do their work. We'd have utterly silly, inane conversations like:

LEONARD: . . . so anyway, the critics didn't like her work, and she was utterly destroyed.

BILL: (cupping hand to ear) Toyed? Toyed? Are you admitting that you *toyed* with her, Leonard?

Does your wife know about this? And here I always thought you were such a faithful, devoted family man.

LEONARD: (laughing) No, no, stop it, I said *destroyed*. She was *destroyed*. She's just an acquaintance I knew from—

BILL: *Deployed*? What is she? A weapon? Some type of destroyer ship? I thought we were talking about a woman. Perhaps she's a *sister* ship?

LEONARD: (giving up and playing along) No, no, she's an actress. A sistership is a *nun*.

BILL: A *none*? Are you saying she's a *zero*? Then the critics were right!

LEONARD: No, they were wrong. I didn't say *zero*, I said *hero*. Or rather, heroine. She's a very good actress.

BILL: Heroin? So now you're claiming *drugs* were involved?

LEONARD: No, I said *thugs*. And there'll be two of them waiting for you in your dressing room if you don't knock this off . . .

BILL: Let 'em try! My Dobermans'll eat them alive!

Well, you get the idea. The makeup people would sigh and roll their eyes at times when it really got out of hand, and I know they probably wondered, "My God, how will they have any energy left for the rest of the day?" But it was our way of waking up. And then De Kelley would wander in, wonderfully laconic and soft-spoken, smiling and shaking his head at our idiocy. De was a stabilizing influence for us both; he was always there to listen to Bill or me gripe about each other (which we would come to do once Spock's popularity took off, as I'll explain later), and always dispensing his oft-solicited wisdom, in classic Dutch-uncle style.

From makeup, it was on to the set or the rehearsal table (though we never had much time to rehearse). Each episode had to be shot in six days or so, so we always worked straight through until about 6:30 in the evening, taking only a short break for lunch, which usually was from the commissary. By then, I'd accumulated several

•

One logical guy

•

calls, most from reporters asking for interviews or people inviting me to public appearances. I tried to return most of the calls during lunch, but it also was necessary to have a phone installed in my car. This was unheard of in the late nineteen-sixties, but I did it because time was at such a premium. During my half-hour commute home, I would return as many calls as possible so that I wouldn't have to stay up all night on the telephone.

In order to save time, I also acquired a red bicycle so that I could save a few minutes getting to the commissary or to my office. Now, I must digress here, because no mention of that bike can be complete without the "Bill and the Bicycle" story.

I've already divulged that my former co-star was an inveterate prankster, but in certain instances, his practical joking became an outright obsession. I'll never understand why, but *my* bicycle became an object of his fixation.

It started fairly innocently—with Bill simply hiding the bike on the set one day, then returning it with a chuckle when I fumed and demanded it so I could pedal to the commissary for lunch. But from there it escalated, as obsessions do: Next thing I knew, Bill enlisted the help of the cameramen to hoist it up on the ropes, so that it hung overhead from our soundstage ceiling.

One might think this was going a little too far; ah, but Bill was just getting warmed up. On different days, my poor bike wound up chained to a fire hydrant, then in Bill's trailer, beneath the watchful eye of one of his most ferocious Dobermans.

In frustration, I took the ultimate step: I locked the damned bike *in my Buick*, and parked the car right next to the soundstage.

Bill, of course, had the Buick towed.

But back to the subject of time conservation. One reason I felt the need to conserve every possible minute was not only because of the long hours working on the series, but because I was traveling almost every weekend. I rarely turned down any paid engagement, because I knew that the series wouldn't last forever. I had seen many of my actor friends go to work on a series for a few years and live up to the level of their income; then, when the series was cancelled, they were once again looking for work, with no steady income and no money in the bank.

I made a private pact with myself that this would never happen to me and my family. I saw *Star Trek* as an opportunity to set aside money for future financial security, and did just that. We maintained a very low-key lifestyle and put away money for the kids' college educations.

So, every time I was offered a paid appearance, I took it. This meant that I left the studio at five or six o'clock on Friday night and took a red-eye flight to my destination. I'd arrive on the East Coast around six or seven Saturday morning, and catch the last flight out on Sunday night. I can remember a time or two when I got back to Los Angeles at two or three in the morning on Monday; I'd go right to the studio, stagger into my dressing room and catch a few hours' sleep on the couch. From there, I headed right into makeup.

I certainly wasn't the only one on the *Star Trek* set with a grueling schedule. Gene Roddenberry worked best in the dark. He'd be on the set all day, dealing with different problems, then after hours, under tremendous pressure, he'd write or rewrite a script from midnight to 5:30 A.M. Very often, we'd show up at the studio in the morning and find a rewrite of a scene we had to shoot that day; it'd be vastly improved because Gene had stayed up all night rewriting it. Then he'd head home and sleep until 11 A.M., and be back at the studio by lunchtime.

The long hours took a toll on us all. I became very concerned about my energy level; to this day, I make it a practice to keep a jar of honey in my dressing room or trailer. On the *Star Trek* set, I'd take copious swigs of honey around three or four in the afternoon in order to keep going. I also learned to eat very light lunches so that I wouldn't become drowsy; in order to succeed at the very fast, very concentrated sort of work required by the series, I had to be disciplined to be at my best.

Of course, not everyone on the set learned to avoid the heavy lunches. On one hot August afternoon, Bill and I were involved in a scene which called for a fight with a few "bad guys," then a dialog between Kirk and Spock. We carefully rehearsed the fight and learned our dialog, so when the time came to roll the cameras, everything went perfectly: Kirk and Spock dispatched the heavies with ease, then segued into the dialog.

Well, *almost* perfectly. As Bill and I exchanged lines, I became aware of a strange rumbling sound nearby. I couldn't figure out exactly what it was or where it was coming from, but from the odd gleam in Bill's eye, I could tell he heard it, too.

But the cameras were still rolling, so we continued bravely on; it wasn't until the very end of the scene that I suddenly realized what had happened. It seemed that one of the stuntmen involved in the fight had dropped "unconscious" to the floor—then relaxed, knowing that his work in the scene was done, and proceeded to fall fast asleep. That strange rumble was the sound of his loud snoring!

There was also a different kind of toll taken by my remaining "in character" as Spock on the set. Of course, I'd laugh a lot with Bill in the mornings, and quite a few times on the set; clowning around is a natural way to ease tension and exhaustion. But sometimes, when things started to get really funny, I'd walk away from the laughter for fear I'd have trouble staying in character. I kept in "Spock mode" even off-camera, because I believe that I can do better work if I make on- and off-stage time one seamless experience; that way, if I'm already Spock by the time the cameras start rolling, I won't find myself fumbling into the character in mid-scene.

So the more consistently I stayed in character as Spock, the more consistent my performance became. However, residing for so long inside the Vulcan's psyche had some definite side effects on Nimoy the human. The character that I developed soon took on a life of his own and began affecting *me*, rather than the reverse! Dwelling inside Spock's head became a pressure cooker; repressing one's emotions, after all, is an unnatural condition. Ted Sturgeon, who wrote "Amok Time," was right—something eventually has to give!

In my case, I found that I soon became prone to occasional eruptions of emotion. Sometimes, I'd sense them coming and would go hide in a private place until the storm blew past. Once, one came over me while I was discussing a script with Roddenberry in his office.

I remember saying to him: "Okay, Gene, here on page fifty-two, Spock is involved in a fight, but I think he would find a way to avoid violence . . . "

And Gene, clad in his typical cardigan and rumpled slacks and frowning down at his own copy of the script, answered, "Come on, Leonard—we need some action there. Spock realizes that, in the interests of time, violence is necessary in this case . . . "

"Well, if you think about it, Gene, there might actually be a more interesting way to further the action *without* a fistfight . . . "

"Leonard, I agree with you in theory, but there isn't any time! I've got the studio breathing down my neck as it is. I've got exactly two days to finish the *next* script!"

"It doesn't have to take a huge overhaul. But Spock wouldn't engage in such violence without a much stronger motivation. I'm sure you could—"

"Leonard, for Chrissake, I *told* you—"

"Gene, calm down. I'm not trying to be difficult. I'm just asking—"

Well, you get the idea. Gene frosted up, I tensed, words were exchanged.

And, very shortly, I was overwhelmed by a sense of frustration that went far beyond this particular script or issue. Exhaustion and stress and the hours I'd spent inside the Vulcan's skin finally got to me—and I found myself struggling to hold back tears as a powerful surge of emotion swept over me.

My "Vulcan training" permitted me to maintain some degree of control. I stood up, and said hoarsely, "I'm sorry, Gene, but I have to leave."

I could see, from the faintly amazed expression on his face that he saw I was on the verge of weeping. To save us both the embarrassment, I hurried out of there and headed straight for my dressing room, where I remained until the storm had blown over.

Spock even intruded on my personal life; it took me most of the weekend to unwind and "de-Vulcanize" myself to the point that I could express emotion easily. By that time, it was almost Monday morning.

WIFE: Sweetheart, what would you like to do this
            weekend?
HUSBAND: Something restful. Other than that, I have no
            preference.
WIFE: Why don't we go to the movies?
HUSBAND: That would be fine. What do you want to see?
WIFE: Well, there's not really anything playing that I'm
            interested in . . .

HUSBAND: Then it's illogical to go. We should seek an alter-
native.
WIFE: Leonard . . . you're doing it again!
HUSBAND: Doing what?
WIFE: Sounding just like Spock!

"The Naked Time" was the seventh episode we filmed, some four
or five weeks after Spock's "birth" in "Corbomite." But I'm including
it here because it was a defining episode for the Vulcan, one that

With Majel Barrett in "The Naked Time"

cemented in my mind—and the viewers'—exactly who Spock was. In a sense, it completed the transformation that had begun with the phrase, "Fascinating . . . "

"The Naked Time" also marked my first big run-in with a writer over the portrayal of Spock.

The episode was written by our line producer, John D.F. Black, who had come up with a very intriguing concept that allowed the characters' inner lives to develop and really come alive for the viewing audience. Anyone familiar with the series will probably recall this episode, as it is still a favorite of the show's fans. The concept was this: The *Enterprise* crew members were infected with a virus that removed their inhibitions and caused their "hidden selves" to emerge. For example, Sulu was swashbuckling about the ship with a sword (and, as we all discovered, George Takei *really did* harbor a secret desire to be Errol Flynn, as we couldn't get him to knock it off after the cameras stopped rolling).

It was a great idea. But in my case John's original draft focused strictly on the humorous, the frivolous. It called for Spock to step from the turbolift into a corridor, where he is accosted by a crewman who runs up and paints a moustache on the Vulcan. Spock then bursts into tears as he staggers down the corridor.

It was a funny scene, theatrical and inventive. But it disturbed me greatly; by this time, I had come to know Spock well enough to know that dignity was an essential part of the Vulcan's personality. The paintbrush incident seemed to me a pointless exercise in stripping that dignity from him—and it also contradicted everything I knew about him. From my own experience, I was certain that Spock would never permit himself to dissolve into tears in front of that crewman; he would maintain control at all costs, and not let down his barriers until he had found a private place.

I relayed the above concerns to John, and asked him to rewrite the scene so that Spock struggles against the virus's effects, then hurries to an empty room where he fights to regain control of himself.

Now, you must understand that writer/producers on a television series have an extremely tough job; to indulge in a metaphor, they're always chasing the rabbit, but are never allowed to catch it. No sooner have they pulled the last page of a script out of the typewriter than someone comes up to them and says, "Here's a problem with the second act; this script is going to need a total rewrite." Of course, they're supposed to be working on the *next* script, without a chance to pause and catch their breath, so they don't appreciate it when the actors won't let them get their work done.

"No way," John told me flatly. "There isn't *time*, Leonard. Just play the scene the way it's written."

But the Vulcan was looking over my shoulder by then; and I was stubborn about not letting his dignity be torn away just for the sake of a brief moment of humor. And equally important, I felt we might miss an opportunity for something deeper.

So I went to Gene Roddenberry. Gene listened very thoughtfully, then said, "You're right. It really is out of character for Spock. Don't worry, I'll take care of it."

I went back to work on the set, and an hour or so later, John Black came over to me and, with a slightly grudging look on his face said, "Okay. Tell me what you have in mind."

"It's about emotion versus logic," I told him. "Love versus mathematics, grief versus pi-r-squared."

Based on that bit of information, John went back and wrote the marvelous scene for Spock that now appears in "The Naked Time." After becoming infected, the Vulcan seeks out a private place in which to ride out his emotional storm; while there, he chants multiplication tables in an effort to regain control. But it's useless. Just as he chides himself, "I am a Vulcan! I am in control of my emotions! Control of my emotions . . . " he finally breaks down, and we learn the source of his grief: He could never bring himself to tell his human mother he loved her. I'm sorry for any frustration the rewrite caused John, but I'm very grateful for the result, because that scene really showed our viewing audience the internal conflict that drove the Vulcan.

The director, Marc Daniels, did a beautiful job of choreographing the very delicate camera dance for this scene. As I stepped into the "conference room" and sat down at the table, the camera did a pas de deux, circling around to my other side.

It was a very unusual technique for a television show, because it was difficult and time-consuming; it would have been a lot easier to shoot in one direction only, because the lighting would have been much simpler. But Marc made a commitment to doing the scene in this more challenging—and artistic—manner.

And while I was in the makeup department being touched up, the set was painstakingly lit. By the time everything was ready and I walked back onto the set, we discovered to our dismay that we only had *minutes* in which to film the scene.

Let me explain something: Like most television series, we had an extremely restricted overtime budget. In other words, we weren't *allowed* overtime. Come 6:18 P.M., we had to pull the plug and get off the set, whether the scene was filmed or not—and tomorrow's schedule didn't allow for us to come back and finish it!

To emphasize that fact, Roddenberry and two or three production assistants wandered out onto the set—letting us know by their silent, ominous presences that they were watching the clock.

We had *just* enough time for *one* take—so it had to go perfectly!

Recalling that moment brings to mind a conversation I had with astronaut Alan Shepard. He told me that, when he was in the lunar landing module, there were some mechanical difficulties, and he had mere seconds to decide whether to make the landing on the moon, or to abort. The signals weren't good, and everyone at NASA was standing by—rather like our esteemed producers—ready to pull the switch and call the whole mission off.

Shepard went ahead and made the landing . . . and somehow, so did we. The clock ticked and the cameras rolled, and through some miracle or magic, the scene went as planned. We got a lovely take the first time out, and at precisely 6:18 P.M., we wrapped.

The episode had an enormous effect on the show's popularity—and on Spock's. The week after the first episode aired, I received less than a dozen fan letters; after the second, perhaps forty or fifty. But once "The Naked Time" aired, the fan mail started arriving in large laundry bags, each containing hundreds of letters.

The Vulcan was alive and kicking; but (if you'll pardon the expression) the most fascinating period of his growth was yet to come.

FOUR

VULCANALIA

or

The Vulcan

Grows Up

SPOCK: *A question.*

NIMOY: Yes, Spock?

SPOCK: *This process . . . This recitation of dialog, display of emotion, being recorded by a camera is your chosen profession?*

NIMOY: Yes. Profession, obsession . . .

SPOCK: *And who will be responsible for the choices made? For example, what shall we put on public display? Character delineation, and so forth?*

NIMOY: It's a process, Spock. Writers, producers, directors and actors all participate. In any case, I'll take a firm hand.

SPOCK: *I certainly hope so.*

A N INTERESTING SHIFT IN NBC's attitude toward *Star Trek*'s resident alien took place after "The Naked Time." Once word filtered through to network executives about Spock's popularity with the viewing audience, they said to Roddenberry, "Say! Why aren't you doing more with that Martian on the show?"

Naturally, Gene was all too happy to oblige. As the first season progressed, the episodes began to reveal more about the mysterious Vulcan's background, and to feature certain of his native skills and traditions.

In preparing to play the character, I had already done some thinking about Vulcan culture and customs, and had made a decision that the Vulcans were a touch-oriented society, that the fingers and hands featured prominently, as they were touch telepaths.

Based on that concept, the Vulcan neck pinch was created. It came about during the shooting of "The Enemy Within," an episode wherein Captain Kirk was confronted by the "evil" half of his personality—his own "Mr. Hyde," if you will. In one particular scene, this "evil" character had confronted the "good" Kirk and was about to destroy him with a phaser blast. The original script called for Spock to steal up behind the "bad" Kirk and strike him over the head with the butt of a phaser.

The scene jarred me when I first read it; it seemed more appropriate for the Old West than the twenty-third century. I could practically hear the Vulcan whispering in my ear:

SPOCK: Barbaric. A Vulcan would avoid unnecessary violence
at all costs. We have, after all, made a thorough study
of the human anatomy, and utilize more scientific
methods, which render the use of force obsolete.

In keeping with the Vulcan emphasis on touch, I spoke to the director, Leo Penn, about my concern. Leo agreed it was valid, and asked what alternatives I might suggest. After explaining the business about Vulcans and how they no doubt were thoroughly familiar with the anatomy of recalcitrant humans, I suggested that they were capable of transmitting a special energy from their fingertips. If applied to the proper nerve centers on a human's neck and shoulder, that energy would render the human unconscious.

Leo asked for a demonstration; since Bill Shatner was the other actor in the scene with me, he was the most available victim. I quietly briefed Bill on what I had in mind, then the two of us made our little presentation for the director. I applied pressure to the juncture of Bill's neck and shoulder, and he most convincingly and cooperatively fell into an "unconscious" heap on the floor. Thus the famous neck pinch was born, in part because of Bill Shatner's talent for fainting on cue.

Even more intriguing than the Vulcan neck pinch was the mind meld, a Gene Roddenberry invention. It debuted in "Dagger of the Mind," in which an apparently insane escapee from a penal colony demands asylum on the Enterprise. The madman, Van Gelder (played by Morgan Woodward), incoherently accuses his captors of sadism; in order to get at the truth hidden beneath the man's tormented thoughts, Spock performs the Vulcan mind meld, joining his consciousness to the human's.

Originally, this was a dull, expository scene in which Van Gelder was interrogated at length in sickbay. In order to make it more dramatic, Gene came up with the Vulcan mind meld—which, in that episode, was portrayed as a very dangerous, risky thing. In fact, Spock reassures McCoy that no harm will come to the doctor— although he states clearly that his own mind is at grave risk. If you watch the episode, you'll see that it also gave me an opportunity to emphasize the importance of touch to Vulcans; Spock uses his fingers and hands to "probe" Van Gelder's face and skull. It was a far more dramatic way to extract information than a lot of questions, and it became a popular device for the show's writers. (However, the more Spock utilized the mind meld, the less dangerous it

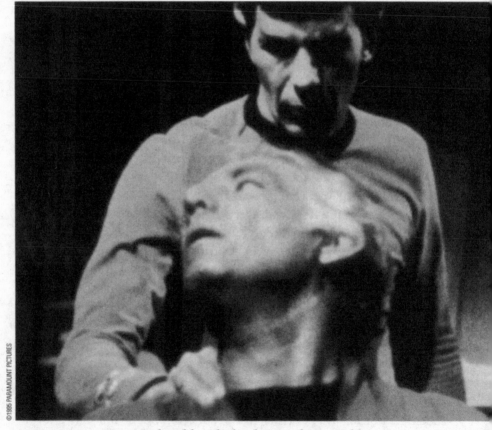

Pre-mind meld with the deranged Van Gelder
(Morgan Woodward) in "Dagger of the Mind"

seemed to become; after a while, the idea that it was extraordinarily risky faded.) I applauded the concept, not only for its drama but because it gave me an opportunity to step outside the character from time to time.

But my favorite use of the mind meld occurred not in "Dagger of the Mind," but in "Devil in the Dark," filmed several months later. In fact, "Devil in the Dark" would definitely be among my favorites, along with others such as "Amok Time," "City on the Edge of Forever," "Journey to Babel," "Naked Time," and "This Side of Paradise."

Why? Not because it featured Spock or provided a unique opportunity for me as an actor—both of which it did—nor because it gave me my first and only opportunity thus far to play a scene with a rock. The episode remains one of my favorites because of its theme. The story deals with the *Enterprise* coming to the rescue of a crew of human miners, who are being attacked and killed by a creature that burrows through rock. The miners all want to destroy the creature (which we later learn is a Horta). Kirk and Spock track the Horta down, and Spock mind-melds with it, only to discover that *it* is a *she*—a mother protecting her eggs from the miners, who are ignorantly destroying the strange "rocks." Ultimately, Kirk explains the situation to the miners, who then form a happy partnership with the Horta—she and her children are protected from harm, and in turn use their natural rock-dissolving ability to assist the miners.

The theme is a powerful one, dealing with racism and intercultural conflict—the fear of the person or thing that we don't know and don't understand. "The Devil in the Dark" illustrates beautifully how unreasoning fear begets violence—and how an attempt at understanding can benefit both sides in a conflict. (Would that it could be accomplished so readily in real life!)

The episode was also significant in terms of the Vulcan's development because it allowed us, through the mind meld, to glimpse a little deeper into his psyche. It also showed a far more pacifistic character than the Spock in "Where No Man," who coldly urges the captain to kill Gary Mitchell. By the time of "Devil," it is established that Vulcans revere all life-forms, and are willing to go to almost any lengths to avoid violence toward them.

We shot the episode in January 1967. I remember it very well, because one afternoon, while we were shooting a scene in which Kirk had a lot of dialog, Bill Shatner got a phone call on the set. Sadly, his father had just passed away in Florida. The producers told him to go ahead and leave, that they were making immediate arrangements to get him on a plane—but Bill just shook his head and gritted his teeth and said, "No, we're right in the middle of a scene, and I'm going to finish it before I walk off the set."

De Kelley and I both said, "It's okay. Just leave, Bill. Just go . . ." But Bill's a scrapper. He was determined not to walk away from the challenge.

And he did finish the scene, though the tension on the set was almost unbearable as we all helplessly watched him struggle to get it done. It was a tough, emotional afternoon; there was really nothing we could do for him except remain close by.

©1995 PARAMOUNT PICTURES

Finally, Bill finished the scene and left, then we went on to shoot the scene where Spock approaches the Horta in order to make mental contact with it. Kirk is supposed to be standing and watching during this time. We wound up filming across the back of Bill's double, so that we got the wide master shot across the double's back, then the shot of me with the Horta. Later, when Bill returned, we got some close-ups of Kirk from the front.

For those of you who enjoy *Star Trek* trivia, there's an interesting inconsistency in the episode. If you carefully watch the mind-meld scene in "Devil," you'll notice that when the camera's looking at Kirk's back, he's holding the phaser down at his side. But when the shot shows Bill from the front, Kirk has the phaser lifted and aimed at the Horta.

When Bill returned from Florida a few days later, De Kelley and I reenacted scenes in order to show him what we'd done, so he would know how to react in the close-ups. I explained to him the mind-meld scene with the Horta, about how I had touched the creature, then cried out, "Pain . . . "

Now, despite the personal tragedy Bill had just endured, his devilish sense of humor was still entirely intact. He folded his arms and said thoughtfully, "So tell me again what I'm reacting to. What *exactly* did you do?"

"Well," I said, "I cried out," (and here I gave a faint imitation of the actual performance) "Pain! Pain . . . "

"Hmm," Bill mused, and adopting a serious "ever the professional" expression, added, "Well, I'd like to see you do it full out, exactly the way you did it when I wasn't here."

Bill, De, me . . . and a rock ("Devil in the Dark")

So I obediently crouched down, closed my eyes, and grasped an imaginary Horta. "Pain!" I shouted, then drew a breath, filled my lungs to their utmost capacity, and screamed out full volume: "PAIN . . . !"

On the set, heads turned, eyes widened in surprise. And Bill, his own eyes filled with a wicked gleam, yelled, *"Jesus!* Will somebody get this poor guy an aspirin?"

Interestingly, the episode shot just before "Devil in the Dark" was one that I was absolutely terrified of doing.

It was originally entitled "The Way of the Spores," by Nathan Butler (a pseudonym of Jerry Sohl), and it featured a romance between Mr. Sulu and a Hawaiian girl, Leila Kalomi. However, Gene Roddenberry felt that the script wasn't working, so he turned it over to his then-secretary, Dorothy (D.C.) Fontana, who had already sold scripts to other television series.

In fact, in 1960, Dorothy had written the episode "A Bounty for Billy" for the television series *The Tall Man*, starring Barry Sullivan—an episode I just happened to appear in. I remember getting a wonderful note from her saying how pleased she was with my performance; I was impressed by her kindness. Dorothy is a very talented, solid individual for whom I have the utmost respect.

But that day in 1967, when she came onto the *Star Trek* soundstage and told me, "Hey, I have an idea for a Spock love story," I was taken aback. Worse than taken aback—I was frightened.

"Look," I told her, "it makes me nervous to hear you even talk about such a thing. I feel I've finally gotten a good grip on the character, and I don't want to lose what we have." The Vulcan was firmly established in my mind—and the audience's—as a cool, distant character, and the very phrase "Spock love story" seemed oxymoronic.

"Trust me," Dorothy said. "There's a way to pull it off properly . . . " And she began to explain the story to me. It seemed that, some time ago, during a brief stay on Earth, Spock had met a woman named Leila, who fell hopelessly in love with him. Now, six years later, they meet again on a planet where native "spores" infect the population; the "symptoms" include the loss of inhibitions and a deep sense of belonging and love . . .

I'm reminded here of a May 1966 memo from Gene Roddenberry about Spock, which said in part:

> Spock's "hypnotic" look strongly affects Earth females and he goes to great pains to avoid too much contact with them. There is a back story on this—many years ago when Mr. Spock first joined the service, he was careless on this score, perhaps even enjoyed this strange ability over Earth women. But it quickly created both personal and professional troubles.

One of which, no doubt, was named Leila Kalomi.

I admit I was intrigued, but still very unnerved by the whole idea. Even after we began shooting the episode—now renamed

"This Side of Paradise"—I found it both scary and liberating to emote as Spock. How would fans react to seeing the cool, rational Vulcan literally swinging from the trees? (However, despite my trepidation, I had to admit that shooting the episode was great fun. Not only did I hang upside-down from tree limbs, I got to smart-mouth my commanding officer and refuse a direct order!)

As it was finally written, "Paradise" not only had Spock kissing a woman—but hinted at much more. (After the first kiss, Spock appears in the next scene wearing civilian clothing, which leads one to wonder what transpired during the commercial break.)

Jill Ireland, a lovely lady, was cast as Leila Kalomi (the vaguely

©1995 PARAMOUNT PICTURES

The Vulcan in love: a spore-smitten Spock with Leila Kalomi (Jill Ireland) and Sulu (George Takei) in "This Side of Paradise"

Hawaiian-sounding name remained, even though the actress was fair-haired and blue-eyed). She was married to Charles Bronson—known even then for his tough-guy roles, before the advent of the *Death Wish* films. The two of them were very much in love, and Charlie was understandably possessive of his beautiful wife—to the degree that he was on the set for Jill's every scene. Now, consider that I was already nervous about the effect this episode might have on the character of Spock—and on top of that, I had to repeatedly kiss Charlie Bronson's wife while he stood by watching!

Fortunately, Dorothy Fontana was right—the Spock love story *could* be pulled off, and quite well; all my trepidation was completely unfounded. To this day, "This Side of Paradise" is numbered among *Star Trek* fans' all-time favorite episodes, perhaps because, like "The Naked Time," it gives another glimpse into the Vulcan's hidden side.

Possibly the single *Star Trek* episode with the most resonance today, "Amok Time" certainly was *the* quintessential "Vulcan" show. Written by science fiction great Theodore Sturgeon, "Amok Time" gave us our first glimpse of Spock's home planet (courtesy of an inexpensive papier-mâché set on the soundstage, outfitted with a large gong) and of other Vulcans. Sturgeon's beautiful script was loaded with Vulcanalia.

The story—a bold one by 1960s standards—dealt with the Vulcan seven-year mating cycle. When Spock begins behaving oddly, Captain Kirk intervenes and learns that his first officer must return to Vulcan for a mating ritual (the *koon-ut-kal-if-fee*), or die. Kirk puts his career on the line to get Spock back to his home planet, and ultimately winds up having to fight his friend to the "death."

Here's another pertinent quote from that same Roddenberry memo of May 1966:

> [Emotional repression on Vulcan] probably led to a need for hypnosis as a part of the sex act, and we may gather from time to time that love on Spock's planet has a somewhat more violent quality than Earth's aesthetics permit mankind to enjoy. (Unless NBC changes its policies somewhat, we probably will not do a script directly dealing with this subject.)

Fortunately, "Amok Time" made it past the network censors, while still hinting that Vulcan sexuality was, like Vulcan's past, tinged with violence and anger.

•

The director was Joe Pevney, who came from a theatrical background back East. He'd actually acted himself in some early black-and-white Warner Brothers films, and had played John Garfield's pal in *Body and Soul*. Joe directed many *Star Trek* episodes, including "Friday's Child," "The Deadly Years," and "The Trouble with Tribbles" (which I, no doubt because of Spock's influence, never really appreciated at the time because it seemed "frivolous"). Joe did a wonderful job of directing the episode and in staging the *koon-ut-kal-if-fee* ritual and the fight between Spock and Kirk.

A great deal of the power and dignity in "Amok Time" springs from the marvelous performance given by Celia Lovsky as the Vulcan matriarch, T'Pau. As a result of his theatrical background, Joe had previously worked with Celia (who was married to the character actor Peter Lorre) and decided she would be perfect for the part. He was right. In fact, many years later, when we were casting for the movie *Star Trek III: The Search for Spock*, I wanted an actress capable of bringing the same proud dignity to the role of the High Priestess as Celia had brought to T'Pau. Sadly, she had passed away by that time; but fortunately, we were lucky enough to get Dame Judith Anderson, who brought the same regal magnificence to the screen.

The words "Live long and prosper" were written by Ted Sturgeon, a wonderful dramatist with the heart of a poet. His exceptional dialog included such powerful exchanges as:

T'PAU: Live long and prosper, Spock.
SPOCK: I shall do neither. I have killed my captain and my friend.

It was a beautiful script.

The now-famous Vulcan greeting was first spoken by Spock, as he approaches T'Pau at the beginning of the mating ritual. At that point, I decided to take advantage of the opportunity to add something special to Vulcan lore; since hands and the sense of touch were important to the culture, some sort of nonverbal greeting using the hands made sense.

For what would soon become known as the Vulcan salute, I borrowed a hand symbol from Orthodox Judaism. During the High

Holiday services, the *Kohanim* (who are the priests) bless those in attendance. As they do, they extend the palms of both hands over the congregation, with thumbs outstretched and the middle and ring fingers parted so that each hand forms two vees. This gesture symbolizes the Hebrew letter *shin*, the first let-ter in the word *Shaddai*, "Lord"; in the Jewish *Qabala, shin* also represents eternal Spirit.

©1995 PARAMOUNT PICTURES

The ritual made an extraordinary impres-sion on me when, as a young boy, I attended those services with my family in an orthodox synagogue. The women sat separately in the balcony, and I sat near the front with my father, grandfather, and older brother, Melvin. The special moment when the *Kohanim* blessed the assembly moved me deeply, for it possessed a great sense of magic and theatri-cality. In Hebrew, they would chant:

"May the Lord bless you and keep you. May the Lord turn His face upon you, and give you peace . . . "

In approximate unison, their voices rose and fell in loud, piercing shouts—fervent, impassioned, ecstatic.

"Don't look," my father whispered. "Close your eyes. You mustn't look."

Being a child, I of course asked, "Why?"

"Because this is the moment that the *Shekhinah*—the holy essence of God—enters the sanctuary."

I had heard that this indwelling Spirit of God was too powerful, too beautiful, too awesome for any mortal to look upon and survive, and so I obediently covered my face with my hands.

But of course, I had to peek.

And I saw the priests enrapt in religious ecstasy, their heads and faces hidden by their shawls, spreading their arms out over the congregation. As they invoked the essence of God, their hands were fixed in representations of the letter *shin*.

•

So it was that, when I searched my imagination for an appropriate gesture to represent the peace-loving Vulcans, the *Kohanim*'s symbol of blessing came to mind.

T'Pau, of course, was supposed to return the greeting to Spock, but Celia Lovsky had a terrible time trying to get her hand in the right position. She finally wound up having to hide her hands and *hold* one in the proper position until the time came to raise it and perform the salute, and the cameraman had to work fast to get a shot of it before her uncooperative fingers went their own ways again.

The notion of the Vulcan hand-oriented society is also shown earlier in the episode, when Spock is under the powerful physical sway of *pon farr*, but still resolutely struggling to control the symptoms. I decided that the stress should be localized in his hands; therefore, Spock often clasps them behind his back, in an effort to control their trembling.

Interestingly, the Vulcan himself intruded on my consciousness over this episode. When I first read through the script for "Amok Time," I was thrilled by it—but I did have some strong reservations about the end-

Live long and prosper: with the regal T'Pau (Celia Lovsky) in "Amok Time"

ing, where Spock breaks into a big grin at the sight of Kirk, whom he'd thought dead (killed, in fact, by the Vulcan himself). At least, I *thought* I was the one with the reservations. Here's part of a May 1967 memo I sent to Gene Roddenberry about the episode:

> Beginning on page 64, approaching the tag of the show, I feel that we may be cheating ourselves of a more powerful payoff to what has been essentially a very strong script. A suggestion would be that because of the nature of Spock's emotional experience with Kirk in the sick bay, that perhaps the two of them be in there alone. *I feel uneasy about Spock showing that emotion over Kirk's supposed death in the presence of McCoy and Christine* [emphasis added]. I think that Spock would go off and do that by himself. But, since he believes Kirk to be dead I think we have an opportunity for him to express that emotion in the presence of the supposedly dead Kirk.

As you probably know, the scene went on to be shot the way it had originally been written, with McCoy and Nurse Chapel privy to Spock's emotional outburst. And I'm glad it was; every time I've been at a *Star Trek* convention where that scene has been shown, the audience goes wild. They especially love it when the Vulcan stiffly explains to Dr. McCoy that he was merely expressing "quite logical relief that Starfleet has not lost one of its finest officers."

It took me a while to figure out *who* really had the objection to the scene. The Vulcan was looking over my shoulder again, and even had me unwittingly speak out on his behalf. *Spock* didn't want McCoy in that emotional scene, because he knew the doctor would make him pay for it later!

SPOCK: *Preposterous. As I explained to McCoy, my reaction was merely one of quite logical relief. I have no need to resort to subterfuge—which is, to Vulcans, tantamount to lying. And as you well know—*

NIMOY: (wearily) Yes, Spock: You're incapable of lying. But as you well know, you're quite capable of "exaggeration." Can subterfuge be far behind?

SPOCK: *(stony silence)*

Perhaps the second most "Vulcan" of the *Star Trek* episodes is "Journey to Babel," in which Mr. Spock's parents appear, and the eighteen-year conflict between him and his father, Sarek, is delineated and resolved. "Babel" was written by Dorothy Fontana, who deserves as much credit as anyone for her wonderful additions to "Vulcanalia." (In addition to "Babel" and "This Side of Paradise," Dorothy penned the script for "The *Enterprise* Incident," in which Spock encounters an amorous Romulan commander.)

Spock's father Sarek was portrayed by Mark Lenard, who had earlier played a Romulan on the series (in fact, that job was one of his very first in Hollywood—and apparently he gave such a fine performance that the next time the producers needed someone for another pointy-eared role, they said, "Say . . . remember that guy who played the Romulan in "Balance of Terror"?). The great dignity that he brought to the role of Sarek earned him a permanent place in the hearts of *Star Trek* fans. Jane Wyatt, whose career goes back to the film *Lost Horizon*, was also marvelous as Spock's human mother, Amanda; both she and Mark are wonderful people and sensitive actors who have made major contributions to *Star Trek*. (I'm sure that Spock will forgive her someday for revealing a terrible family secret to an overflowing crowd at a huge New York *Star Trek* convention. When pressed by the audience to reveal Spock's first name—after all, who would know better than his mother?—Jane smilingly replied: "Harold.")

Although Mark had already appeared in the series, I didn't actually have a chance to meet him and work with him until we shared a scene in "Babel." The first time we three appeared together was the moment Sarek and Amanda arrive on the *Enterprise* and greet the captain. Mark was very curious about Vulcans and wanted to know as much as he could about them, so we discussed this at length on the set.

"I have this notion that Vulcan society emphasizes tactile contact," I told him, "and I'm always on the lookout for opportunities to use the hands and fingers, as a symbol, a benchmark of the race." I talked about the Vulcan mind meld, and demonstrated the salute—which, fortunately, came easily to Mark. (Not everyone is so talented, as De Kelley—who, as Dr. McCoy, said of the salute: "That hurts worse than the [dress] uniform!"—can testify. Bill Shatner can't do it either; obviously, it's something only true Vulcans do well.)

The question came up as to what public sign of affection, if any,

.

Sarek and his human wife would display. Handholding was clearly out, but perhaps finger-to-finger contact of a ceremonial, dignified nature might work . . .

Mark and Jane took my comments to heart, and came up with the wonderful gesture where Amanda rests her first two fingers lightly upon Sarek's two fingers. It worked beautifully, and added to the texture of one of the series' best episodes.

Since this chapter deals with "Vulcanalia," I feel it's only fitting to include a couple of interoffice memos to Gene from our hard-working associate producer, Bob Justman, and production executive, Herb Solow, concerning things Vulcan. These illustrate the lengths to which our dedicated producers were willing to go in order to flesh out the show's more technical aspects—in this case, the concept of Vulcan proper names.

To: Gene Roddenberry   Date: May 3, 1966
From: Bob Justman   Subject: Star Trek Planet Vulcan
                                       Proper Names

Dear Gene:

I would like to suggest that all proper names for citizens of Mr. Spock's Planet Vulcan follow a set routine.

To wit: all names begin with the letters "SP" and end with the letter "K." All names to have a total of five letters in them—no more and no less.

Therefore: Mr. Spock aptly fits this pattern. Other names would be as follows:

Spook	Spurk	Spenk	Spakk
Spuck	Sponk	Spawk	Spekk
Spack	Spilk	Spauk	Spikk
Speek	Spalk	Speuk	Spokk
Spouk	Spelk	Spuik	Spukk
Spaak	Spolk	Spouk	Spark
Spilk	Spulk	Splak	Sperk
Spiak	Spirk	Splek	Spirk
Spunk	Spark	Splik	Spork
Spank	Spork	Splok	Spurk
Spink	Sperk	Spluk	Spxyx

Hope that the suggestions are of immense help to you. I remain,

                        Your humble and obedient servant,
                                Robert H. Justman

To: Gene Roddenberry   Date: May 5, 1966
From: Herb Solow   Subject: Planet Vulcan Proper Names

Dear Gene:

In an industry that is founded on the uncontrollable appetite for creativity, it is indeed heartwarming for the management of a major studio to receive a copy of a memo that deals with such an intensely competitive and accurate discussion of proper names on the planet Vulcan.

However, with time being of the essence, with our schedule calling for production of our series to commence in three very short weeks, I feel enough time—rather more than enough time—has been spent devising names for Mr. Spock's relatives. With a deep respect for creativity, I feel we should go on to something of greater importance.

H.F.S.

P.S. Have you thought of the name Spiik? Or Sprik? Or Sprak? Or Sprok? Or Spruk? Or Spudk? Or Spidk? Or Spuck? Or Spisk? Or Spask? Or Spesk? Or Spask? Or any of the other seventy-eight I have already devised?

P.P.S. Please refer to Mr. Justman's May 3 memo and you will find that the fifth name in column one is the same as the sixth name in column three. I understand that you science fiction people with your technical jargon have a word to describe this happening. It is known as a "mistake."

P.P.P.S. What do you say if all the people on the planet Vulcan are lawyers (interesting idea) and they all have a firm name like Spook, Speek, Spork, Splik, and Roddenberry? (The last name is necessary to keep the audience aware at all times that this relates to science fiction.)

P.P.P.P.S. Also note that in the May 3 memo the eighth name in column two is the same as the eighth name in column four. Also the tenth name in column two is the same as the ninth name in column four. There are probably others, but my time is too valuable to waste it pointing out that the seventh name in column one is the same name as the third name in column two.

Amusingly, the "S——k" pattern for male Vulcan names *did* become part of *Star Trek* canon—Spock's father's name was Sarek, and the founder of Vulcan pacifism was called Surak—so Justman's humorous memo had more influence than he probably anticipated. (Vulcan females tended to have names that began with "T'P," perhaps in honor of that grand matriarch, T'Pau.) Of course, the rules for Vulcan male names were loosened a bit to allow any name beginning with the letter "S"—after all, as Justman and Solow no doubt realized, there are a lot more Vulcans than there are S—−−k combinations.

(Speaking of *Star Trek* appellations: I've always been struck by the fact that Roddenberry christened his characters with names that tended to feature the "k" sound. Compare, if you will, Kirk, Pike, Spock, Scott, McCoy, Sarek, Picard . . . All very tough, short, strong-sounding names, and certainly very different from Roddenberry. If one wanted to get psychoanalytic about it, a case could be made that these officers were part of Gene's fantasy life, representing the "tough leader" he always wanted to be.)

Bob Justman and Herb Solow were only two behind-the-scenes members of the large *Star Trek* family. And, like every family, ours had its good moments and bad, its squabbles and disagreements.

But that's another chapter . . .

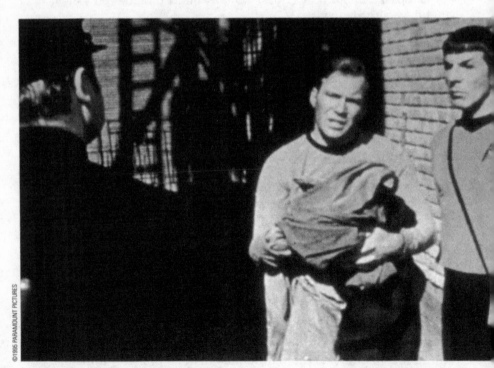

©1995 PARAMOUNT PICTURES

"My friend got his ears caught in a . . . er . . . automatic ricepicker . . ." Kirk and Spock face a 1930s policeman in "City on the Edge of Forever"

FIVE

SPOCKAMANIA

or

It's Pear Blossom

Time

in Medford

NIMOY: I was overwhelmed by all the attention. Overwhelmed, flattered, excited—and terrified.

SPOCK: *After a time, you may find that having a thing is not so pleasurable as wanting it. It is not logical, but it is often true.*

IN *I AM NOT SPOCK*, I had a brief conversation with the Vulcan on the subject of celebrity:

NIMOY: Spock . . . how does it feel to be popular?

SPOCK: *I do not have feelings.*

NIMOY: I'm sorry. I didn't mean to offend you.

SPOCK: *I am not offended. I understand your tendency to judge me by your human standards. It would however, facilitate matters if you would refrain from doing so.*

NIMOY: I'll try . . . Are you aware that you are popular?

SPOCK: *I am aware of a certain public interest that exists.*

NIMOY: People like you. Do you care about that?

SPOCK: *To be concerned one way or the other is a waste of energy. And popularity does put one in strange company.*

NIMOY: How do you mean?

SPOCK: *In your culture, popularity may be achieved by bizarre beings and in strange ways. One can achieve popularity by appearing nude in your magazines. Certain animals, dogs, mammals, etc., have become popular through weekly exposure in your television dramas. Would it not be better to honor real achievement?*

NIMOY: Can't popularity and achievement go together?

SPOCK: *Victor Hugo said, "Popularity? Why, it is the very crumbs of greatness."*

NIMOY: That sounds pompous.

SPOCK: *Possibly, but Mr. Hugo was only human.*

NIMOY: Let me put it this way, Spock: If you are popular among humans, doesn't that say something positive about the human ability to value a culture and a lifestyle alien to its own?

SPOCK: *That does seem logical.*

NIMOY: Coming from you, Mr. Spock, I consider that a great compliment!

Perhaps Spock was unfazed by celebrity, but I can hardly make the same claim. In fact, I was so concerned and affected by it that I found myself riffling through a *Bartlett's Quotations* in search of insight on the subject—and found the above-mentioned quote from Victor Hugo. That phrase became a touchstone for me, reminding me to stay focused on the work at hand rather than its side effects. Popularity was bound to fade, and what would be left behind would be the quality of the work (if it was there).

Now, normally in Hollywood, you can find instructors in every field imaginable. There are people who can teach you how to speak, how to sing, how to do accents. Want to play a hillbilly from West Virginia, even though you hail from the Bronx? No problem! Hire a dialect coach. Want to cut a record album, even though you've never sung outside the shower? Again, no problem; there are people who can teach you how to sing from pop to opera—and voice lessons are only the tip of the iceberg.

They can teach you horseback riding, archery, swimming, tennis, sailing, boxing. They can teach you how to take a punch, how to fall, how to laugh, how to cry. Did I mention fencing? That, too; if you're going to appear in a swashbuckler, you'll need to learn foil or saber. I have no doubt that as long as there have been actors, there have also been instructors to teach them the necessary skills.

But there are no classes in celebrity to help you cope with its impact on your life, and the lives of your co-workers, family, and friends. Frankly, I wish there *had* been such classes available back in 1967, because they might have kept me from making mistakes such as *I Am Not Spock*.

At a recent *Star Trek* convention, a teenage girl asked the question, "How did you prepare for what happened to you when you became famous?"

My answer? "I didn't."

In fact, when Gene Roddenberry called to let me know that *Star Trek* was going to become a regular series, I had no inkling of how it would change my life outside of getting a regular paycheck. As I mentioned earlier, I was so naive that I didn't even bother to change my phone number, which was listed in the directory. (I soon realized my folly and corrected that mistake!)

The first hint of the Vulcan's popularity came with the laundry bags full of mail after "The Naked Time" aired. I was both relieved

If this is Saturday, this must be . . . um . . .

and pleased to know that Spock had fans; after all, not so long ago, NBC had wanted to ditch the alien.

So while the fan mail kept mounting, I began to get calls from different organizations, all asking me to make public appearances. "Great!" I thought, and accepted every offer I could. One call came from Medford, Oregon, inviting me to be grand marshal of the annual Pear Blossom Festival Parade in April 1967.

Let me digress a moment here to mention an earlier experience I'd had on a parade route. Around Thanksgiving of 1966, very shortly after *Star Trek* went on the air, Bill Shatner and I were invited to participate in the "Santa Claus Lane" parade down Hollywood Boulevard. The parade features many film and television stars, usually riding in open convertibles.

Bill and I were happy to be invited and get the publicity, and we

Leonard Nimsy—er, Nimoy—promoting his record album, 1968

FROM THE COLLECTION OF LEONARD NIMOY

both enjoyed waving at the enthusiastic crowd, but as we neared the announcer's platform, he boomed: "And here come the stars of *Star Trek*, William Shatner and Leonard Nimsy!"

Nimsy?!

Bill turned to me at once and said with a grin, "You'll remember that as long as you live—and maybe you should."

Well, he was right; I *still* haven't forgotten it. And when I agreed to go to Medford, Oregon, I decided to go in costume as Mr. Spock, as the parade organizers requested.

I never made *that* mistake again.

The parade went smoothly enough. I was very grateful to see the huge turnout—the largest in the festival's history—and although it was rather strange to be in costume as Spock while smiling and waving as Leonard Nimoy in the back of a convertible, I enjoyed myself a great deal along the parade route.

The problem came after, when I was taken to a nearby park. A table was set up on the bandstand so that I could sign autographs. But instead of the hundreds I'd hoped to see, there were thousands of people there. They surged forward so quickly that I was terrified someone would be crushed to death; and then they started pressing against the bandstand so hard it began to sway beneath my feet! The people with me soon realized we were in trouble. Fortunately, the local police came to the rescue and pulled me through the throng!

The incident became a media event, and no one was more surprised than I. Later that afternoon, as I was contemplating what had happened in the relative safety of my hotel room, I got a phone call from the head of NBC's promotion department, who said, "From hereon out, we'll make sure you have security."

So, as I said, I made sure *never* to appear publicly again in Vulcan guise. But the crowds still kept coming.

Only a few years before my sudden encounter with fame, I had given private acting lessons to the teen idol Fabian (who was preparing for a role in a *Dr. Kildare* episode directed by Marc Daniels). I remember Fabian telling me about his first experience as an "object" of adoration. His promoters had made a big hulla-baloo about his coming to Los Angeles, so by the time his plane landed at the L.A. airport, the tarmac was filled with screaming kids. He'd been whisked into the waiting limo, but it was soon surrounded by hysterical fans. It was a hot summer's day; the windows steamed up so that the driver couldn't see to make the getaway, and the fans swarmed the car, rocking it and eventually breaking a window before their beloved idol, Fabian, finally escaped them.

He had been honestly terrified; but at the time, it was hard for me to entirely understand his fear. To be surrounded by screaming admirers sounded a little scary, sure, but it must also be a great ego boost.

At least, I thought so until it happened to me. I came to absolutely *hate* the phrase, "We've arranged security for you," because most times it meant trouble. In my experience, "arranged security" people usually sent out signals that they were *expecting* trouble—which of course alerted fans that something was going on. I became firmly convinced that a lot of the "crowd hysteria" was induced by the very people who were supposed to be protecting me from it: the security guards, who were understandably overwhelmed by adrenaline when surrounded by a screeching crowd.

Perhaps my most exciting "escape" occurred not long afterwards in a Long Island department store (Modell's Shoppers World, to be precise), where I was promoting an album I'd recorded for Dot Records entitled "Leonard Nimoy Presents Mr. Spock's Music from Outer Space."

I was signing autographs at a counter, closed in on either side by portable gates. At some point, the crowd started pushing so hard that the gates started to collapse. Unfortunately, the crowd was noisy, and out of control; I tried standing on a counter and talking to them to quiet them down, but there were just too many people. Finally, the manager grabbed my arm and said, "Let's get out of here!"

We pushed our way through the throng and started running. Fortunately, we made it up to the manager's office and locked the door behind us, thinking we were safe at last. But then we realized we had a *new* problem: we were now trapped in the office! There was no way out of the building except down and out through the crowd . . .

But the manager was a resourceful man, and said, "Wait a minute. We can't go *down* because of all the people. But we can go

The musician: "I don't know, but if you hum a few bars . . . "

up. There's a back stairway that leads to the roof . . ."

He placed a call to the fire department, who sent a hook-and-ladder truck to the back of the building (out of sight of the crowd). I went up to the roof, climbed down the provided fire ladder, and made good my escape!

During that same promotional tour, the crowd in another store got carried away; the security guards pushed me into the freight elevator, away from an overly enthusiastic mob. But the fans kept reaching for me, so the elevator doors wouldn't close.

There happened to be one elderly gentleman on this particular elevator, and as I lunged inside, gasping for breath, he gazed saucer-eyed at the shrieking horde behind me.

"What's going on?" he cried out. "Who are they after?" And he stared at me a minute, as though wondering what crime I had committed to provoke a mob to chase me, then lifted a gnarled finger and pointed it at me. "It's *you* . . . They're after *you!* Who *are* you?"

I smiled and said, "Would you believe Kirk Douglas?"

He scowled at me, then shook his head. "Noooooo," he replied, "Kirk Douglas, you *ain't.*"

Thinking about that particular tour for the record album reminds me of a promise I once made myself when I was around twelve years old. At the time, I was a great fan of Danny Kaye; I went to see him on stage in Boston, and waited outside the stage door with a group of other kids, hoping to get an autograph. We were there a very long time before Mr. Kaye finally emerged, escorted by two associates. "No autographs!" they told us, and waved us aside as they walked briskly past. But I was determined, and followed. By the time Mr. Kaye and his group got to their car, I was the only one left.

Once again, I asked for an autograph; but he never responded, never looked at me, only got in the car and rode away. Frustrated, I swore to myself that if I ever were in the same position, I'd *never* turn down anyone asking for an autograph.

I remembered that vow somewhat wryly during the record tour—especially at one appearance, where I wound up signing no fewer than eight thousand autographs in one sitting, from ten in the morning till six at night. (Even then, to my disappointment, I wasn't able to keep my promise to myself—it had become physically impossible to sign all the autographs requested!)

"Escaping" from crowds soon became a way of life. A part of me enjoyed the adventure; a part of me hated it. I was both extremely flattered and extremely unnerved by the attention. Suddenly the simplest things—going out to dinner, or a mall, or the theater— became complicated. Every time my family and I went anywhere, we had to plan: "How will we get there? Get in? Get out? Can the car wait outside the door? Is there a side entrance, or can we enter through the kitchen?" I wound up seeing a *lot* of restaurant kitchens and service elevators in hotels.

Travel became more complicated as well. I couldn't simply walk through the airport and get on the plane; I had to be met curbside by an airline representative, who would escort me to a private waiting room. I'd always preboard, because it meant I could get on the plane without dozens of people seeing me. So I'd follow the representative up some side stairs and a walkway, and get onto an empty plane; otherwise, there'd be a steady parade of people to my seat. (Of course, sometimes even after taking care to preboard, I'd wind up cringing right after takeoff, when the captain cheerily announced, "Guess who's flying with us today, folks? None other than *Star Trek*'s Mr. Spock!")

Despite the Vulcan's popularity, a great deal of the time the character I played was erroneously referred to in the media as "*Dr. Spock,*" because his title was often confused with that of the famous pediatrician. In fact, in 1968, I had the honor of meeting Dr.

Benjamin Spock, at a gathering sponsored by the American Civil Liberties Union. (At the time, believing that we should be out of Viet Nam, I became active in political campaigning on behalf of Eugene McCarthy, the leader of the "dove" movement. I also worked on behalf of Cesar Chavez's United Farm Workers and Martin Luther King's Southern Christian Leadership Conference, in addition to the ACLU.)

Benjamin Spock was also very active in the peace movement. In 1968, he had been arrested for interfering with draft board activities and at the time I met him was still awaiting trial. He was a vigorous, energetic, athletic-looking man, strongly committed on social issues, and I was eager to speak with him. I introduced myself with, "How do you do? My name is Leonard Nimoy, and I play a character named *Mr. Spock* on the TV series *Star Trek*."

He smiled as he shook my hand and replied briskly, "I know. Have you been indicted yet?"

Now, ever since the ear-touching incident with Maura McGivney, it had not escaped my attention that the majority of Mr. Spock's fans were women. And, for some mysterious reason, they found the Vulcan compellingly attractive. There was a lot of amusing speculation about this—including theories about Spock's "satanic" good looks—but one of the most entertaining articles was written by the famous science-fiction writer Isaac Asimov and entitled, "Mr. Spock is Dreamy." (Coincidentally, it appeared in *TV Guide* the very same month the fateful 1967 Pear Blossom Festival took place.) The humorous essay's premise was that Spock was sexy to female viewers precisely *because* he was smart (while Dr. Asimov bemoaned the fact that *he'd* been playing dumb all these years, based on his observation of television sitcoms, which always portrayed a stupid husband who was loyally adored by his smart wife). In the article, he said:

> For years and years, I have done my best to be a stupid husband . . . But it hadn't occurred to me that Mr. Spock was sexy . . . that girls palpitate over the way one eyebrow goes up a fraction; that they squeal with passion when a little smile quirks his lip. And all because he's *smart*!
> If only I had known! If only I had known!

I enjoyed the piece immensely, and sent him the following letter:

May 8, 1967

Dear Mr. Asimov:

I am not sure, perhaps times have changed. When I first came to California to start a film career, the current rage was Marlon Brando, who had just won the hearts of the American females by playing a stupid, insensitive boor—perhaps you're right, I certainly hope so.

At any rate, the article was marvelous, and I would expect the response would be excellent.

Many thanks,

Sincerely,

Leonard Nimoy

"What does it mean—fanzine?"

Shortly thereafter, I received the following reply:

May 17, 1967
Dear Mr. Nimoy,

Thank you for the unexpected pleasure of your letter of the 8th.

Actually, I don't *really* think being unusually intelligent gets more than a small percentage of the ladies, say a few thousand all told. But then, what normal man needs more than a few thousand—especially if all are going to tell?

My fan mail makes it quite clear that what *really* gets the girls is your (or rather, Mr. Spock's) imperviousness to feminine charm. There is the fascination of trying to break you down that appeals to the hunter instinct of every one of the dear things.

This is the worst news possible for me, for although I am perhaps in the top percentile as far as intelligence is concerned, I am the most pervious man (with respect to feminine charm) that any woman has ever met. I am so laughably simple a conquest that few bother. They just laugh.

Yours,
Isaac Asimov

Over the years, female interest in Spock took a decidedly . . . interesting twist, when fans turned their creative talents—and their erotic fantasies—toward the production of "fanzines." One such publication sports a cover that reveals Spock stripped to the waist, a bare leg peeking out from his flowing toga, his hands manacled. The title? "Spock Enslaved!"

•

I am, of course, terrifically flattered—and reminded of a young college student at Bowling Green University, who rose to ask, "Are you aware that you are the source of erotic dream material for thousands and thousands of ladies around the world?"

I lifted my glass of water from the podium and toasted her with, "May all your dreams come true!"

At the same time, I know it's not me, but Spock they want. The Vulcan, of course, remains silent—and, unlike Dr. Asimov, impervious—on the issue. I can pretty well imagine the following scenario between Spock and one of the "dear things" mentioned in Asimov's letter:

SHE: Mr. Spock, may I offer you something to drink? Scotch, bourbon, brandy, a martini?

SPOCK: Madam, my mind is in precisely the condition it should be. I see no reason to alter that condition with stimulants or depressants.

SHE: Would you excuse me while I slip into something more comfortable?

SPOCK: Since the costume you are now wearing is certainly not functional, and you inform me that it is not comfortable, I fail to comprehend the reason for buying or wearing it.

Perhaps Asimov was right that Spock's unconquerability only served to make his female fans that much more determined. In fact, the "underground network" of fan-to-fan communications often made the CIA look like a bunch of amateurs.

I recall one public appearance I made in Billings, Montana. I'd just arrived at the hotel and turned the key in the door, only to find the phone already ringing. When I picked it up, a young feminine voice asked, "Mr. Nimoy?"

When I responded affirmatively, she said, "My name is Mary, and I'm one of your biggest fans. I just wanted to say hello and tell you how much I enjoy you on *Star Trek*!"

Startled, I asked, "How did you find me?"

"Oh," she said, "I heard you were going to be in Billings, so I just called all the hotels until I got the right one."

I thanked her and explained I had to hang up, as I was due to make an appearance in a few minutes. I then changed clothes and headed out the door, but before I could make my exit, the phone rang again.

I picked it up and heard: "Mr. Nimoy? My name is Patricia. I'm in Chicago, and I just wanted to say hello."

How did she find me?

"Mary in Denver called me . . ."

As much as I appreciated the well-intentioned enthusiasm of most fans, once in a while an individual's determination would lead to unpleasant consequences. In 1967, one fifteen-year-old girl from Houston stole her mother's car and passed $1,500 worth of bad checks trying to get to Hollywood to see me. Needless to say, I made a point of *not* seeing her, as I had no wish to encourage criminal behavior.

And then there was the time *Sixteen* magazine published my home address.

Yes, you read that sentence correctly: my *home* address. I hadn't seen the article, but realized what had happened after a flood of mail started coming to the house. After a few days, the postman refused to deliver the mail because there was so much of it; the post office finally hauled it to us by truck, and for weeks we lived with a literal mountain of mail in the living room, sometimes so high that it was taller than I was. And then there was the occasional young fan skulking about the shrubbery, hoping to catch a glimpse of me coming or going . . .

Fortunately, even the most persistent of the fans were always good-natured; I was more worried about my family's privacy being endangered than I was about our physical well-being. But there was *one* incident that made my blood run cold.

It happened in 1978, while I was shooting the remake of *Invasion of the Body Snatchers* in San Francisco. Because most of the scenes were set at night, we filmed on the city streets until the wee hours of the morning. One night after finishing a scene, I was on my way back to my trailer when I heard a woman's voice behind me, asking, "May I have an autograph for my fourteen-year-old son?" It was dark, so I didn't get a clear look at her; I merely signed the piece of paper she handed me, thanked her, and went into my trailer for a short break.

We finally finished shooting around midnight, and I went back to the motel where most of us were staying in order to take a fast shower and change clothes before rejoining several cast members for a late supper. But when I entered my motel room, I realized that I'd been burglarized. Someone had taken my clothing, luggage, driver's license and credit cards. Even more distressing was the fact that the sheets were all tousled, as though someone had been in the bed. The more I searched through my room, the more things turned up missing.

Shaken, I called the police. They informed me that there was little they could do except mail me a form to fill out; I agreed to this, and gave them my name and address.

I then went to dinner, and told the other cast members what had happened. When I returned to my room an hour or so later, the phone was ringing. When I answered it, a feminine voice asked, "Mr. Nimoy?"

"Yes," I answered cautiously.

She chattered on in a friendly fashion, saying that we had met before at some particular event (which I couldn't recall). And then her tone changed abruptly and she said, "I suppose you're missing some things from your motel room by now."

A chill settled over me; I was quiet for a moment, then responded, "Yes, I am."

"We really have met, you know. Do you remember earlier this evening, when you signed an autograph for my fourteen-year-old son? That was me . . ."

I realized in a flash what had happened: The woman had obviously watched me walk into my trailer to rest between scenes. And when I'd left to go back to work, she'd gone in, found the key to my motel room (with the motel's name prominently displayed), gone to the room, spent some time in my bed, and taken my things.

The conversation took a decidedly eerie turn.

"I suppose you'd like your things back . . ."

"Yes," I said firmly. "I would."

"Well, then, why don't you come and pick them up?"

"No," I answered. "You figured out how to get them; you can figure out a way to put them back where they belong."

She hesitated. "If I bring them to you . . . how do I know I won't be surrounded by police?"

"You don't. You should have thought about that before you took them."

She laughed suddenly. "I'm you right now."

"I beg your pardon?"

Her answer caused another shiver to course down my spine. "I'm you. I'm wearing your clothes."

I ignored the fear her words evoked and demanded, "Where are you?"

"Not far away."

"*Who* are you?"

"A nurse. I really *do* have a fourteen-year-old son. And we are in the same business, in a way. I've written a screenplay; Richard Brooks, who did *Looking for Mr. Goodbar*, is going to direct it . . ."

The conversation drifted into vagaries from there, with nothing settled, although I kept insisting she return my things.

Just to check out her story, I called Richard Brooks, who was on the Paramount lot at that time. He wasn't in, but I told his secretary the story, and gave her my number.

An hour later, Richard himself called me back and asked wonderingly, "What the hell is this all about?"

I told him the strange story, and he said, "Believe it or not, I think I've got her name and address for you. A screenplay has just arrived in the mail unsolicited, from a woman who says she's a single-parent nurse. I won't read it, because I don't want her accusing me of stealing her story. Do you want the name . . .?"

"You bet," I said; after I took it down and thanked Richard, I called the police. Within half an hour, I was visited by a very intelligent, sensitive police officer who asked whether I wanted to file charges or simply wanted my things back. Since I had no desire to file a complaint and testify in court, he offered to call her as an officer and explain to her that she was a suspect—and if she wanted to return my belongings, there would be no charges.

He made the phone call. Within minutes, while we were still discussing the situation, someone knocked on the door. I opened it to discover the bellman, with all my missing belongings in his arms.

Fortunately, almost all encounters with fans are much more pleasant. And lest I ever take the subject of popularity too seriously, there's always the Victor Hugo quote . . . and the encounter with a certain admirer in 1971, when I was appearing at the Coconut Grove Playhouse in Miami. I was stepping from an elevator into the hotel lobby when an elderly gentleman grabbed my arm.

"Hey," he shouted, "look who's here! I know you! I watch you on television all the time. I've got to have your autograph!"

While we fished for pen and paper, he noticed a friend of his passing through the lobby.

"Charlie!" he yelled. "Come here quick! Look who I found!"

Charlie obediently approached, just as we had located some paper and I was on the verge of affixing my name to it.

"Charlie," my new acquaintance proclaimed gleefully, "Do you know who this is? You see him all the time on television! This here is Kreskin!"

I cheerfully signed "Kreskin" to the piece of paper, shook hands with the two men, and left.

SIX

THE
STAR TREK
FAMILY

NIMOY: When Spock became enormously popular, I felt very proud, and hoped all my "fathers" at *Star Trek*—the producers and studio executives, especially the Creator himself—would be pleased. To my deep disappointment, they were anything *but*. They were nervous, paranoid, even hostile—but not pleased.

SPOCK: *I quite understand. I have labored under similar concerns.*

NIMOY: You, Spock? Really?

SPOCK: *Indeed. My father never approved of my decision to enter Starfleet. In fact, our familial ties were completely severed for no fewer than eighteen years. During that time, we never spoke as father and son.*

NIMOY: You know, for once, I think you really *do* understand . . .

I'VE SAID MANY TIMES and in many places that, when I became a series regular on *Star Trek*, I felt I had at last found a professional "home" and "family." After sixteen years of being an "orphan," always moving from job to job, it meant a lot to me to finally have regular work, a place where I belonged. Not a morning passed that I wasn't grateful to wave cheerily at the studio guard and hear his warm welcome as he opened the front gate so I could drive through. In the past, I'd been a stranger at studio gates, always having to stop and explain my business there, and hope that the gate would swing open for me.

I really did see my fellow actors as my brothers and sisters, and the directors, producers, and studio heads as parents. And I felt blessed to be surrounded by such a talented and creative group of people.

But even in the closest families, there are bound to be misunderstandings and tensions. And the *Star Trek* family was certainly not immune.

Fortunately, most of our disagreements were minor and a natural, normal part of the creative process—the types that were resolved and quickly forgotten.

But—and this is a very large *but*—a certain very unpleasant tension developed between me and my "fathers," one that hadn't existed when I first came to work on the *Star Trek* set. It was born of the Vulcan's success; and, like Spock's popularity, it grew and grew until it was impossible to ignore.

One of the first hints of the studio's new attitude regarding Spock's popularity came a few months after the Medford, Oregon, incident. I requested some office supplies—pens, pencils, and paper—from Desilu in order to handle the increasing volume of fan mail. (By that time, it had grown to roughly ten thousand letters per month.) I thought it was a very minor, routine request—what's a few boxes of pens and pencils to a major Hollywood studio, right?

Wrong. Apparently those writing utensils meant a lot more to the studio than I ever imagined. Here's the formal response I received from studio business executive Ed Perlstein:

DESILU PRODUCTIONS INC.
INTER-DEPARTMENT COMMUNICATION

To: Leonard Nimoy   Date: June 12, 1967
From: Ed Perlstein   Subject: Fan Mail

Dear Leonard:

For the past several weeks I have been consulted with respect to the operation in regard to your personally handling your fan mail and have iterated myself many times with regard to the agreement that I made with respect to our obligations to you in this connection. For purposes of clarification to you and the others receiving copies of this memo, I would like to iterate the agreement that was made.

1. Desilu, in addition to your compensation, agrees to pay you $100 towards your secretary and equipment needs for your personally handling the fan mail.
2. All equipment is to be furnished by you other than that specifically enumerated herein below. We agree to furnish you the following:
   a. The photographs of you that we select.

•

b. All postage with respect to fan mail which the studio would normally cover under its existing fan mail facilities.

c. Stationery designated by Desilu for fan mail and not your own personal unapproved stationery. Envelopes will be furnished by Desilu.

It is not intended nor was it specifically agreed that we would furnish you with *pencils, pens*, etc., which we assumed you would furnish yourself as we also contemplated that you would furnish your own typewriter and other equipment.

From the requests that you have made and which I have rejected and which we will charge you for items such as staplers, staples, pens, pencils, pencil sharpener, memo pads, special stationery, applications for membership in Leonard Nimoy Fan Club and any expense in connection with fan clubs is something that we are not responsible for as this goes beyond the *Star Trek* series and which I personally consider a personal item of expense. [Author's note: Do not attempt to translate this sentence from bureaucratese into grammatical English. Permanent confusion could result.]

This is not a witch-hunt but rather a business letter asserting rights on behalf of profit participants, including the network, the producer of the show, Desilu Studios and other profit participants. None of the profit participants or interested members have raised nor are aware of your requests nor have they raised any specific beef concerning your requests and concerning the charges. As I said, there have been many inquiries regarding proper classification and charges and it has come to the point where in my opinion this memo is necessary.

If you have any questions concerning this memo, pro or con, then I would welcome your reply and for this purpose I invite you to use, free of charge, an inter-office memo.

I urge you once again to consider this memo in the vein it was intended for clarification of those charges which are properly to be absorbed by Desilu and that which is to be considered personal and your personal items of expense.

Wow.

I must have read the memo over a dozen times just to be sure Ed wasn't somehow joking, or that I'd misunderstood. I thought all I'd done was ask for some pens and pencils—but clearly the studio saw something much more ominous happening. My request was seen as the nose of the camel—"Give him a few pencils, and next thing you know, he'll start making outrageous demands, because he thinks he's a star."

The last thing I wanted to do was seem unreasonable. So I thought the matter over carefully, and the next day, with tongue firmly in cheek, wrote the following reply to Perlstein's memo:

To: Ed Perlstein   Date: June 13, 1967
From: Leonard Nimoy   Subject: Fan Mail

Dear Ed:
   I want to thank you very much for taking the time to send me your memo clarifying—or attempting to clarify—our agreement as regards to: fan mail, supplies, etc. My impression is that there are two (2) primary issues raised in your memo, and I should like to deal with them forthwith so that we may arrive at a satisfactory understanding.
   The first issue seems to be that which has to do with the provision of pens, pencils, etc. I hasten to assure you that my secretary and I have managed to steal enough pens and pencils from various offices around the studio, so we will no longer need to make requests in this area for some time.
   The second area deals with those expenses and I quote from your memo: " . . . in connection with fan clubs . . . that we are not responsible for, as this goes beyond the *Star Trek* series and which I personally consider a personal item of expense." In this area we may have to create a subdivision, since not all of the 160 fan clubs could, in all fairness, be considered completely personal. I list herewith a few examples of some of the clubs which might fall out of the "personal" category:

   "Crew of the *Enterprise*"—Mobile, Alabama
   "Star Trek Association"—Los Angeles, Calif.
   "Spock"—Los Angeles, Calif.
   "The *Enterprise* II"—Oceanside, Calif.
   "The *Star Trek* Club"—Jackson Heights, New York
   "*Enterprise*, Inc."—Great Neck, New York
   "*Star Trek*"—Elmira, N.Y.
   "Vulcanian Enterprises"—Brooklyn, N.Y.
   "Star Trekkers"—Brooklyn, N.Y.

Those are some examples of the clubs which I feel fall most predominantly in the *Star Trek* area, and cannot in all fairness be considered "personal" clubs.

Then there are those which I feel we should split. For example:

"Nimoy Enterprise"—San Jose, Calif.

"Leonard 'Spock' Nimoy Fans, Inc."—B.C. Canada

"Yomin Enterprises"—Pontiac, Michigan

(The name of the ship in this case being spelled forward and my name being spelled backward—perhaps we ought to go for a 75% vs. 25% split of the expense.)

In fairness to all parties involved may I suggest that we arrange for a periodic audit of the fan club files in order to determine where the expenses should rightfully fall. Perhaps, Price-Waterhouse would be available for such an audit, and we could arrange for a dramatic presentation of the findings in a sealed envelope.

Yours for fair and equitable allocation of expenses,

Leonard Nimoy

Now at this point, Robert Justman, our production manager and eventual co-producer, got into the act. (You might remember Bob as the initiator of the S———k Vulcan-proper-names memos.) Bob has a marvelously wry sense of humor, and his delightful response did much to relieve the tension.

To: Ed Perlstein   Date: June 14, 1960
From: Bob Justman   Subject: Fan Mail

Dear Ed:

I have received copies of correspondence between Leonard Nimoy and yourself recently. With respect to Mr. Nimoy's memo of June 13th, I should like to report to you that I have noticed that pens and pencils have been disappearing from my office at a phenomenal rate. I don't have proof, so I don't think that I can logically accuse anyone of these thefts. However, I staked out my office the other night in an attempt to identify the guilty party.

Unhappily, some unknown assailant sneaked up behind me and clamped a fiercely vise-like grip upon me somewhere between my neck and shoulder. I lost consciousness within a split second and did not awaken until several minutes later. To my dismay, I noted that there were more supplies missing from my office.

Whoever attacked me and stole my supplies must have been endowed with a quite superior sense of hearing, as I am certain that I made no noise and, in fact, was quite careful to breathe as lightly as possible.

There is one very strange fact which has emerged from this incident. I had rather cleverly concealed a naked razor blade within my pencil box, so that whoever would be stealing my pencils would have an opportunity to slice open his or her finger. Upon investigating my now empty pencil box, I discovered a slight amount of the oddest green liquid present on the razor blade and around the bottom of the pencil box. I can't imagine what it can be. It certainly isn't blood, as we all know that human blood is red.

Incidentally, getting back to fan mail. This past season, I have received three fan letters. I answered them post-haste. Please send me fifteen cents to cover postage.

Sincerely,

Bob Justman

How could I resist? I—or, more correctly, Spock—immediately dashed off the following:

To: Ed Perlstein   Date: June 15, 1967
From: Spock   Re: First Aid

Dear Mr. Perlstein:

I should like to file a complaint about the first aid facilities here at the studio.

It seems that late one night last week, while doing some very important work in my office I had a minor accident and cut a finger. I went to the first aid office only to discover that they are closed after shooting hours. I think it highly illogical to assume that accidents only take place during shooting hours.

What can be done?

Spock

Now, the same thing happened when I tried to put a telephone in my dressing room: The studio flat-out refused.

Please note that I didn't say the studio refused to *pay* for my telephone. No, they refused to let *me* pay to have one installed.

You see, on the entire *Star Trek* soundstage, there was exactly *one* telephone. *One* telephone, which was used by the fifty or so odd people—cast and crew—who worked there. Now, shortly after the show started airing, I started receiving several calls during the day, mostly requests for personal appearances. Since I couldn't come to the phone while we were rehearsing or shooting, the message slips would pile up. By the time we got a break, there'd be a line of people waiting to use the phone. The nearest available one was a pay phone offstage, down the street.

So, I asked the production manager if the studio would be willing to put a phone in my dressing room. He promised to pass the request along. A week or so later, when I asked again, he told me that Herb Solow, the head of Desilu, wanted to discuss the issue with me.

I assumed that Solow wanted to discuss finances; my contract with the studio had no provision for a telephone, so I told the production manager not to bother Solow—I'd just pay for the phone myself.

Turned out that wasn't good enough—Solow *still* wanted to talk to me about the phone issue. One day, Herb came to my office, and said, "Look, Leonard, we simply can't let you have the phone."

"No problem," I told him. "I've already decided to pay for it myself."

"No, no," he said, "there are other actors who've requested phones, and we told them no. If you get one, then they'll all be jealous."

"Herb, didn't you hear what I just said? I'll just let them know that *I'm* paying for the phone . . . "

He shook his head. "We still can't let you do it."

I felt as though I'd just been transported from the *Star Trek* set into the twilight zone. "But why?"

"They won't believe you. They'll think we're paying for it, and I just don't want any hard feelings . . ."

The phone became an amazingly major issue. But I persisted and, eventually, Herb listened to reason and permitted me to have a telephone installed in my dressing room. And I paid for it myself.

Fortunately, the studio's paranoia didn't infect everyone, and most people on the set combatted it (and chronic exhaustion, the other occupational hazard of working on a series) with good humor.

I'd like to take a moment here to express my appreciation of associate producer Bob Justman, not only for his wonderfully witty
memos (including the above), but for the sincerely interested ear
he always made available to anyone concerned about the quality of
the show. Bob was deeply involved in *Star Trek*'s production almost
from its inception. After the day's shooting was done, I'd often head
for Bob's office to discuss the characters, scripts, makeup—or simply to blow off steam. Bob served as my sounding board. He had a
great talent for listening—I always came away knowing I'd been
heard out—and for responding appropriately to a complaint or suggestion. Bob never blew me off with the standard answer of "Well,
we just don't have the time to fix it"; if he thought my concern had
validity, he'd do whatever it took to make things right. Bob was passionately concerned about the show's quality, and if something
needed correcting, he'd see that it got done.

And he did it with grace and a remarkable sense of humor. And
although Bob was typically soft-spoken, he could be amazingly
determined at times—especially when Roddenberry was late with
a scene rewrite. Bob was well known for walking into Gene's office,
climbing atop his desk, and standing there until Gene finished the
rewrite—which Bob then snatched and carried off to the waiting
director. (Eventually, Gene had an electronic lock with a remote
switch installed on his office door, so that when he saw Justman
coming, he could shut him out in time!)

Bob was probably as close to Gene Roddenberry as anyone.
Unfortunately, I never had the close personal relationship I would
have liked to have with Gene. We didn't hit it off as friends, perhaps
because his sense of humor and mine simply weren't compatible.

For example, during *Star Trek*'s early days, Gene and Majel were
avid gemologists; they bought unfinished gemstones and polished
them, then resold them. One day, I expressed an interest in buying
a stone to set in a ring, as a present for my wife. I picked out a lovely unfinished opal, and Majel quoted me a very reasonable price,
and said, "We'll polish it up for you. Just come by tomorrow after
shooting and pick it up."

So at the appointed time, I went to Gene's office—still wearing
my Spock costume—and found him sitting at his desk frowning
down at the opal, now nicely polished.

"Great!" I said, but Gene didn't smile. In fact, he was scowling.

"We've got a big problem here, Leonard. Majel made a serious mistake. This stone is worth a lot more than she quoted you."

Completely caught off guard, I stammered, "Well . . .I don't know what to say, Gene. What sort of price did you have in mind?"

"At least five, six times the price she told you." And he fixed a stern, penetrating gaze on me.

I didn't quite know what to say; embarrassed and uncomfortable, I hemmed and fidgeted for a moment, trying to decide whether to pay the price, try to bargain, or forget the whole thing.

In the midst of my turmoil, Majel suddenly popped out from under Gene's desk, rolling with laughter, and Gene's frown turned into a broad grin. I realized then that I'd been had. Gene and Majel thought it was a terrific joke, but to be honest, I was simply uncomfortable.

That's a typical example of Gene's sense of humor; he enjoyed putting people on the spot. The infamous prank he played on John D.F. Black, on John's first day of work, has been told many times in other places. Briefly put, Gene arranged for a woman to play a starlet, who confessed to Black, in his office, that she'd do *anything* for a guest starring role on *Star Trek*—at which point, she stripped her clothes off in front of the mortified Black. At that precise moment, Gene and some of the office staff arranged to rush in and "catch" John with this unclad actress. Maybe it's the influence of the Vulcan on me, but I never understood what was funny about putting people in uncomfortable, embarrassing situations.

Even so, on the *Star Trek* set, Gene and I had a courteous and cordial—but strictly professional—relationship. With Spock's burgeoning popularity, however, I believe Gene felt somewhat threatened by the thought of losing control of his creation.

Over time (as I'll discuss in future chapters), our relationship began to deteriorate—a fact that has always frustrated and saddened me. I sincerely wanted to be on good terms with Gene, but I never seemed to find that one thing I could have said or done to break through the emotional wall that separated us.

It's also very difficult for me to reflect on the fact that Gene is gone now, and there is no longer any chance of mending our relationship.

I can only honor his memory here by saying that, to this day, I remain deeply respectful of Gene's creativity, his talent, and his sharp intelligence; working with him was always rewarding. If I had a valid suggestion on a script, he'd take my idea, amplify it, and make it better. If I had a concern or a problem with a story or scene, he'd understand it and deal with it appropriately and swiftly. He maintained a strong vision of what *Star Trek* should be about—and that included keeping a certain alien on the *Enterprise* despite the network's objections. For that, I'll always be grateful to him.

There was a second Gene involved in the series—one who, unfortunately, died before he had the chance to see *Star Trek*'s rebirth in syndication. I'm speaking about Gene Coon, who came to us from *Wild, Wild West* and served as a writer-producer on our show for the first and second seasons. Coon was an imaginative talent who added much to *Star Trek* lore; the Klingons and the Prime Directive were but two of his contributions.

Coon was a sensitive, kind man—once you got to know him well. But on the surface, he came across as a crusty Jimmy Cagney/Spencer Tracy type, the sort of guy you'd see cast as the tough 1940s newspaper editor, handing out guff to young reporters. I always picture Gene Coon sitting behind his typewriter. If you went up and asked him a question, chances are he'd just look up at you and grunt, then go back to pounding the keys.

It's with fond amusement that I recall the time Gene Coon suspended me.

Yep. Suspended. As in "thrown off the set."

Suspension is something that happens very rarely in our business. Technically, an actor can be suspended—which means that he or she is basically "fired" until a resolution of the matter is reached—for refusing to perform. Take a hypothetical situation: If an actor shows up for work and in the middle of shooting, keeps saying, "I don't understand how to do that scene," even after the director explains it again and again, the actor is costing the studio money. Let's say that actor does it for *so* many scenes in a row, it's clear he's refusing to work. Then, in desperation, the producers might suspend him.

But such a thing is only done in extreme circumstances, after very serious conversations among all the parties involved—the actor, the agent, the lawyer, the producers, and ultimately (in the case of a television series), the network. Normally, if the actor is popular, the network's attitude is "Just don't lose him—do whatever you have to in order to fix the problem." So the studio would be reluctant to go to the network unless they have extremely strong cause, such as an actor arriving for work too drunk or drugged to perform.

So suspension is a very drastic step. And Gene Coon did it to me.

It might seem odd that I smile when I think about it, but it's illustrative of Gene's no-nonsense, tough-guy attitude. He didn't do it out of ill will or spite; he just did it because he was busy and couldn't be bothered with trying to talk it over with me.

At any rate, I've forgotten the particular episode that sparked the incident. Suffice it to say that I thought there were problems in a particular script Gene was working on—Spock was asked to do something entirely out of character.

So I marched into Coon's office and said, "Gene, I have a problem with this scene. I can't play it the way it's written."

Gene looked up from his typewriter, scowling, and said, "Whaddya mean, you can't do it? You can't, or you *won't?*"

Now, I realized that saying I *wouldn't* play the scene was the same as refusing to play it—and so I very carefully replied, "No. I'm not saying I *won't*—I'm saying that I can't. It's antithetical to Spock. He just wouldn't behave the way this scene has him behaving."

Gene blinked at me a second, then grunted and fixed his attention back on the typewriter keys.

This was typical Gene Coon–speak for letting me know the discussion was at an end, so I left the office, wondering whether the grunt meant my concern had been registered or not.

Well, the scene was coming up in a couple of days, so I didn't think much more about it. I was busy working on the set when someone came up to me and said, "Your agent's on the phone."

I had no idea what the call was about, but knew it must have been important for me to be interrupted on the soundstage, so I took the call.

"What happened?" my agent said, in a tone of dismay. "Did you have a run-in with Gene Coon?"

It took me a second to figure out what he was talking about; I would hardly have called our brief conversation a "run-in," but I answered, "Yes, I guess so. I can't play this particular scene . . . "

"Look," my agent said, "he wants to suspend you."

My first reaction was disbelief; my second reaction was to grin. After all, we were all exhausted from the strain of working on a series—and if Coon wanted to play hardball, that was fine with me. I could use the rest. "Well," I replied, "ask him whether I can leave now, or whether I have to wait until the end of the day."

"I will," my agent said, and hung up.

Fortunately—or unfortunately, depending on your point of view—I never did get kicked off the set. Shortly after I spoke with my agent, I got a call from Gene Roddenberry.

"No one's suspended," Roddenberry said wearily. "If anyone's going to be suspended around here, *I'll* do it."

I couldn't help feeling a little disappointed at losing my chance to go home early. But Gene Coon was great, and there were no hard feelings between us about the suspension business. I respected Gene because he was a very direct, honest man and a hard and consistent worker. He was the kind of person who didn't parade his amazing accomplishments—he just simply did the impossible, and did it well.

Of course, a chapter on family squabbles wouldn't be complete without addressing the so-called Shatner/Nimoy feud—at least, that's what the movie magazines called it, and once Spock's popularity took off with the fans, all the gossip columns and tabloid magazines insisted that Bill Shatner and I detested each other and weren't on speaking terms. After all, the same thing had supposedly happened earlier on the popular sixties series *The Man from U.N.C.L.E.* Robert Vaughn was considered the lead of the show—until co-star David McCallum's popularity with the female fans mushroomed. The fact led to tensions on the set.

Were there similar tensions between Bill and me on the *Star Trek* set? Of course. We're human (even if a part of my psyche is claimed by a Vulcan).

Was there hatred? No. Sibling rivalry? Yes. We were like a pair of very competitive brothers, and there were times when I complained to Gene (or Bob Justman, or De Kelley) about Bill, and times when Bill complained to Gene (or Bob or De) about me. Many times, Gene was effective in his role as Daddy, solving the conflicts between two squabbling kids. And there were times when he wasn't.

For example, there was the time Paramount's publicity department arranged to have a photographer come to get some pictures of Freddy Phillips working his makeup magic to turn

Fellow actor William Shatner reacts graciously to news of Spock's mushrooming popularity

Bill and I have a little script discussion over who gets the last line

me into a Vulcan. I agreed to do it, and touched base with all the producers, to be sure it was okay; I confess, I didn't check with Bill because I couldn't see where it would be a problem for him, even though at the time, he had the makeup seat next to mine.

To make a long story short, since I got in there first, I was getting made up, and the photographer had his camera out and was snapping away. Bill came in around 7 A.M. ; by 7:10, we noticed that the photographer had disappeared. We thought he'd gone to get some film—but it turned out that Bill had gone to the assistant director and said, "I won't continue while this is going on. Get rid of this guy."

So the photographer had been ordered off the set. Was I angry? Of course. Were we being insensitive to Bill in arranging the shoot? Probably. Papa Roddenberry finally had to come out and smooth everyone's ruffled feathers. The photographer was finally called back, and the shoot proceeded without further incident.

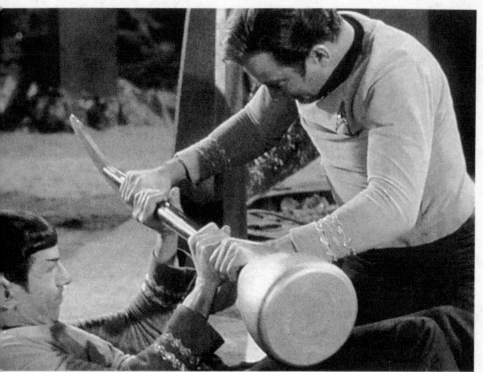

RAMOUNT PICTURES

A major area of conflict was Bill's concern that Spock was getting ahead of Kirk in terms of problem solving. Of course, the Vulcan's primary function as science officer was to do research and provide data—but Bill worried that Kirk would seem unintelligent by contrast. And so lines of dialog that had logically been Spock's soon became Kirk's.

I addressed the situation in a memo to Roddenberry dated February 21, 1968, which says, in part:

> It would be as if Shakespeare had written "To be or not to be . . . " to be played by two characters instead of one . . .
>
> KIRK: To be . . .
> SPOCK: . . . or not to be . . .
> McCOY: Yes, that is the question . . .
> KIRK: I've made my decision . . .
> McCOY: (angrily) Jim, you've endangered thousands of
>   lives!

SPOCK: (his eyebrows slowly rise . . .)

Believe me, I know that peace and harmony are vital in a series situation, but must it be reduced to this:
(Spock enters bridge, approaches Captain's chair . . .)

SPOCK: Captain, I believe I found the . . .
KIRK: The answer, Mr. Spock?
SPOCK: Yes, Captain. I am convinced that the planet is—
KIRK: Infested, Mr. Spock?
SPOCK: Yes, Captain, with a rare and unique disease which is capable of—
KIRK: Making itself invisible to our sensors, Mr. Spock?
SPOCK: Precisely, Captain.
KIRK: Exactly what I had expected, Mr. Spock. Good work. What are the odds?
SPOCK: Approximately 47.3 to 1, Captain.
KIRK: I'll take that chance. Prepare phasers, Mr. Sulu.

©1995 PARAMOUNT PICTURES

Please Gene, let Captain Kirk be a giant among men, let him be the best damned captain in the fleet, let him be the best combat officer in the fleet, let him be the greatest lover in the fleet, let him be capable of emerging unscathed from a brawl with five men twice his size, but above all, let him be a LEADER, which to me means letting your subordinates keep their dignity.

Roddenberry tried to smooth that one over, too, but the conflict kept recurring. Those were hectic, exhausting times, and both Bill and I were under enormous stress—as I've said, celebrity's not an easy thing to cope with, and there are no classes in helping you to deal with it—so some tension was inevitable.

But here's the bottom line: Our deep, sincere respect for each other outweighed any conflict. We sorted out a lot of things in those early years, and have become very good friends. And as I've said before (and will no doubt say again), if it hadn't been for Bill Shatner's dynamic portrayal of Kirk, the character of Spock could never have worked so well. It's the synergy, the chemistry between the two (and De Kelley's Dr. McCoy) that helped make *Star Trek* magical.

One of the wisest things I think Gene Roddenberry ever did was to consult Isaac Asimov on the friction between Shatner and myself, and the problematic popularity of Spock. Asimov advised him to make Kirk and Spock loyal, inseparable friends, so that when the audience thought of one, they'd automatically think of the other.

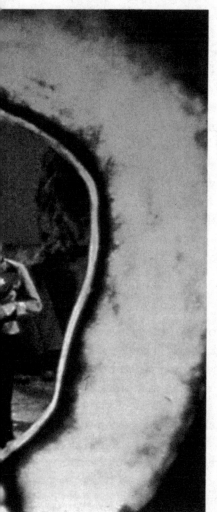

The advice worked with the viewers—and maybe even with Bill and me, because we certainly came to appreciate our friendship more as time went on.

Even if it *was* really mean of him to keep stealing my bike.

But back to the subject of fun and games. Since I'm discussing the *Star Trek* family, I may as well give credit to my right-hand woman, Teresa Victor—an extremely loyal, dedicated worker—for helping me win one of my minor skirmishes with the studio. At the end of the show's first season, I renegotiated my contract, and the

Bill and I contemplate some of the less subtle Freudian imagery used on the show

new terms included an office. I hired Teresa and she moved into the office, which consisted of two tiny rooms with a bathroom in between. Each room had a window, but there was no cross-ventilation, so when summer came, the rooms became unbearably hot. On hot days, the office became practically uninhabitable by the afternoon.

So I asked Herb Solow's assistant, Morris Chapnick, about getting an air conditioner. Morris promised to look into it.

Days passed; Teresa was still sweltering in the little office, so I called Morris and asked, "What's happening on the air conditioner?"

"I checked your contract," he answered, "and it doesn't call for anything except office furnishings."

"That's true," I said, "and the contract doesn't specifically mention an air conditioner, but the office is virtually unusable without it."

He sighed and said, "I'll see what I can do."

A couple of days later, a small exhaust fan was installed in one of the tiny windows. Naturally, it had no effect. Teresa struggled along for another few days.

By that time, Los Angeles was enjoying a typical summer heat wave; I stopped by the office and was incensed on Teresa's behalf to find her perspiring in truly unbearable heat. The little room was like an oven. So I said to her, "Teresa, lie down on the floor. You're fainting from the heat."

"I am?"

"Yes, you are," I said firmly. "In fact, in just a few seconds, you're going to be unconscious."

She caught on right away, and lay down with a grin while I proceeded to call the studio nurse. I told her I'd wandered into my office to find my poor secretary passed out from the heat. The nurse arrived quickly and applied some cold compresses, which prompted Teresa to "revive." (Teresa's performance was so convincing, it made me wonder whether she'd missed a calling as an actress!)

My next call, of course, was to Morris Chapnick. And the story I told him was later verified by the studio nurse.

In two days, we had the air conditioner.

SEVEN

PREMATURE BURIAL

.

"Brain and brain! What is brain?!"
—Kara, "Spock's Brain"

I N THE MIDDLE OF *Star Trek*'s second season, NBC began hinting that the series would be cancelled. Apparently *Star Trek*'s ratings weren't good enough to convince the network heads of its popularity, despite the truckloads of mail and the media attention it generated. The network wisdom held that *Star Trek* had attracted a "cult" audience, intense and vociferous, but limited in number. (Five years later, during my contract at Universal, I heard the same from studio president Sid Sheinberg. He said, "The *Star Trek* viewers are intense and vocal. They'd kill for the show, but there just aren't enough of them to justify making a movie.")

Fortunately, a concerned fan by the name of Bjo (pronounced "Bee-jo," short for "Betty Jo") Trimble listened to a different drummer. She and her husband mounted a massive write-in campaign, and the resulting onslaught of letters had the desired effect: NBC agreed to renew *Trek* for a third season.

When it did, the network executives promised Roddenberry an excellent time slot: Monday nights at 7:30. Buoyed by the vote of confidence, Gene vowed to personally oversee every script and make the show's third year its best ever. *Star Trek*'s future had never looked so bright.

But a number of unfortunate events conspired against its success—and against the quality of the episodes.

First and foremost, NBC broke its promise to Gene, and switched *Star Trek* from its enviable 7:30 Monday night slot to 10 P.M. on Fridays—a time when its young viewers were bound to be out socializing. (*Laugh-In*'s producer, George Schlatter, reportedly refused to let the phenomenally successful show be moved from its 8 P.M. slot to 8:30, as the network planned.) Infuriated, Roddenberry threatened to leave the show if the time slot wasn't changed. NBC called his bluff—and so Roddenbery was forced to make good on his threat. While he technically retained executive producer status (his name appeared in the credits), he left the lot and moved to MGM to pursue other projects.

Dorothy Fontana soon followed suit, leaving to pursue her freelancing career. Gene Coon had already departed during the second season, which left only one production-end veteran: Robert Justman.

Surprisingly, Justman wasn't asked to fill Roddenberry's shoes; both Gene and the network decided that task should go to Fred Freiberger (who, like Coon, had served a stint on *Wild, Wild West*). In fact, when he was preparing to shoot the first *Star Trek* pilot, Roddenberry's first choice for associate producer was Freddy Freiberger—but Fred reluctantly turned down the offer, as he was unavailable at the time.

Bob Justman was understandably disappointed at being passed over; he was also burnt out after two seasons of hard work. He went to the studio and told them he wanted off the show—but the Powers that Used to Be refused to let him out of his contract. Reluctantly, he stayed on—but only for a time. He finally managed to leave later on in the season.

On top of everything else, NBC seriously slashed *Star Trek*'s budget. The tougher time slot and reduced funds were hardly an ideal situation for Freiberger as a newcomer; morale was not at its highest after Gene's departure.

But I, for one, was looking forward to Fred's arrival. He and I had been friends since the late 1950s; any concerns I had about the effect of Gene's absence on the series were laid to rest. "Great!" I thought. "Terrific! Freddy's an old friend that I really can talk to, so things'll go smoothly this season . . ."

Unfortunately, the moment of his arrival was the best moment we had. Our friendship soon became strained, because Freddy came to *Star Trek* with some very strong ideas about how it needed to be changed. He echoed NBC's original reaction to "The Cage," in that he felt *Star Trek* was too cerebral for most viewers. Fewer ideas, more physical action, more fight scenes—that's what Fred felt the show needed, and he set about to give it that imprint.

Star Trek's third season debuted with "Spock's Brain," an ominous portent of things to come.

The episode began with a beautiful young woman mysteriously appearing on the *Enterprise* bridge, and rendering everyone uncon-

Guest star Marj Dusay (Kara) contemplates the effect of "Spock's Brain" on her career

scious via a strange device. When the crew comes to, they discover Spock in sickbay—minus his brain.

Thus begins a desperate search through the galaxy for the missing gray matter. It leads the captain and his brave crew to a planet undergoing an Ice Age. Oddly, the primitive cavemen on the surface are all just that—cave*men*; not a single female can be found. That is, until the *Enterprise* crew discovers an extremely sophisticated underground civilization, populated by gorgeous women whose intelligence is even scantier than their minitogas. Spock's brain, it seems, was purloined by their exceptionally witless leader, Kara, so that it could take care of the underground civilization—which was obviously too stupid to fend for itself.

Kirk beams down into this civilization with Bones *and* Spock—who has been outfitted with a metal device on his cranium so that he can accompany them. The doctor has a little "remote control" that operates Spock; he accompanies them, blank-eyed as a robot. Kirk eventually finds the head bimbo/organ swiper, Kara. The term "cerebral" might have applied to her special brand of thievery, but certainly not to her. ("Brain and brain!" she cries out, stamping her foot in frustration because she's too dense to understand exactly what it is the captain keeps demanding. "What *is* brain?" I think the question for that third season might well have been, "What happened to *Star Trek*'s brain—and heart?")

After a brief struggle in which Kirk overpowers the armed Kara, Dr. McCoy reinstalls the Vulcan's brain, with the help of an omniscient computer bank known as "the Teacher." (The Teacher was also responsible for advising Kara on stealing the brain in the first place.) During the surgery, Spock comes to and tells McCoy how to finish the job, which allows the good doctor to quip, "I should never have reconnected his vocal cords."

There was little acting challenge in walking around pretending to be brainless; I just let my eyes glaze over, and functioned in automaton style. But frankly, during the entire shooting of that episode, I was embarrassed—a feeling that overcame me many times during that final season.

The episode had logical holes in it large enough to accommodate a starship. But beyond the questions about why the population hadn't died off when males and females were entirely segregated, and why Spock's hair was never *once* mussed up, even during brain surgery, the larger question remains: What was the point of the story?

When the series was really cooking, the stories dealt with some exciting and profound and even important ideas relative to the human condition. And, just as important, at the same time, the characters were developed. We learned about them and came to care about them as they struggled with difficult choices. Sadly, during the third year (which should have been seized as an opportunity to further develop the characters and examine new facets of their relationship to each other), the clear definitions between the characters—especially the three central figures of Kirk, Spock, and McCoy—began to erode. Spock again fell in love and ate meat (in "All Our Yesterdays"), brayed like a donkey and did the flamenco (in "Plato's Stepchildren"), and openly discussed the Vulcan seven-year mating cycle (which, in "Amok Time," a mortified Spock had at first refused to discuss even with his closest friend, Kirk) during an uncharacteristically flirtatious conversation with a woman ("The Cloudminders").

Now, perhaps it's amusing to sit back and criticize *Star Trek*'s third season, especially the sillier episodes, such as "Spock's Brain." But it's not my intent to simply gripe about the decline in the show's quality, or criticize Freddy Freiberger, or tell a bunch of entertaining anecdotes about what a mess the third season was. *Star Trek* and the character of Spock are dear to my heart; watching their gradual erosion was painful. The point these inferior episodes make is this: Some work—especially in the sciences or arts—simply fills time and space. Yes, it might temporarily appease the bosses and pay the bills—but with the passage of time, that work is forgotten.

I'm reminded here of the time I met Phillipe Halsman, the extraordinary photographer who did countless covers for *Life* magazine. About twenty years ago, I got to visit his studio and discuss his work, which, since I was an amateur photographer, greatly intrigued me. I asked Phillipe about how he got involved with photography, and he said, "Well, my career is rather like the story about the prostitute. When someone asked her how she got into her business, she said, 'First I did it to please myself, then I did it to please my friends, then I did it for the money.'" That's what his career had become, and he possessed a rather wistful cynicism about it. He had started with love, and ended up with commerce.

Have I acted for the money? Sure, at times. Would I rather do it for the love? Obviously. There's a fulfillment there that makes everything else pale in importance.

Because meaningful work—that done with care and attention and love, for its own sake rather than the sake of public approval (including Nielsen ratings)—endures. *Star Trek* episodes such as Harlan Ellison's poignant "City on the Edge of Forever" or Theodore Sturgeon's poetic "Amok Time" are just as powerful and meaningful to today's audiences as they were to viewers back in the 1960s. For me, drama is something of a spiritual crusade, and it's important that mercenary concerns take a back seat to the love and concern for the quality of the work. I know without a doubt that this was true for every other cast member: Bill and De and Jimmy and George and Nichelle and Walter. Perhaps that's why *Star Trek* has endured.

In all fairness, there were a few excellent episodes during that last year—most notably "The *Enterprise* Incident," by Dorothy Fontana. The story centered around Kirk's sudden, apparently irrational order to warp into a forbidden area of space claimed by the Federation's Vulcanoid enemies, the Romulans. Kirk is taken prisoner by the female Romulan Commander (played wonderfully by Joanne Linville), who sets about wooing Mr. Spock. Spock apparently yields to the commander's charms and betrays Kirk, ultimately killing him with the "Vulcan death grip" when the outraged captain attacks him. The "dead" captain's body is transported back to the *Enterprise*—where, to most everyone's surprise, he revives. Kirk then assumes Romulan guise and sneaks back over to the enemy vessel to steal their new cloaking device (capable of rendering a ship invisible). All the while, Spock is permitting himself to be seduced by the commander. However, Kirk and Spock are both found out at the last minute—but manage to escape, thanks to Mr. Scott's intervention with the transporter. The Romulan commander is inadvertently beamed over with Spock; she is, of course, outraged by the Vulcan's duplicity—but he privately tells her that she underestimates herself. He was indeed moved by her touch.

(Just as an aside: If you put Dorothy's scripts together as a group—especially "Incident," "Journey to Babel," and "This Side of Paradise"—she gave us, by far, the best stories where we interacted with women who were fully developed characters in their own right. That's not to say that that was her primary intent as a writer, or that that was her only contribution to the show. But *Star Trek* was a product of the sexist sixties, and that was sometimes reflected in the writing, where women characters were often treated as stereotypical love interests or altogether ignored. Dorothy's scenes not only avoided such stereotypes, but were dramatically intriguing.)

©1995 PARAMOUNT PICTURES

Episodes like "The *Enterprise* Incident" made it exciting to go to work. Like all of Dorothy's scripts, it had an edge to it, an adult level of complication, and social commentary. The character's lives were being affected, their ethics violated, even their spirituality touched. Scripts like these added to the moral structure of the *Star Trek* universe. The durability of such fine work is endless; I felt that the more of it we were able to do, the more we added to the show's life span.

With all that in mind, when scripts started showing up that contradicted everything I knew about Spock and *Star Trek*, I felt it my duty to speak up. For example, in the script "All Our Yesterdays," Spock and McCoy are accidentally sent back into a planet's Ice Age, where Spock falls in love with Zarabeth, a beautiful young woman who was cruelly exiled there to a solitary life.

Why did Spock fall in love with

Zarabeth, and to please her, agree to eat meat? In the original draft, no particular reason was given. When I discussed this with Freddy, it turned out that he'd forgotten that Spock would never permit himself to behave in such a manner (unless under the influence of those spores from "This Side of Paradise"). Fred did listen and agreed that a solution was needed. Ultimately, some lines were added to suggest that, because he'd been transported to the past, the Vulcan was reverting to the violent behavior of his ancestors.

Not the soundest logic, but at least it allowed me to play the scene without feeling I was violating the character's basic premise.

"All Our Yesterdays" was only one example of the many meetings that Fred and I had over script problems. Sometimes Fred listened, and we compromised.

Here's an excerpt from the first memo I sent Fred concerning a particular script—in this case, the first to air during the third season, which would be renamed "Spectre of the Gun."

A touching exchange with the Romulan commander (Joanne Linville) in "The Enterprise Incident"

A frostbitten Vulcan forgets himself with Zarabeth
(Mariette Hartley) in "All Our Yesterdays"

To: Fred Freiberger   Date: May 6, 1968
From: Leonard Nimoy   Subject: "The Last Gunfight"

Dear Fred:

   As per our phone conversation, here are whatever ideas I could put together. Aside from the other problems discussed, I believe that Spock should start working on constructing his device (whatever that is going to be), no later than scene #31. Perhaps on Page 18, where Kirk says, "I have no intention of letting a bunch of primitives kill my people and myself." At this point, if not earlier, I believe that we must begin to introduce the concept that we are here because of a scientific or telepathic force, and that we must find a scientific or telepathic way in which to combat it. If Kirk begins to initiate his relationship activity at this point, Spock should begin to initiate his scientific activity.

To me, it makes more sense that Spock would be trying to build a communicator, or some kind of electronic signalling device, rather than a phaser. I think that his primary aim should be to get out of here, rather than to win a fight, since we must accept that we cannot do that. If we continue to play the idea that we could win this fight, then we deny the whole premise—which is that we are the "Clantons" and we will lose in any fight.

Perhaps this idea could be dramatized in Spock wanting to use the gunpowder from the bullets in order to build his equipment. The others might be interested in maintaining the use of their weapons, while Spock points out the futility of weapons in trying to beat the history involved.

I am sorry I can't be more helpful. It seems in this case I must choose the role of "The Devil's Advocate"! Wish you the best, and will be in touch when I get back.

Peace!

Leonard Nimoy

As you can see, Fred and I still enjoyed a comfortable relationship at that time. (You can also see that one of the toughest things I had to do was convince the writers and production staff that Spock was committed to nonviolence!) But the quality of the scripts, and the apparent familiarity of the writers and producers with the character of Spock, quickly went downhill—as did my ability to convince Fred of the relevance of my concerns about the fact.

Perhaps at this point, I should explain further why I thought it was *my* responsibility to look after the character. You see, after a television series has been on the air for a period of time, the staff will undergo a good deal of turnover. Writers, directors, and producers all come and go; only the actors, usually, remain. So the actor is ultimately the "keeper of the flame" for his or her character. It often falls to the actor to point out to incoming producers and directors any inconsistencies in the character, because the staff may not be familiar with what's gone before. Therefore, if the actor doesn't take on the responsibility, a character "drift" is likely to take place, and not necessarily for the better. So, feeling as stongly as I always have about the development of character, I felt I was responsible to protect Spock from disintegration.

•

The one thing that certainly *did* disintegrate was my relationship with Fred. After a while, I believe he felt that I was simply being difficult, and he grew frustrated. In the case of the episode "Is There in Truth No Beauty?" Fred simply refused to address some concerns I had about a particular scene in which Spock has a discussion with Dr. Miranda Jones.

The scene in question was meandering and pointless—a long and frankly dull conversation about Spock and Dr. Jones's respective personal philosophies. There was no event, no drama, no reason for the scene to exist. It needed to be given a purpose, or be cut. I sent Freddy a memo, and tried to discuss it with him, but was resoundingly ignored.

Now it was my turn to be frustrated. So I called Gene Roddenberry at his office on the MGM lot, and explained the problem. He agreed with me that the scene needed a rewrite, and promised to take care of the situation. Very shortly afterwards, the rewritten script pages arrived. The scene was no longer meandering, and now had two very obvious functions: one, to say good-bye to the character of Dr. Jones, and two, to bring attention to a medallion Spock was wearing, called an IDIC. The term stands for Infinite Diversity in Infinite Combinations, and was meant to reflect the Vulcan belief that

Wearing the IDIC medallion ("Is There in Truth No Beauty?")

many diverse life-forms can join together peaceably to create meaning and beauty. Simply put, it's a statement against bigotry and hatred.

Certainly, I was all in favor of the philosophy behind the IDIC— but not the fact that Gene wanted me to wear the medallion because he wanted to sell them through his mail-order business, Lincoln Enterprises. Where the scene had been problematic creatively for me, it now was problematic ethically. While I wouldn't argue with the IDIC concept, I was troubled that I had opened the door and let in a new kind of animal while trying to get rid of another.

"Dagger of the Mind" revisited: "Whom Gods Destroy"

Although I didn't appreciate Spock being turned into a billboard, I at least felt that the IDIC idea had more value than the content of the original scene. We filmed the scene as Gene had rewritten it. But the whole incident was rather unpleasant; Roddenberry was peeved at me for not wanting to help his piece of mail-order merchandise get off to a resounding start, and Fred Freiberger was peeved at me for going over his head. I certainly didn't make any friends over the issue.

The final straw for me came near the season's end, with the episode "Whom Gods Destroy." The story deals with a high-security insane asylum, which unbeknownst to the visiting crew members of the *Enterprise* is actually controlled by the mad inhabitants—who hope to use the starship's appearance as an opportunity to escape.

The concept was strongly reminiscent of an earlier episode we'd done, "Dagger of the Mind" (cited as Spock's first use of the Vulcan mind meld). But at the end of the third-season version, "Whom Gods Destroy," one of the mental patients is a shape-shifter who assumes Kirk's appearance. Now, as Spock approaches, armed with a phaser, he finds two Kirks, and is forced to figure out which one's really his captain.

In the original draft of the script, the phony Kirk catches the Vulcan by surprise and knocks him out. I went to the production department and said, "Look, you can't have Spock walk into a room where there are two Kirks, and not have him ask subtle, pointed questions to determine which is the real captain. And you certainly won't have him being overcome by the wrong guy!"

Well, the producers had decided that the fight between two Kirks was just too nifty an idea to pass up (even though we'd done it with far more sophistication and dramatic complexity in the first season, with "The Enemy Within"). They insisted on keeping that confrontation as is, but we did reach an accommodation in terms of Spock.

Sort of. In the rewrite, Spock was still attacked by the false Kirk and falls to the floor—but the audience is let in on the fact that the Vulcan isn't *really* knocked cold, but is watching the fight between the two Kirks.

When it's all over, and the good Kirk (luckily for our side) wins, he asks Spock, "Why didn't you help me?"

And the Vulcan replies, "I thought you'd want to handle the situation yourself." It was a tongue-in-cheek send-up of the whole encounter, which wasn't particularly fulfilling or satisfying for the viewers, but at least it didn't destroy established character traits.

I had grown so frustrated by the time the episode was being shot that I sent a plaintive memo over Fred Freiberger's head, to Gene Roddenberry and Doug Cramer, then head of Desilu. If you compare it with the first one I sent Fred, you can see the difference in my level of anger. My memo came to be known as "The Letter":

To: Gene Roddenberry, Doug Cramer   Date: October 15, 1968
From: Leonard Nimoy

Gentlemen:
During the first season of *Star Trek*, a character named Mr. Spock was established in the series. This character had pointed ears, extremely high intelligence, was capable of brilliant leaps of deductive logic, could contact people's minds, could tick off data about Earth, space, time, etc., as though he had memorized libraries on the subject, was extremely powerful physically, had a great deal of pride, and a few other things, which in general made him a smart ass.

Now we all know that nobody, but *nobody* likes a smart ass, and above all a continuing character in a TV series must not only be liked, but well liked! Therefore, I can well understand the efforts this season to change this character's image, so that he will be more acceptable to the American public.

Now we are embarked on re-doing a show that we did during the first season when it was originally entitled "Dagger of the Mind," with guest star James Gregory. A story of a planet which supports a mental institution. The title has been very cleverly disguised, and we are now calling it "Whom Gods Destroy." Since evidently the show was effective the first time around, we have managed to retain much of the story line for the second shooting.

I note one major difference which is evidently indicative of the drastic change in the Spock character. In "Dagger of the Mind," Spock picked up some valuable information by mind-melding with a man whose mind was terribly disturbed, and Spock was able to gather information from him only through the mind-to-mind contact which Vulcans are capable of. In our current episode, Spock is confronted with what would seem to be a rather simplistic situation. He walks into a room, phaser in hand, and is confronted by two "Kirks." One is obviously his real captain and the other is an impostor. Question: Can Spock handle the situation using his deductive logic, the phaser in his hand, his previous experiences with Kirk, his mind meld, or any of the other imaginative techniques that a smart ass Vulcan would normally use? The answer is: NO.

Not only is he unable to cleverly, dramatically, and fascinatingly arrive at a solution, he also proves to be a lousy gun hand, since he allows the two men to become embroiled in a brawl while he stands there holding a phaser, not sure whether he should shoot one or both, or maybe just let them fight it out and "hope that the best man wins."

Now I'm given to understand that a fight between the two "Kirks" is absolutely vital to our series. I guess I can understand that from a production point of view. It seems that most series are cutting down, or cutting out violence, and I guess *Star Trek* will corner the market with this kind of sub-rosa activity.

My primary interest in contacting you gentlemen is my concern over my lack of experience in playing dummies. Perhaps you could arrange to get me educated in this area. Maybe if I watched some "Blondie" episodes and watched Dagwood as a role model, I could pick up some pointers. Or better still, I could get right to the bottom line by wearing some braids and feathers and learning to grunt, "Ugh, Kimosabee"?

Any suggestions?

Hopefully,

Leonard Nimoy

Fred, naturally, sent me a memo letting me know how unhappy he was that I had again gone over his head. I wasn't happy that I'd done it, either—but I felt I had no choice. The alternative was to watch the character of Spock slowly deteriorate.

By the end of the third season, I was still under contract to Paramount for an additional two years. However, I was so distressed by the problems with the scripts that I was prepared to resist coming back to work—which would probably have led to suspension from my contract, and legal proceedings.

I steeled myself for the probable confrontation—but as it turned out, my worries were unnecessary. NBC failed to renew *Star Trek* for a fourth season, and my resolve to defend the character of Spock became moot.

EIGHT

FROM
FIVE-YEAR
MISSION
TO
MISSION:
IMPOSSIBLE

.

NIMOY: Spock, how did you feel when *Star Trek* was cancelled?

SPOCK: *Please . . . I must remind you . . .*

NIMOY: I know, I'm sorry. I mean, did you have any reaction? You were set
         aside . . . relegated to nonexistence.

SPOCK: *Simple nonexistence, like death, is not to be feared. That is a human*
         reaction.

NIMOY: Let me rephrase the question, then: What did you *think* about the
         cancellation of *Star Trek*? About the "end" of your existence?

SPOCK: *I thought it rather . . . premature. A regrettable situation, like the*
         needless death of a child. But there was nothing to be done. To have
         indulged in anger or despair would simply have been a waste of
         time.

NIMOY: Did you ever entertain hopes that *Star Trek* might return? That you
         might be . . . reborn?

SPOCK: *I would not use the term "hope." It was merely logical that* Star Trek
         return. When the demands of the fans reached critical mass, my
         rebirth was inevitable.

NIMOY: Well, you could have fooled me! I was sure you and the show were
         finished.

THE SEVENTY-NINTH and final episode of *Star Trek*,
"Turnabout Intruder," was filmed during December 1968
and January 1969. During its filming, we were all aware
that the show would be cancelled; although we hadn't
received official notice from NBC, the time had already passed for
the network to notify us that the series would continue for a fourth
season. Technically, however, NBC had the right to exercise its
option to renew us shortly before a fourth season would have

begun—and had that happened, we would have all been called back to work.

But it didn't. On the last day of shooting "Turnabout," we all stepped onto the soundstage with a sense of finality. I honestly remember little of that last day, except a feeling of heaviness. And of course, I remember the episode very well. The story offered Bill Shatner an interesting acting challenge, because it called for Captain Kirk's body to be taken over by a vengeful woman's mind. My recollection of the script was that it was something of a one-note joke, rather gimmicky, but Bill approached the challenge with typical zest and energy, which I admired. He was less serious and reflective than I; he didn't question whether he should be doing it, he simply said, "Well, we're doing it, so I'm going to attack it!"

However, even Bill's enthusiasm finally gave way after the final scene was shot and it was time to call it a wrap. There was no formal wrap party, no official event to mark the show's passing. We each drifted off the *Star Trek* soundstage for what we were sure would be the last time, and went our separate ways.

It was a few months later that I got the official notification from the network, at the time our contracts finally expired. "Leonard, hello," a warm but solemn voice said over the phone. "This is Dave Tebet at NBC. Leonard, I have sad news; it falls to me as the network's head of talent to call you and tell you that *Star Trek* won't be coming back for another season."

"I suspected as much," I told him, and thanked him; Dave expressed his sincere regret once more, and we hung up.

(A quick aside: I bumped into Dave Tebet two years later, when I was working in London on the film "Baffled"—which, ironically, was intended as a pilot for NBC, Dave's network. I was having lunch with my wife in Mayfair, at the White Elephant, when I passed Tebet having lunch with Tony Curtis. As we passed, I greeted him with a bright, "Hello, Dave!"

He looked up at me blankly, then went right back to his conversation with Tony without missing a beat. I had to laugh, because it was such a perfect example of the "then-we-loved-you, now-we-don't" mentality in Hollywood. More on that later.)

I had terribly mixed feelings about *Star Trek*'s cancellation, including a sense of relief because I wasn't happy with what the show was becoming. Of course I didn't want the series to end; I wanted to keep working, and was happy to do good stuff. At the same time, I didn't want to see *Star Trek* sink to a level where we were tearing away at the standards we'd set.

A short time after we finished shooting "Turnabout," I was still occupying office space with my secretary, Teresa Victor, on the Paramount lot. Ed Milkis, who'd been *Star Trek*'s production assistant, called me and said that since the show was cancelled, they'd be needing that space. So when could I be out?

I asked for a couple of weeks, since I had to go out of town; but as soon as I was back, I promised Eddie I'd vacate. "Fine," Ed said. "No problem. I think we can handle two or three weeks."

But within a few days, he called me back. The situation was now urgent: A new writer had been hired for *Mission: Impossible* and needed the space. "How fast can you be off the lot?" Ed asked bluntly.

I asked if we could stick to our original agreement, but Ed said, as tactfully as he could, that they really needed the office space yesterday, if not sooner.

The next day, two workers and a van arrived at the office. They loaded everything into the van, and we wound up moving all the equipment and supplies to Teresa's house for emergency storage until we found a new location.

So that—I thought—was that. *Star Trek* was over, and I had no plans whatsoever for the future. I knew, however, that I was very interested in playing as many different roles as possible, in order to broaden my base as an actor.

In the meantime, around the time *Star Trek* was cancelled, trouble began brewing on the *Mission: Impossible* set. The series had been renewed for a fourth season, and Martin Landau and his wife, Barbara Bain, had reached an impasse in their contract-renewal negotiations with Paramount. Since the couple was perceived to be the heart of the show, they had hoped to negotiate on that basis from a position of great strength. But the studio bucked at their contract demands, and closed the door on them.

When that happened, my agent called me to say, "You have to go back to work, Leonard. They're offering you a job on *Mission: Impossible.*"

I was immediately concerned, because I was friends with Marty and Barbara. *Mission* had been sold by Paramount and begun production at the very same time as *Star Trek*. In fact, the *Mission* and *Trek* soundstages were adjoining. So I saw Marty quite often around the set.

"Look," I told my agent, "I won't be used as a negotiating ploy against Marty and Barbara."

"No, no, it's not like that at all," he said. "The studio had already stopped negotiating with them. It's over, done."

"Are you sure?" I asked. "I don't want to find out later that I'm out, and they're going back to work . . . "

My agent was adamant: The studio had absolutely decided to let Marty and Barbara go before offering me the job. And he turned out to be correct, as I later learned from an article in the *Los Angeles Times*, where Marty and Barbara told their story.

So it was that I wound up replacing Marty Landau—the man Gene Roddenberry had in mind as a second choice for Spock, had I been unavailable for "The Cage"—on *Mission: Impossible*. The situation was ideal for an actor; I was permitted to "test the waters" by signing an eight-episode contract, and scripts were made available to me for my approval.

When the deal was done, one of the first people I called was Ed Milkis, who'd help me move off the Paramount lot after *Star Trek* was cancelled. It was time for that truck and two drivers again, to help move me *back* onto the lot. I laughingly commented to Ed that we could have saved a couple moves if I'd been allowed to stay on the lot a few weeks longer.

Ed's reply was classic Hollywood: "Well, Leonard, we didn't love you then. But we love you now." (I recalled that line with amusement two years later in London, when met by Dave Tebet's blank stare.)

Working on *Mission: Impossible* was at first very exciting . . . But soon, quite frankly, it became boring. (In fact, to this day, there are long periods of time where I forget I ever did the show!) It was exciting to me because my character, Paris the Great, was a master of disguise; therefore, I got to play a multitude of characters: old men, Asians, South American dictators, blind men, Europeans . . . And *Mission* was refreshing television for the time because it was very cinematic. You had to stay glued to the screen to follow what was happening (whereas *Star Trek* had a lot of dialog; you could usually follow it by listening from the other room). *Mission* was also very clever, like the movie *The Sting*; each episode, all the series regulars used their different talents to pull a fast one on the villain of the week.

In fact, the third script Paramount submitted to me was a beauty; in it, I played a revolutionary leader loosely based on Che Guevara. I did some research on the character, worked with the wardrobe and makeup people, got myself some cigars, and in general, had a marvelous time with the part. And I guess the fun I had must have showed, because when Paramount and CBS saw the footage of the episode, they offered me a longer four-year contract. Enthused at the time, I agreed.

But then, before I knew it, I was playing the South American dictator again. And the Asian, and the old man, and the blind guy . . .

The other thing that led to my boredom was the character I played, Paris. (I often wondered if the one-word name was chosen because of my success with the monosyllabic moniker Spock.) Paris is more correctly termed a "non-character," because we knew absolutely nothing about him. Whereas Spock's internal life had been rich and clearly defined, Paris had no internal life at all. On *Mission*, none of the characters did; nor did they have any interaction with each other. The focus was on their skills and activities as part of the *Mission* team. In each episode, Paris simply reached into his bag of theatrical tricks, but we never saw what made him tick, or what personal conflicts he faced. About the closest we came to a personal, private moment with Paris was in a scene where Paris came home to his apartment one night, dressed in a tux, just as the phone rings. (It's Mr. Phelps, of course.)

And, frankly, I missed Spock. I missed him during *Mission* and afterwards, until 1979, when we filmed the first *Trek* motion picture. I've never been totally free of mental "echoes" of Spock ever since we did *Star Trek*, and certainly, from time to time, I'd hear his voice commenting quite logically on a particular situation.

•

©1995 PARAMOUNT PICTURES

Having a revolutionary good time on the Mission set

•

However, I don't mean to sound like I'm complaining here, because my experience on the *Mission* set was a very pleasant one. The cast—Greg Morris, Peter Lupus, Lesley Anne Warren, Peter Graves—were a great bunch of people. And frankly, this series seemed like a cakewalk after the grueling workload on *Star Trek*. On *Trek*, most every scene featured Kirk and Spock, so Bill Shatner

Paris the Great

and I had to be on the set and at work most of the twelve-hour shooting day, five days a week. But on *Mission*, the work was split among five people. The "team" was all gathered in each episode's opening scene and again in the last scene, as everyone drives off after the mission's accomplished. In between, the characters went their separate ways. So while Greg Morris was off tunneling through walls installing electronic devices, for example, I had some free time.

In fact, I had plenty of time. So much so that I started writing poetry and indulging my passion for photography. I even started working out, swimming every morning before going to work. I thought I was totally comfortable, relaxed, and happy, glad to be free from the pressure of *Star Trek*, with all its dialog to be memorized and the early morning makeup calls . . .

But then something interesting happened to me during *Mission*'s first season. One Saturday night, when I went out to dinner with my wife, I began to feel discomfort in my stomach. I managed to get through dinner and then home to bed, but was awakened around two in the morning with severe stomach pains. By 3 A.M., I was on the phone to my doctor, and by 4 A.M., I was in a hospital bed being tranquilized.

It seemed I had suddenly developed a gastric ulcer.

Now, if *ever* I should have gotten an ulcer, it should have been during *Star Trek*, not *Mission*; but when I ponder it, it makes me wonder—was the lack of fulfillment on *Mission* actually more stressful for me than the tough but meaningful grind on *Star Trek*?

At any rate, I followed my doctor's orders and went on a new dietary regime. Within a year or two, I experienced a total recovery and to this day have no further stomach problems.

And I went back to work on *Mission*. But midway through my second season, I finally realized I had done it all: I had played all the different parts that I had wanted to play, and the fun had begun to wear thin for me. There was no challenge, no excitement left. So I called my agent and asked him to request my release from the series.

Now, if there's one thing in this world Hollywood agents pray for, it's the chance to land their clients in a television series, because it means steady work in a notoriously undependable business. Actors fight hard to get *into* series, not to get *out*.

So my agent ignored me for a couple of months. He assumed, quite rationally, that I was totally crazy, or that I'd had a disagreement with someone—which, of course, he hoped would blow over. He did a good job of waiting me out, and after I reassured him time after time that I really had decided to leave the show, he finally talked to the studio.

I left the series on very good terms with the studio. *Mission* continued for three very successful years without me (in fact, it amuses me to think that no one really noticed when Paris disappeared).

As for Spock and *Star Trek*: Even though those "echoes" of the character continued to remain with me, I still had no inkling that the show would ever be revived. (Interestingly, shortly after the show was cancelled, it was reported in some papers that NBC had offered me my own series based on Spock. Where they got the information, I can't imagine, because it was utterly false. The downside was that these reports lit the first fires of resentment among fans who were mourning the death of *Star Trek* and came to blame me for their deprivation.)

Shortly after I left *Mission,* I signed a one-year contract to act and direct at Universal. Sid Sheinberg, who was head of production at that studio, said, "We've just hired Gene Roddenberry to write a project for you."

The Questor Tapes was about a robot created by a multinational group of scientists. During his creation, he realizes that his existence will lead to an international struggle over who owns him; therefore, he finishes himself and runs off in search of his creator (a favorite Roddenberry theme).

Gene sent me the first draft of the script. I read it and gave him some comments and suggestions, saying, "Let's talk some more."

The contract I had signed with Universal was with the understanding that I was to star in this new series. Until that happened, I worked in various guest-starring roles at the studio. It was there that I did my first directing, an episode of *Night Gallery*, "Death on a Barge." I hired Lesley Anne Warren, who gave a lovely performance as a vampire, in a story with Romeo and Juliet overtones.

One day at the studio, I was in the makeup department for another job when I noticed a life-mask and some photos of me on the wall. I knew that the *Questor* pilot required the robot character to appear in various stages of development; it seemed they'd found an old life-mask of me, and were using it in order to make the necessary appliances for the pilot.

So I naturally thought, "Great! I guess they'll be calling me in soon to do the appliance work."

But I never got the call. Perhaps it's just as well, because I was sincerely beginning to enjoy my flexibility as a guest star. I wasn't sure I was ready for the grind of another series.

So one day, I was at the studio again for makeup, and thinking about why I hadn't gotten the call for *Questor*. I mentioned this to an actor sitting beside me, James McKeechan. "Well," James said, "I think we can get an answer for you pretty fast, because I know the director, Richard Colla."

So he picked up the nearest phone, called Dick Colla (who was on the lot), and asked him to come over and meet me.

Colla showed up looking rather sheepish. "This is very embarrassing for me, Leonard. We've just cast someone else."

I was very surprised, but laughed to put him at ease. "Please relax, Dick," I told him. "You've actually done me a big favor. I'm not so sure I'm ready for another series."

"Well, I'm glad you feel that way, because frankly," Colla said, "we were having meetings about casting, and I said I thought it was too obvious to have you playing this character, because he's so Spock-like. So I suggested that we should consider hiring someone else. The idea took root, and we've hired Robert Foxworth."

I thanked him and again told him not to feel uneasy about it. Later, I called Gene Roddenberry.

"Hi, Gene," I said. "I'm sitting here having a drink to the success of Robert Foxworth."

There was a brief silence as Gene digested this, and then he said, "Well, I'm outraged. It's a terrible thing! I'm the executive producer, and they've been asking me to look at films of different actors, and asked me to look at Foxworth. I had no idea what their intentions were—I just looked at the film and said, 'Well, he's a good actor, I guess'—and before I knew it, they offered him the job." He paused, then added: "Of course, he hasn't accepted it yet. And if he doesn't, we'll be back to you immediately."

"It's all right," I assured him. "Save yourself a phone call. I'll just assume I'm out of this."

And that was the end of my involvement in the *Questor Tapes*. It's just as well, because Dick Colla was right—the main character was somewhat Spock-like, and I didn't want to repeat myself.

After all, Spock and things Vulcan were forever relegated to my past, or so I thought, back in 1971.

Little did I know that my relationship with *Star Trek* and the Vulcan were only really about to begin.

NINE

IDENTITY CRISIS

NIMOY: Spock . . . What did you think about *Star Trek*'s rebirth in the 1970s? You were gone, and then came back bigger than ever.

SPOCK: *Your question's premise is faulty. For one thing, I never went away.*

IN LATE 1971, after my departure from *Mission: Impossible*, I permitted myself some time off to indulge my personal love of photography for a few months.

One day, while I was developing some film, the phone in my dark room rang. It was an old friend, motion picture producer Euan Lloyd. "How would you like to go to Spain?" he asked.

It turned out Euan was producing a Western, *Catlow*, starring Yul Brynner and Richard Crenna. My old acting teacher and partner, Jeff Corey, was also to appear in the film, and Sam Wanamaker, whose work I respected, would direct.

I agreed to do the project, which required me to leave for Spain on April 7. Now I started growing a beard, since Sam Wanamaker thought it would be appropriate for my character. By late March, when I headed to New York for a political fundraiser, I was sporting some serious facial hair.

While I was in New York, I decided to meet with my theatrical agent, Eric Schepard. In the past, I'd always been too tied up with television to be available for theatrical roles, but now that I had some time, I was interested.

Eric and I met at his office at the International Famous Agency, and talked about my future.

"Look," he said, "I know of a great role. Would you be interested in playing Tevye in *Fiddler on the Roof*?"

(*Fiddler*, of course, is the wonderful musical about a shtetl, a community of Russian Jews. Naturally, because my parents had come from such a village, I was immediately intrigued by the idea.)

I laughed, wondering if my new beard had sparked Eric's imagination. "Of course I'd be interested."

"Great," Eric said, and made a phone call to Stephen Slane, a theatrical producer. Slane and his director, Ben Shaktman, happened to be in New York, where they were in the process of casting for an upcoming summer production of *Fiddler*.

Within an hour, I met with both men and did a very clumsy audi-

As Tevye in Fiddler on the Roof, *1971*

tion for them; at the time, I hadn't seen the play, and knew very little of its storyline or music. But that night, I went to see the Broadway production of *Fiddler*. I was more determined then that I wanted the part.

In the morning, when I spoke with Slane, he told me he felt I was capable of the role; but the director, Shaktman, had reservations. A tall, skinny Tevye who was best known for playing an alien with pointed ears was *not* what he'd had in mind. When I learned of his concerns, I called Shaktman and poured out my heart, telling him my family's background and my deep, personal identification with the characters in the play. He agreed to let me do a second audition, which was far more successful. Within a matter of days, he called to ask whether I was still interested in the role.

I left for Spain to do *Catlow* with the script of *Fiddler* tucked into my luggage. My role in *Catlow* was quite small, which permitted me a good deal of free time. I spent it either photographing the local scenery or lying on the beach, listening to tape tracks of *Fiddler* songs. (I must have been a strange sight for the Spanish locals: Mr. Spock with a beard and bathing suit, listening to Semitic songs on a cassette recorder!)

I should mention here that my family always understood that an actor's profession was nomadic. Despite that, we worked hard to keep the family together, and so during that Spanish summer of '71, my wife and two kids came along with me. Charlie Bronson was filming in town, and he'd brought along his wife, Jill Ireland, and their children, one of whom was around Julie's age; we actually wound up splitting the cost of a tutor with them.

Despite the fact that we were filming in remote towns on Spain's southern coast, where there was virtually no television, *Star Trek* still managed to catch up to me. One day, I was sitting in the chair of *Catlow*'s makeup trailer, practicing my truly bad Spanish on a friendly young makeup artist from Madrid.

Fortunately, his English was much better than my Spanish; and that day, he said to me, with a gleam in his eye, "I have something to show you." He reached into his cabinet, pulled out a cigar box, and opened it.

Lo and behold, nestled inside were a pair of Mr. Spock's ears! Not a cheap plastic imitation, mind you, but an authentic foam-rubber appliance, made from the mold cast from my own ears. (All right, you trivia lovers: Want to know how many pairs of ears I went through during those seventy-nine episodes? A whopping 150, almost two per episode. The Vulcan lives on, but his ears weren't good for much more than a few days.)

I was dumbfounded. I hadn't even expected him to know about *Star Trek* and Mr. Spock—but to see a pair of ears here, in a cigar box in rural Spain . . .

How did this happen? It all had to do with a man named John Chambers. Chambers, a true master among makeup artists (who later won an Academy Award for his work on *Planet of the Apes*), had supplied *Star Trek* makeup man Freddy Phillips with Vulcan ears during the series. Well, it turned out that he'd come to Spain to teach makeup artists about appliances, and he'd brought some examples of his work—including several pairs of Spock ears. My Spanish makeup man just happened to have worked for him as an assistant.

(A similar thing once happened to me in London, when I was visiting at the home of a Paramount sales representative there. I was chatting with him and his teenage son when the boy left the room, then returned with a Mr. Spock uniform, complete with boots. "How nice," I thought, "and what a really authentic-looking copy!" Until I looked at it more closely and realized it *wasn't* a copy. It turned out to be one of *my*—or rather, Spock's—actual uniforms that I'd worn on the set! It still amazes me how pieces of Spock are scattered all over the world. All I've got from the series— other than that calm voice inside my head—are some photos and one pair of ears, mounted in a plastic box.)

On June 10, 1971, I finished work on *Catlow* and flew from Spain back home to Los Angeles. By June 24, I was in New York again, preparing for a seven-week tour of *Fiddler*.

Fiddler opened in Hyannis, Massachusetts, to a sold-out crowd who gave us a standing ovation at the play's end. Reviews were equally as enthusiastic. The next seven weeks were, simply put, glorious; there are times when one realizes that a very special event is taking place in one's life. *Fiddler* was such a time for me. I can compare it to the best of *Star Trek*: I walked with pride and a special spring in my step because the vehicle, the company, and the time all came together to create a special magic. I felt a deep kinship and gratitude toward the entire theatrical company—who, in their kindness, gave me and my wife a very special gift, a pair of pewter candelabras inscribed with a phrase from *Fiddler*'s Sabbath prayer song: "Favor them, O Lord, with happiness and peace."

Fiddler was only the first experience in my extremely enjoyable theatrical career. I went on to appear as Fagin in *Oliver*, Arthur in *Camelot*, and the Siamese monarch in *The King and I*. In addition to the musicals, I also appeared in numerous dramas, including *The*

FROM THE COLLECTION OF LEONARD NIMOY

A pensive King Arthur in Camelot

Man in the Glass Booth, which was performed at San Diego's Globe Theatre.

   Glass Booth was especially exciting for me because it does what all good drama should: provoke its audience to think, to question themselves and their values. It deals with a man who has been accused as a Nazi war criminal, and is taken back to Israel for trial. The man, Goldman, doesn't deny any of the accusations against him. If anything, he revels in the part he played in the Holocaust, taunting his infuriated prosecutors.

As *Goldman in* The Man in the Glass Booth

FROM THE COLLECTION OF LEONARD NIMOY

Ultimately, though, a woman who had been an inmate at one of the Nazi extermination camps reveals Goldman's secret: "He's one of us," she says. "He was no Nazi. He's a Jew! I recognize him as an inmate in the camp where I was imprisoned." The point was that Goldman *wanted* his accusers to execute him—only later to find that, in their haste toward vengeance, they had killed an innocent man. The play caused some outcry from a small, very vocal group who called it anti-Semitic; in response, the director and myself held an open seminar at a local temple. The exchange was lively and interesting—and, it turned out, the overwhelming majority of the people (most of them Jewish) didn't find it at all anti-Semitic.

It was during my theatrical experiences that I became increasingly aware of a strange phenomenon: a surge of interest in the defunct *Star Trek* series. The show had gone off the air in 1969, but by 1971, many television stations had picked it up in syndication and were running episodes on a daily basis. *Star Trek*—and Spock—were dead (or so I mistakenly thought), yet here they were, gaining new fans.

And almost every review of the plays I worked in contained a reference to Spock or *Star Trek*. In fact, the review of *Glass Booth* in San Diego bore the headline: NIMOY GREAT SANS EARS.

I have to admit, this caused me something of an identity crisis. I didn't want to be known as a one-note performer; I was involved in theatrical work precisely so that I could be known as an actor with a great deal of range. I was trying to convince audiences of precisely what the San Diego critic said—that I could act *without* the ears.

Still, the Vulcan was always with me—even the night when, at a theater-in-the-round, I was deeply engrossed in my character and moving slowly down a darkened aisle, preparing to make my entrance onto the stage. From one of the nearby seats, a little voice whispered: "Hi, Mr. Spock."

And, I confess, there were times when I was annoyed by Spock's continuous presence. I recall quite clearly the time I gave a performance as the mad emperor in *Caligula* in Austin, Texas. There was a line in the play I dreaded, when Caligula says: "We are resolved to be logical."

The logical but crazed Caligula, 1975

Night after night, I approached that line like a reluctant horse approaches a hurdle; I didn't want to say it, but knew I had to. And once I uttered those fateful words, I could hear—or almost hear, in the silence—the little laugh that said, "He's here. Spock is here . . . "

SPOCK: *Greetings. You've been away.*

NIMOY: Yes. Doing a play in Austin, Texas. *Caligula.*

SPOCK: *Ah. The Roman emperor. He was mad, was he not?*

NIMOY: Yes. The play was written by Camus . . .

SPOCK: *The French existentialist. A contemporary of Sartre and Gide . . . And what did the play concern?*

NIMOY: Caligula, in his madness, wants to "change the scheme of things" . . . to teach his people to demand more of themselves and each other.

SPOCK: *And how does he propose to do that?*

NIMOY: (hesitantly) By insisting they base their actions on logic rather than emotion..

SPOCK: *Brilliant! I must reread my Camus.*

NIMOY: (triumphant) But Caligula is mad—and even he, in the end, realizes he's lost his way.

SPOCK: *Unfortunate. A fine idea gone astray in the hands of an unbalanced human.*

The resurgence of interest in *Star Trek* caused me a great deal of conflict. Because, at the very same time that I was struggling to avoid being typecast as a Vulcan, I really did miss Spock. I was glad for his return, and for the opportunities that *Star Trek*'s newfound popularity brought me.

Now, 1972 was a landmark year for the show, because in January, the very first national *Star Trek* convention was held in New York City. It was an entirely new concept, this gathering of fans to celebrate *Trek* for a weekend. The organizers crossed their fingers and hoped for 500 attendees.

They got 3,000.

The conventions were a particularly dramatic manifestation of what was happening to *Star Trek* in its resurgency. At my first convention in 1972, I walked into a hall so crowded, there was some concern the fire department would close it down.

The thunderous wall of noise that greeted me took me completely by surprise. The screams, the applause, the electric response to my every move, my every word, my every gesture, was simply extraordinary. It was a physical shock, like being knocked breathless by a huge ocean wave; for several seconds, I literally could not speak because of the emotion. (Not that the applauding audience could have heard me anyway!) It was a wonderful, warm, welcoming homecoming.

What made it even more touching was the fact that the conventions were so genuine, so grass-roots. There was no hype, no commerciality, no Hollywood promoters organizing the events; these were people who came together simply because of their love of *Star Trek*.

Why did the *Star Trek* phenomenon occur? Why did the series attract such a large and devoted audience?

Like everyone else, I can only speculate. But some things seem clear.

For one thing, *Star Trek* offered hope to a generation who had grown up haunted by the specter of nuclear war. A significant portion of its viewers remembered the 1962 Cuban missile crisis, when the country was readying for World War III. Kids were being taught to "duck-and-cover" beneath their school desks if they saw an atomic flash. Grim end-of-the-world scenarios were shown in popular books and films, such as Nevil Shute's *On the Beach* and Pat Frank's *Alas, Babylon!* At the same time, our paranoia toward Soviet Russia had reached an all-time high—which may explain why space aliens were generally portrayed in films as evil monsters, bent on conquering Earth.

And in the midst of this paranoia and fear came a bright message of hope in the form of *Star Trek*, which said, "Yes, we *will* survive the atomic age. We *will* contact other intelligent life on other planets, and they'll be our friends, not our enemies. Together, we'll work for the common good."

Suddenly, a whole generation who'd grown up with these terrible tensions and fears turned on their television sets to discover *Star Trek* there, every weekday.

The 1970s were still times of great cultural upheaval as well; this was the era of Vietnam and Watergate, of drug abuse and sexual revolution. Society was undergoing a rapid change; Americans were learning to mistrust their political leaders. And in the midst of those undependable times, there were the *Star Trek* crew: utterly trustworthy, predictable, incorruptible—people who could be counted on to tell the truth and behave ethically, with dignity and compassion and intelligence.

Sid Sheinberg was right; the *Star Trek* fans I spoke to at the conventions were indeed intense and vocal. And there were *thousands* of them, everywhere I went. A lot more than Sheinberg or I, or anyone else, had suspected. I soon began to realize that it wasn't a question of whether *Star Trek* would return in some guise; it was a question of how and when.

As early as 1972, NBC was beginning to have a change of heart. The network started talking to Roddenberry about the possibility of bringing back the series. However, the original sets had been trashed, and executives decided that rebuilding them—and replacing all the props and costumes—would be just too expensive. The project was dropped.

However, in early 1973, *Star Trek* reappeared on the small screen in animated form. The show, produced by Dorothy Fontana, lasted two seasons, and drew praise from critics.

Paramount—which had bought *Star Trek* rights from Desilu—finally determined to bring the series back to life with the original cast. By 1975, the studio was talking to Gene Roddenberry about developing a new *Star Trek* show for television. But as the fans' enthusiasm grew, so did Paramount's, and Gene's; before long, the TV series idea had become a motion picture.

Roddenberry's first draft of a movie script, *The God Thing*, was rejected. For the next three years, a score of writers had input into the project, but none of the scripts were deemed acceptable.

Finally, by 1978, the Paramount executives decided that *nobody* was going to come up with a *Star Trek* idea suitable for the big screen. At the same time, the studio had plans to launch a fourth network. Why not bring back the original cast in a new series, *Star Trek: Phase II*, the cornerstone?

I'll confess that when I first heard about the new show, I had major reservations. (Remember, only a few years earlier, I had foolishly given my book the title *I Am Not Spock*.) I was still very concerned about being perceived as a one-character actor, and still war-weary from the unpleasant struggles from *Trek*'s third season. But I was at least willing to hear what Paramount and Gene Roddenberry had to offer.

And here it was: a recurring role wherein Spock appeared in two of every eleven episodes.

Quite honestly, the offer confused and startled me. Only *two* out of every eleven? I was being offered a parttime job. It made little sense for me to be technically tied up with a series and having to be unavailable for other challenging work, while at the same time making such a small contribution to the show.

I—and that ever-present calm, rational voice in my head—struggled to make sense out of it.

SPOCK: *Let us examine the possibilities. Perhaps we will dis-cover a hidden logic here.*

NIMOY: Okay. I'm willing.

SPOCK: *Is it possible they believe you are reluctant to return, and therefore are offering you something less than full involvement for your own convenience?*

NIMOY: Not likely. My agent asked if we could choose the number of episodes I'd like to do—and the answer was no.

SPOCK: *Is it possible your salary per episode is prohibitive?*

NIMOY: It hasn't even been discussed.

SPOCK: *Then we must face the possibility that my contribu-tion is judged to be nonessential.*

NIMOY: That's crazy, Spock! If that's what they think, then they're crazy!

SPOCK: *(calmly) I appreciate your support. Nevertheless, we must deal with this very real possibility, however unpleasant.*

I passed, and another actor, David Gautreaux, was hired to play the "new" Vulcan science officer, Xon. (Too bad Bob Justman was-n't around to write memos exploring all the new paradigms for male Vulcan names!) Unfortunately, my "refusal" to return to this new *Star Trek*, coupled with *I Am Not Spock*, was perceived as an utter rejection of the Vulcan. All the other cast had signed on; I was the lone holdout.

Ultimately, however, *Star Trek: Phase II* never warped out of spacedock. Only weeks before shooting was to begin on the new show, the project was scrapped—but not because Paramount had lost faith in it. To the contrary, they had more faith than ever, because of a totally different science fiction phenomenon with an extremely similar title:

Star Wars.

TEN

THANK YOU, GEORGE LUCÁS

SPOCK: *I should like to use this platform to publicly state for the record that*
         I do not imbibe fermented alcoholic beverages brewed from barley
         malt and hops—
NIMOY: You mean beer?
SPOCK: *I believe I just said that.*
NIMOY: Never even tasted it?
SPOCK: *Indeed not.*
NIMOY: Pity. A glass or two might've eased your dark mood throughout most
         of the first movie . . .

I'D LIKE TO LAUNCH right into the story of *Star Trek: The Motion Picture*. But in order to set the stage properly, I first have to dispense with the matter of the beer-guzzling Vulcan.

Beer? you ask. Spock drinks *beer?*

No one was more surprised to learn it than I.

The story of *ST:TMP* (affectionately pronounced "stimp" in fandom) rightly begins in London, where my wife and I were vacationing in 1975. In a hotel bar, to be precise, where I went shortly after we checked in one evening. The bartender grinned at the sight of me—friendly sort, I thought—then winked as he said knowingly, "I'll bet you want a Heineken, Mr. Nimoy."

Now, I'm not much of a beer drinker, so I was completely taken aback. "No, thanks," I answered pleasantly, and ordered my usual, wondering where on earth he'd gotten the notion that I'd want a beer—much less that particular brand.

I soon found out.

A few nights later, we went to see Henry Fonda, who was performing onstage in *Darrow*. (I had worked with Fonda three years earlier on a television movie entitled *The Alpha Caper*.) After the performance, we joined him and his wife for a late dinner. At some point during the conversation, Henry said, "You know, Leonard, I hope you're being paid for all those billboards around town."

"What billboards, Henry?" I had no idea what he was talking about.

"Do you mean to tell me you don't know about all those Heineken billboards?"

I recalled the strange question the bartender had asked me. "No. I sure don't. Can you show me one?"

He did. Turns out they were all over London—and they were large, prominent, and eye-grabbing.

There, larger than life, were three Spocks, facing the viewer in "see-no-evil, hear-no-evil, speak-no-evil" fashion. The leftmost Spock had exaggeratedly long ears that drooped down like floppy dog ears. The center Spock was lifting a glass of beer to his mouth, while his ears were half-erect and showing signs of life. The final Spock sported totally erect ears and a look of smug satisfaction.

The bold caption read:

HEINEKEN. REFRESHES THE PARTS OTHER BEERS CANNOT REACH.

The infamous beer-guzzling Vulcan

A familiar voice whispered in my ear.

SPOCK: *What does it mean?*
NIMOY: It's an advertisement to sell beer.
SPOCK: *I am not certain I fully understand the implication. "Refreshes the parts other beers cannot reach"? My ears, for example? Is this an attempt at humor?*
NIMOY: It's a joke, Spock, with a sexual subtext.
SPOCK: *Ah. (pause) Not exactly what I would call a dignified presentation in so public a place. Did you authorize this?*
NIMOY: No! Certainly not! It's a giant pain in the ass!
SPOCK: *A strange place for the discomfort to manifest itself.*
NIMOY: It's a figure of speech, Spock. Let me deal with this.
SPOCK: *Please do.*

I pulled out my trusty Nikon and took some quick shots of the billboard, then went back to the hotel and made a few phone calls. I soon learned that the Heineken billboard deal had been made back in Hollywood.

Now, I'd seen my Spock image used commercially before—such as on a box of Kellogg's Corn Flakes (which had also come from England). I'd been amused by it, finding it campy and even flattering; the notion of whether it was legal for my image to be used without my permission had never even occurred to me.

But it occurred to me when I saw those billboards. So when I returned to Los Angeles, I contacted my trusty business manager, Bernie Francis, who arranged for me to discuss the issue with a lawyer. "Do they have the right to do this?" I wanted to know. "Do I have any approval over how my likeness is used?"

The lawyer studied my old *Star Trek* contract, and asked Bernie just how much business was being done with my likeness. Bernie went over the books and discovered some explosive information: We hadn't received a single check for use of likeness in *five years*. The checks prior to that had been so negligible, we hadn't paid any attention when they stopped coming.

If you note the dates, you'll make the same interesting deduction we did: The money stopped coming just around the time *Star Trek* became a huge success, thanks to syndication!

The next bombshell came from the lawyer: It seemed that, once *Star Trek* was cancelled, Paramount had no legal right to license my likeness from that time on. So not only had Paramount been marketing me as Spock for almost ten years without the right to do so, for the last *five* of those ten, they hadn't sent me any of the proceeds.

You'd better believe there were a *lot* of phone calls between my office and Paramount. The studio claimed—and I believed them—that the billboards caught them by surprise. They said—and I believed them—that they too had found the ads to be in questionable taste, and had rejected them. Apparently, someone at a London agency had acted without approval.

Fair enough, I told them, but what about the inappropriate merchandising of my likeness for almost ten years—with no payoff to me for five?

All just a misunderstanding, the studio said—but we couldn't agree on what Paramount owed me, or on what my original contract had intended. I wound up having to file a lawsuit.

Add to this legal unpleasantness the *Questor* and *Star Trek II* incidents, and perhaps you can understand why I wasn't chomping at the bit to get involved with Paramount and *Star Trek* again.

But I knew I'd be hearing sooner or later from the studio. You see, in the summer of 1977, when I was in New York appearing in *Equus*, my agent called me to say, "Look, you've got to get yourself to a theater and see this new *Star Wars* movie."

So I slipped into a matinee showing in midtown Manhattan. And frankly, what I saw blew me—and all the other moviegoers in that same theater—away. *Star Wars* is a wonderfully inventive, entertaining film, complete with great images, a fun story, and incredible special effects. Along with everyone else, I laughed and cheered and had a great time. And I said to myself, "You're going to be getting a call from Paramount!"

Indeed I did. Fortunately for us all, it came from a young man named Jeffrey Katzenberg, who said, "Would you mind if I came to New York to talk to you? I'd love to see you in *Equus.*"

How could any actor refuse?

Jeff, it turned out, was refreshingly direct. He has a jockey's build, endless reserves of energy, a quick mind, and strong opinions, which he has no trouble voicing.

But the weekend he came to New York, he mostly listened carefully while I talked. He didn't posture, but gave the impression that he wanted to be truly helpful and fair. We frankly discussed the difficulties I was having with the studio. After several hours of talks, he asked whether I'd be willing to look at the script. I told him I didn't feel comfortable doing that while the lawsuit was still going on. He accepted that, and we parted on good terms.

In the meantime, I finished the play and went to work on

Equus, *the Helen Hayes Theater, Broadway, July 1977*

Invasion of the Body Snatchers in San Francisco, a remake of the 1950s science fiction classic. Paramount, of course, called again, but I reiterated my position that it didn't seem appropriate to discuss a new contract in the midst of a lawsuit.

The tension was building: Word was out that a *Star Trek* movie script was being written, and that other original cast members had signed on. Did I want the *Enterprise* to sail without me?

No. But I had faith that the matter would soon be settled.

Soon, director Robert Wise (of *The Sound of Music* and *The Day the Earth Stood Still* fame) was signed to direct. Unbeknownst to me, Mr. Wise was working on my behalf. He believed Spock to be important to the film, to the degree that his own contract with Paramount required the studio make its best effort to settle our differences.

Then word came that the entire cast had now signed their contracts. The script was finished, and everything was in place—except for Spock.

Paramount called again. Would I read the script?

I held firm. The lawsuit had to be resolved before I would read a script or sign a new contract.

Finally my lawyer called. "Look, Paramount's actually showing some willingness to reach an agreement. Would you read the script if they settled the lawsuit?"

Yes.

Four days later, on a Friday evening, the lawsuit settled; my lawyer came to my house with a check. An hour later, the script arrived. I sat down and read it through that night.

There were two problems. For one thing, the story simply wasn't very good.

For another, Spock didn't appear in it.

The following morning, Saturday, Gene Roddenberry, Robert Wise, and Jeff Katzenberg came to my home to discuss the script and my involvement in the film.

But before they came, I had another visitor.

NIMOY: Spock . . . Is that you?

SPOCK: *I am quite certain that it is I. Do you not recognize me?*

NIMOY: Well, of course, but you seem somehow . . . I can't really describe it . . .

SPOCK: *I experience myself as unfocused. But I do not find this condition surprising. Unpleasant, discomforting, perhaps—but not surprising.*

NIMOY: Why not?

SPOCK: *We have been quite preoccupied with the ancillary aspects of our relationship for some time.*

NIMOY: I'm sorry. All this stuff had to be dealt with. The fans, the press, the merchandising—they may seem strange to you, but they're part of what this is all about.

SPOCK: *I will try to understand. But then there is the other matter—the matter of identity.*

NIMOY: Whose identity?

SPOCK: *Ours.*

NIMOY: I don't understand.

SPOCK: *The separation of personalities. The rejection. The book.*

NIMOY: You mean, *I Am Not Spock?* That was just a play of words, ideas. I was just trying to find a way to come to terms and explain . . . us. Our relation-ship. Did you feel rejected? I'm sorry.

SPOCK: *I would not describe my experience as a "feeling."*

NIMOY: I didn't mean to offend—

SPOCK: *No offense taken. I am more concerned now with the gentlemen you are about to receive, who want me to make an appearance in their film. Perhaps I should be meeting with them instead of you.*

NIMOY: Spock, you're not even in the script yet.

SPOCK: *I am well aware.*

NIMOY: Then maybe I should meet with them and find out what we can do about a proper entrance for you . . .

SPOCK: *Very well—if you think it best. I must admit, however, that I look forward to being done with this business and getting on with the creative work. These past few years have been wearing.*

NIMOY: I know what you mean.

•

SPOCK: *I believe your guests have arrived. Perhaps you should*
         go greet them.

NIMOY: What do you mean? I didn't hear the—*The doorbell*
         rings—doorbell. (sighs) All right, Spock. Let's go
         see what they have in mind.

I answered the door to find Gene Roddenberry, Jeff Katzenberg
and Robert Wise; we exchanged greetings, and I was introduced to
Mr. Wise, whom I hadn't met. Compact and gray-haired, Robert
Wise is a calm, soft-spoken man—a true gentleman whose personal dignity has always inspired me to refer to him as Mr. Wise. I have
enormous respect for both him and his body of work, which
includes the Academy Award–winners *The Sound of Music* and *West
Side Story*; my personal favorite (the one that probably best recom-
mended him for *ST:TMP*) was the classic *The Day the Earth Stood
Still*. The movie concerns a group of technologically advanced
aliens who come to Earth not to conquer, but to warn us about toy-

The gentlemanly Robert Wise on the ST:TMP *set*

ing with atomic weapons. To convince us skeptical, war-loving humans of their abilities, they cause all power on the planet to cease (except in situations where life might be threatened, such as in hospitals) for a short time. It was a landmark film, which provoked us to think about how compassionate, peaceful outsiders might view us and our little planet.

(I have no doubt that the pro-extraterrestrial group in Nevada—and their alien friends—would have only good things to say about Mr. Wise and those involved in the making of that film.)

At any rate, we shook hands and took our seats. Gene and I greeted each other cordially, and the tone of our conversation remained pleasant, but in all honesty, he appeared agitated, haggard, and preoccupied. I got the impression that he had only come reluctantly, at Katzenberg's insistence ("You *will* be there, Gene, to help us get this guy on board!"). Perhaps he also instinctively knew I would have problems with the story.

And I think we both were grateful for the buffering presence of the other two men. After the unpleasant *Star Trek: Phase II* and *Questor* incidents, Gene and I were more uncomfortable than ever with each other.

Once the small talk was done, Jeff got right to the point.

"So, Leonard, did you read the script?"

"Yes. I read it last night."

"What did you think?"

I'd known the question would come. My gut instinct was to reply, *I think it's pretty bad*—but there seemed little point in complaining. In one of my more admirable moments of diplomacy, I evaded answering by throwing out a question of my own. "Is this the story you plan to shoot?"

"Yes," Jeff, Gene, and Mr. Wise chorused at once.

"Of course," Jeff hastened to add, "there will be some modifications . . ."

He and Mr. Wise quickly outlined them.

"And what are your intentions for the character of Spock?" I asked.

Katzenberg and Wise both turned in their seats to look at Gene, who fidgeted a bit in his chair, a man put on the spot.

"Well," Roddenberry said, with a hint of defensiveness, "when the five-year mission was over, Spock returned to Vulcan to purge himself of all vestiges of human emotion. And in his effort to achieve pure logic, he winds up suffering the Vulcan equivalent of a nervous breakdown."

I heard a soft voice inside my head:

SPOCK: *"Nervous breakdown?" Is this an Old-Earth colloquial-*
         ism? What does it mean?
NIMOY: Trust me, Spock—you don't want to know . . .

I drew a deep breath and replied, "I'm not sure how many of our audience would look forward to seeing Spock mentally disabled." In truth, I had no stomach for it myself; it seemed to violate the character's inherent dignity. It also showed that Spock hadn't really been worked into the story. One of the first unwritten rules of good drama states that every character has to fulfill an essential purpose in the story—otherwise, that character is unnecessary and should be cut. Spock's return to Vulcan was all very nice, but it had nothing to do with the plot about V'Ger (short for Voyager, the damaged Earth probe which supposedly hooked up with an alien probe and became superpowerful, thus causing problems for our heroes). How did the character fit into the big picture?

"It's only one idea," Gene assured me, with a quick glance at the other two men, and Katzenberg and Wise hurried to echo him. "We can discuss others, if you like . . . "

At that point, Jeff stood up and announced that he had another appointment, and motioned for Gene to come with him—which Roddenberry did, with obvious relief. (Actually, Jeff and I had earlier agreed that if things didn't seem to be working out, I would sit and talk privately with Bob Wise—and I'm certainly glad now that I did.)

Once Mr. Wise and I were alone, I asked some questions: "Do you believe in this script? What do you think about Gene's suggested story line for Spock?"

I didn't want to seem impudent or rude in front of this quiet, dignified director whose work I respected; and he clearly didn't want to say anything that might offend me. So we had an awkward but cordial conversation.

"There's a lot of work yet to be done on the script, and on Spock's storyline," he allowed, but beyond that, was not terribly forthcoming about details. We talked a bit more, while I tried to discern his intentions; but in the end, I had no definite guarantees about how the script or the Spock story might be improved.

Yet I liked this pleasant man, and trusted him; his manner suggested that he had integrity. So when our conversation came to an end, I said honestly, "I really don't know what to do."

"Come aboard," he said, with such disarming sincerity that I decided to go with my instincts.

"All right," I said. "I'll do it."

Because, in the end, I also realized that I had no desire to face the public reaction if it were announced that I was the lone hold-out from the original cast. I'd already weathered one firestorm with *I Am Not Spock*, and was in no hurry to kindle another one.

We shook hands, and Mr. Wise departed. But I still wasn't alone . . .

SPOCK: *You have made a decision that affects us both.*
NIMOY: In other words, "A fine mess you've gotten us into
this time, Ollie . . . "
SPOCK: *I beg your pardon?*
NIMOY: Never mind.
SPOCK: *How shall we proceed?*
NIMOY: Well, we'll start by recapturing the look. The make-
up, the ears, the haircut. And there'll be
discussions about the writing . . . Are you okay
about this?
SPOCK: *It is somewhat unsettling, particularly for one who is
most comfortable with control . . .*
NIMOY: You're telling me!

A few weeks after that meeting, the entire cast, plus
Roddenberry and Robert Wise, all appeared at a huge press confer-

ence on the Paramount lot. Also
in attendance were Michael
Eisner, then head of Paramount,
and *his* boss, Charles Bluhdorn,
chairman of the parent company
Gulf & Western.

Bill Shatner, Gene Roddenberry,
Mr. Wise, and myself all met for a
chat in Michael Eisner's office,
then made our way out to join the
cast at a long dais table in front of
a vast swarm of press people.

Michael Eisner is a tall, angu-
lar, gangly man who can respond
with a quip faster than the
Enterprise can go into warp drive.
Of course, that made him perfect

*The reunited cast, flanked
by Robert Wise
and Gene Roddenberry*

to face this particular situation. He made some opening remarks announcing *Star Trek*'s return as a major motion picture, with the original cast, then solicited questions.

When someone asked Robert Wise what the film's budget would be, he answered, "Around fifteen million dollars."

"Hmm," Eisner said. "Does he mean a *round* fifteen million, or around fifteen million?"

The quip brought a big laugh from the assembled horde; no one would have guessed then that the cost would soar to $45 million!

Finally, one of the reporters asked, "Mr. Nimoy: After a long delay, you were the last member of the cast to sign on. Can you tell us what took so long?"

I had anticipated the question, and that morning, in the shower (where I do some of my best creative thinking), I'd come up with an answer. I'd decided that I wanted to start fresh (cleanliness pun intended), without referring to any past acrimony. So I said—without the Vulcan's approval, of course, "We've been trying to come to an agreement for some time, but the mail service between Earth and Vulcan is very slow."

It drew the laugh I'd hoped for. Later, after the conference had ended, Charlie Bluhdorn hugged me exuberantly and said, "You did your profession proud today."

It was a happy moment for me. The original crew was back together for the first time in eleven years, and spirits were high . . . though we would soon be warping into troubled space.

Soon the preproduction process began; I dragged out old photos of Spock and took them to the barber. Freddy Phillips, my friend and makeup artist from the original *Star Trek* days, was hired and made new molds of my ears. Numerous press interviews were scheduled, and the questions always included: "How does it feel to be back together after eleven years?" and "Has this ever happened before? A film to follow a television series?"

(Answer number one: "Great!"

Answer number two: "Well, yes—a very cheap *Batman* movie that failed.")

One thing ST:TMP wasn't was cheap. It was decided that we'd have the best special effects around, so millions were spent on that alone. Brand new costumes were designed—I thought they were sleek, even cool, although others referred to them as the "monochrome pajamas." Molds were made of our feet, and boots custom built, even though they were totally hidden by our jumpsuits.

And we recreated the transporter effect entirely from scratch. Back in the sixties, when we did the original show, the transporter effect was designed to be a simple, fast, low-cost way to get on and off planet surfaces. Since shots of the *Enterprise* herself landing or taking off were prohibitively expensive, the "beaming" effect was designed around a simple dissolve. We actors would gradually "disappear" from our place and gradually "reappear" in another, with a few cents' worth of glitter thrown in. However, for *ST:TMP*, a camera unit and special effects crew spent countless days and hours shooting tests in the transporter room—as though it had never been done before.

However, there was one expenditure of which I totally approved (and which we could never have afforded on the series): A huge group scene in which Kirk addresses the entire *Enterprise* crew. Four hundred faithful *Star Trek* fans (including Bjo Trimble, the woman who spearheaded the "Save *Star Trek*" letter-writing campaign) were rewarded for their support by being summoned to appear as extras in that scene.

Everything we did made news: Persis Khambatta, the former Miss India, who had long ago been cast to appear in the scrapped *Star Trek II* series, was cast as the new navigator, Ilia, and had her head shaved for the role. The pictures of her being shorn appeared everywhere. So did the gathering of fans to play extras.

In the meantime, the writing continued. Could we create a role for Spock which would be successfully grafted onto the existing story? Actually, yes. The nervous breakdown idea was dropped, but it was decided we would indeed find Spock engaged in the ancient and mystical Vulcan rite of *Kolinahr,* the pursuit of total nonemotion. This he would abandon when he sensed he was needed aboard the *Enterprise*—at which point he became involved in the main storyline about V'Ger.

Spock's reappearance aboard the *Enterprise* was extremely dramatic; he beams aboard wearing a black cape as stark and severe as his manner. When this scene played in the theaters, the audience was holding its collective breath, hoping at last for some fun, some

Spock's dramatic entrance onto the Enterprise *bridge*

sign of the old camaraderie between the Vulcan and the *Enterprise* crew, or of the bantering between McCoy and Spock.

It never came. Spock remained dark and moody until the very end of the picture, stepping off the transporter pad to sweep past an eager Chekov, and coldly ignoring any friendly overtures from his crewmates.

Once filming commenced, it seemed like we actors stood forever on the bridge of the *Enterprise*, staring at a blank screen, which later would be filled with wondrous special effects. The work was very tedious, and, frankly, not much fun. What was this gloom? This depressed atmosphere? This lack of attack, fun, élan?

I think it came out of a sense that we were doing something Historic and Important. Somehow, although the TV shows depended heavily on the day-to-day energy of the creative community— writers, directors, and actors—the movie seemed to have been taken out of our hands. And our energy was sapped by an unwarranted reverence. We were passengers along for the ride on a voyage we could never quite fully manage or understand.

•

But we all pitched in and worked hard. Bill Shatner and I offered numerous suggestions on how scenes that weren't working might be played; some of those suggestions were accepted, and others weren't.

One which *was* accepted dealt with a scene near the end of the film, when the V'Ger probe (now embodied by the actress Persis Khambatta) was doing some foot-stamping on the bridge, saying: "You *will* obey me!"

Now, originally, the script called for us to have a long conversation, trying to reason with the V'Ger probe. It was tedious, not very exciting—so instead, we had Spock say:

"Captain, V'Ger is acting like a child. I suggest we treat it like one."

And Kirk responds with, "Okay! Everyone off the bridge!" And they leave the probe to have a tantrum by itself, basically ignoring it as a parent might ignore a kicking, screaming child. It was quick

Kirk, Spock, and the V'Ger probe (Persis Khambatta), prior to the foot-stamping on the bridge

©1985 PARAMOUNT PICTURES

V'Ger's alter ego

and clean and active, and certainly more interesting than having Kirk and Spock have endless, drawn-out verbal battles with V'Ger.

Some of the revisions Bill and I suggested were shot as alternatives; much was left out of the film. Later, when *ST:TMP* was released in home video, many of those scenes were added, including one improvisation of mine where Spock sheds a single tear on the bridge, saying, "I weep for V'Ger as a brother."

I discovered through those efforts that Spock could play V'Ger's "alter ego," which I hoped might shed some insight on the story, and help the audience to care about what was happening. In fact, when the video was released, I received many comments from viewers, who said, "Oh . . . So *that*'s what the movie was about!"

At any rate, while Bill and I were busy improvising, Gene Roddenberry and Harold Livingston kept a steady stream of rewrites coming at all hours, and Bob Wise chipped away at the moment-to-moment shooting issues.

Finally the last day of filming arrived; we were scheduled to shoot the final "tag" scene on the *Enterprise* bridge. The dialog called for Kirk to tell McCoy that he (the doctor) would be returned to Earth, where he'd been planning to retire. McCoy refuses the offer on the grounds that, once on board, he might as well stay. Kirk then turns to Spock and offers to return him to Vulcan; Spock declares that that is unnecessary, since his business on Vulcan is finished. The implication was that the crew was together again and would fly off together toward the next adventure. It made sense and was a neat wrap-up, but not particularly fun.

In the final rehearsal before filming, I at last heard a Spock voice in my head that captured the right "feel" of the characters and relationships from the series.

So I decided to take a chance. With the cameras rolling and Bob Wise and Gene Roddenberry watching, our scene began in earnest.

Kirk delivered his line, and McCoy gave the appropriate response; then Kirk turned to Spock and offered to return him to Vulcan.

And I—or rather, Spock—replied, "I have decided to stay with the *Enterprise*, Captain. If Dr. McCoy is to remain on board, my presence here will be essential."

It drew a good laugh on the set—but when I saw the whispered conversation between Gene and Bob Wise behind the camera, I knew it was doomed. Bob walked over with the decision: "The feeling is that the joke is inappropriate in light of what's gone before."

The scene was filmed as written.

SPOCK: *Did I say something inappropriate?*
NIMOY: No, no, Spock. I think it was a good idea.
SPOCK: *Then why was it rejected?*
NIMOY: It was an artistic decision. Out of our hands. It might have worked; we'll never know.
SPOCK: *A pity.*

The decision was made that, fiery hell and high water notwithstanding, the movie *had* to open in theaters on December 7. There turned out to be plenty of *both* unfriendly elements: By the time

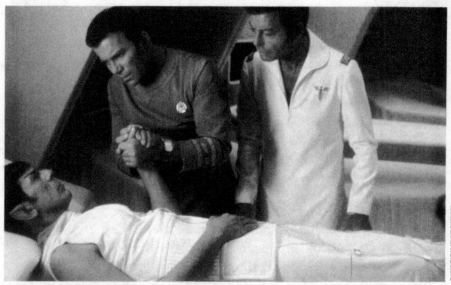

A moment of friendship between the first officer and his captain, which appeared only in the video release

shooting was almost completed, Robert Wise discovered that the special effects company that had been hired had done an unacceptable job, especially considering the five million dollars they'd been paid. Two other effects houses were hired and went to work seven days a week trying to get the film finished. They did a magnificent job—perhaps *too* magnificent, because the film wound up overburdened with endless shots of the effects. Unfortunately, Bob Wise simply lacked the time to edit the effects as they came in, and so the movie wound up being the special-effects extravaganza Paramount wanted—but little else.

A number of us involved in the film were flown to Washington, D.C., for a gala red carpet premiere of the film, followed by a party at the Smithsonian's Air and Space Museum. The promotion was laid on thick, and the public's expectations were enormous. As I sat in the theater to see the movie for the first time, along with the premiere audience, the atmosphere was electric with anticipation.

"Please," I thought silently, "please be good."

Bill Shatner was sitting in front of me; just as the lights dimmed, we reached to each other with a good-luck handshake—and then the film began.

What do I remember of the movie that I saw? Incredible shots of the *Enterprise*, looking more massive and awesomely beautiful than she ever had.

And then *more* shots of the *Enterprise*, looking massive and impressive.

And *more* shots . . .

Eventually, the special effects became downright tedious. A great cheer went up from the audience when the ship went into warp speed, but unfortunately, the story itself never really took flight—and the chemistry that had existed between the characters was never taken advantage of.

Did the film do business?

Yes. The hype and expectation brought out a large audience for a short period of time—and then it was over. It didn't perform as well as *Star Wars* by any means, although it did respectably.

But by then I felt I'd taken off the Spock ears for the last time. The *Star Trek* movie so longed for and so greatly anticipated was done. "And that," I thought, "is the end of that."

ELEVEN

MOVIE
MADNESS

or

If It's Tuesday,

This Must Be

Beijing

.

NIMOY: Once I completed *ST:TMP*, I figured that was it—no more Spock. The
         monkey was off my back!

SPOCK: *I find the comparison unflattering, to say the least.*

NIMOY: Not to mention premature . . .

O NCE *ST:TMP* WAS OVER AND DONE, I felt liberat-
ed: No longer would I have to deal with questions like,
"Why won't you do *Star Trek* again? Are you sick of
Spock?"

With a sense of relief, I immersed myself in other projects—the
theater, and speaking engagements at universities. After one of my
lectures, I was invited to the home of a couple who taught art at the
university; we got to talking about touring programs such as mine,
and they mentioned a one-man play about Vincent Van Gogh,
based on the more than four hundred letters he'd written to his
brother.

I was immediately intrigued, because I'd been interested in finding such a one-actor vehicle along the lines of Hal Holbrook's wonderful presentation that permitted audiences to spend an evening
with Mark Twain. It seemed a fascinating challenge. At the same
time, this particular play about Van Gogh struck me as unique,
because it didn't feature Vincent himself, but rather Vincent's
brother, Theo. And it seemed to me that audiences would be able
to much more quickly accept such a character, rather than an actor
claiming to be the brilliant and eccentric Van Gogh himself.
(Besides, Kirk Douglas had already given a marvelous performance
as the artist in the film *Lust for Life.*)

I contacted the author, Phillip Stephens, and bought the rights to
the play. The original version contained two acts: In the first, Theo

is in his apartment, waiting for his brother to come visit, and reminisces about their childhood together. It ends with Theo saying, "Ah! Here's Vincent! I must go now . . . " The second act picks up after Vincent's tragic death from a self-inflicted gunshot wound.

Two things moved me about the material: Theo's unswerving love for his brother and confidence in Vincent's talent (it was Theo who financially supported Vincent and his painting); and Vincent's own passion for art and desire to leave behind something of value. Vincent toiled for years to perfect his craft, and approached it with a love and zeal that can only be called spiritual. He summarized his feelings with a quote from Ernest Reynaud that has great meaning for me: "To act well in this world, one must sacrifice all personal

As Theo Van Gogh in Vincent

desires . . . " He believed he had been born not to seek happiness, but rather to leave behind a legacy to benefit all humankind. The focus of his life was, first and foremost, The Work.

SPOCK: *An approach I find quite logical. With the exception, of course, that I should not wish to limit my contribution merely to* humankind.

NIMOY: Well, then, we're finally in agreement on something, Spock! But Van Gogh himself could hardly be accused of logic. He was a very eccentric, emo-

In Auvers, France, in the room where Vincent died in Theo's arms

tional individual. In fact, his neighbors in Arles, France, used to taunt him, calling him a madman—even throwing garbage at his windows—all because he was different. "Alien," if you will.

SPOCK: *I, for one, can certainly understand the difficulties inherent in being so. But did his own brother not say, "You were blessed by that difference; that difference gave you beauty?" Certainly his unique perspective brought something glorious to the universe—a fine example of the Vulcan philosophy of IDIC, how infinite diversity among beings can add beauty and meaning. Vulcans might not approve of his emotionalism—but we can certainly appreciate his contribution to art.*

NIMOY: Spock, you amaze me! There's hope for you yet!

SPOCK: *Thank you.*

I did some further research and began revising the play. After reading a letter Theo had written to their mother after Vincent's death—a letter in which Theo admits that he was too overcome to speak at his brother's funeral—I created the fiction that Theo has rented a hall about a week later and invited anyone who would come listen to him talk about his beloved brother. He speaks of Vincent's struggle to become a great artist in order to give something of beauty to humankind, and argues against the popular notion that his brother was crazy. (Because Vincent cut off part of his own ear, he has been stereotyped throughout history as the "typical mad artist." In fact, two doctors diagnosed Vincent as suffering from debilitating epileptic seizures.)

My vision was that with a few props—mainly the letters—and a bit of wardrobe, I could travel light and do performances in reasonably small venues. But once I began to do further research and revise the play, I realized that more was needed. For one thing, the production cried out for a visual presentation of Vincent's work. His paintings, particularly the late oils, were so breathtakingly vibrant that I began putting together a collection of slides. Ultimately, the show included one hundred thirty images, tracing the development of his talent from the crude early drawings to his final dazzling masterpieces. His is a powerful body of work, particularly when one considers that he completed over one hundred paintings during his last seventy days on earth—yet only one of his pictures ever sold during his lifetime.

The first performance of *Vincent* took place in Sacramento. I flew up that day, did the performance that evening, and flew home again, curious as to how the critics would receive it. The next morning, I got a call announcing the verdict: The response was so overwhelmingly positive (despite the obligatory "ear" comments) that I decided to extend *Vincent*'s tour. For three years, I performed *Vincent* in thirty-five cities, giving over one hundred fifty performances. Eventually, it was videotaped for the A & E Network; Paramount Home Video was good enough to do the video distribution.

It was a most rewarding continuation of the "alien connection."

Speaking of which, during the time that I was touring with *Vincent*, I got an interesting call from Harve Bennett.

Harve and I had already worked together—on a television movie, *The Alpha Caper*, in 1972. Although the project wasn't terribly rewarding or memorable, it provided me the opportunity to work with Henry Fonda. (I was a great fan of his and I was nervous. A few seconds after being introduced to him, we immediately went into one of those long takes that are an actor's nightmare. It was a scene in which Fonda and other actors had a lot of dialog—and then, near the end, everyone else turned to me for *my* lines. Now, in scenes like this, you know that if you blow it, everyone's going to hate you because they'll have to do the whole take over again. I was really sweating by the time my lines came around—especially because I was working with Fonda for the first time. Luckily, I didn't blow it!)

If there's one thing working with Henry Fonda on *The Alpha Caper* taught me, it's that every seemingly trivial event often leads to more interesting events, sometimes in the strangest ways. I did my work on *The Alpha Caper* and thought, "Well, nothing will ever come of that . . . " But because I knew Henry and went to see him in *Darrow* a few years later, he pointed out those Heineken billboards to me.

And then, of course, there was Harve Bennett, producer of *The Alpha Caper*. Coincidentally, during its filming, Harve came up to me and revealed that he had been regularly renting my small plane—which I leased out when I wasn't using it. (Life is full of strange connections.) Harve's a jovial man, a military buff and tennis player with an athlete's build who was known for producing the television miniseries *Rich Man, Poor Man; The Mod Squad;* and the series *The Six Million Dollar Man,* among others.

So one day, many years after *The Alpha Caper* and some time after *ST:TMP*'s release, Harve called me and said, "Hi, Leonard. I've been hired by Charlie Bluhdorn and Michael Eisner to work on another *Star Trek* movie. Now, I know you're not interested, but I'm just trying to talk to everyone involved so I can get a good feel for what *Trek* is all about. Could we meet for lunch?"

I accepted, and we had a good talk. Harve was well aware of my turbulent experiences with Paramount, and his approach was that he simply wanted to ask questions, not pressure or demand. And ask he did: Was there a future for *Star Trek*? Could I help him understand what had gone before? Who were the players, what was the game, and where were the bodies buried?

He operated on the assumption that I'd had enough and wouldn't be interested in any future involvement.

Was he correct? Possibly. For the moment, I was intrigued and flattered, because he was validating my contribution.

Was he also being seductive when he said, "I'm sure you don't want to be involved"? Maybe.

I told him what I could about the series, the continuing interest of the fans, and the making of the movie. We said good-bye, but I left feeling it wasn't quite over.

Did I want to be involved?

Let's just say I didn't want to be passed over, ignored, left out. I guess I wanted the decision to be mine.

At the same time that I was intrigued, I was also worried, because word was out that Paramount wanted to have another *Star Trek* movie—but this time, they were approaching the idea with a tight fist. Harve was a TV producer, and the project would be made by Paramount's television department. That meant the budget would be strictly controlled; the first figure tossed around was eight million dollars, less than a fifth of what had been spent on *ST:TMP*.

It sounded as though somebody at Paramount wanted to get one last squeeze out of the *Star Trek* cow—and if that was true, I wanted no part of it.

On the other hand, I knew that, for all the millions spent on the first movie, it had failed to recapture the magic of *Star Trek*. Furthermore, the series had always been shot on a tight budget. Good story, good directing, and good acting were possible without spending mountains of cash.

And Harve had asked the right questions, and listened well. Maybe there was hope . . .

At any rate, I went about my business, touring with *Vincent* and lecturing, and occasionally answering questions when Harve called.

"Leonard, do you know Sam Peeples?"

Yes. Sam had written for *Star Trek* early in its first season, and legend has it that he first suggested to Gene Roddenberry that Spock be half-human. If that's true, then I'm eternally in Sam's debt.

Clearly, Harve was dealing with writing issues by this time. I asked no questions, merely waited to see what developed. And tactfully let it be known that I simply wouldn't be interested unless the idea was exciting to me; I had no desire to participate in another *ST:TMP*.

So one evening, I invited Harve and Jeff Katzenberg to a gathering at my home; and at one point, I recall pouring Harve a drink at the bar, and asking, "So how's it going?"

I remember with crystal clarity his answer, because it shocked me so. He leaned forward and responded to my question with one of his own: "How'd you like to have a great death scene?"

I laughed nervously, and said, "Let's talk."

Did I want to see Spock killed? No. But I couldn't help being intrigued by the idea; after all, if this was indeed going to be one last squeeze of the cow, the final *Star Trek* effort, then it would make sense to go out gloriously.

But a lot would depend on the script.

Before long Paramount contacted me, and we started contract negotiations. Harve told me the story he had in mind—one that was energetic and more in keeping with the flavor of the original series. I was interested, but I felt it was important that I also find new ways to broaden my career; I wanted a commitment from Paramount to employ me in other projects.

"No problem," Harve said enthusiastically. "I'm also producing a Paramount TV movie about the life of Golda Meir. You'd be perfect for the part of her husband, Morris Meyerson."

The deal was done: I would play Spock again, for a negotiated salary. In addition, Paramount agreed to two "pay or play" commitments at a preestablished price. One of those commitments would be my performance as Morris Meyerson opposite Judy Davis and Ingrid Bergman in *A Woman Called Golda.*

And so I figured that, once my tour with *Vincent* was done, I

As Morris Meyerson, with Ingrid Bergman
in A Woman Called Golda

•

would fly to Israel and remain there a month, then fly home and have a month back in the U.S. before *Star Trek II* began filming.

But, as I said before, one event leads to another, and things are sometimes connected in strange ways. *Star Trek II* had led to *Golda*, and soon *Vincent* would lead to something else very exciting . . .

On a bitterly cold, snowy night, I did a performance of *Vincent* at the Guthrie Theatre in Minneapolis. The evening was special because of the unusual audience: A departing NBC affiliate was being replaced by another local station. To publicize the event, NBC had brought several hundred personnel from around the country to Minneapolis to welcome the new station into the fold.

The network bought out the Guthrie on the final night of their three-day celebration. After a big dinner party and a cocktail reception in the theater lobby, these several hundred well-fed and well-oiled participants were to watch my one-person show.

As it turned out, there was a major snowstorm that night, and the crowd arrived a half hour late. Then they lingered in the lobby, drinking and schmoozing, refusing to respond to the blinking lights that indicated curtain time.

Back in my dressing room, I was furious. I wasn't looking forward to performing for a rowdy crowd who hadn't chosen to be here, and considered me a refreshment on their schedule. The curtain finally went up almost an hour late—but I must say that when I made my entrance, the lengthy ovation shocked me and moved me almost to tears.

The irony didn't escape me—these were the people from NBC, the network that had cancelled *Star Trek*. The show went well and, for the most part, the audience behaved themselves.

Among them, as fate would have it, was the producer Vincenzo LaBella, who was preparing the *Marco Polo* miniseries. Apparently he didn't dislike what he saw that night, because some time after, he called to offer me a role in *Marco*: that of Kubla Khan's devious aide, Achmet. The job would shoot for a month in Beijing—too exotic of a locale for me to resist. I accepted.

But the *Marco* company ran into a lot of preproduction difficulties in China; delay followed delay until my agreed-upon work dates had come and gone. It seemed impossible to go to Beijing within my schedule.

By then, I was finished touring with *Vincent* and was preparing to go to Israel for *Golda*. As I said earlier, the plan was to work in Israel a month, then have a month back in the States before beginning work on *Star Trek II*.

But my agent, Merritt Blake, was as tenacious as a dog that wouldn't let go of a bone: He was determined to figure out a way for me to make all three commitments. I was sitting in a New York hotel room, a few hours before going to JFK for a 9 P.M. flight to Tel Aviv when Merritt called.

"Great news!" he said. "Harve Bennett and LaBella and I have worked out your schedule. You'll do the job in Israel, then fly directly to Beijing for a month of work, then fly back to L.A., where you'll immediately begin work on *Star Trek II*!"

Stunned and excited, I hung up the phone and immediately went out to shop for luggage and clothes that would be appropriate for the colder Chinese weather. I had just enough time to do that, then make my nine o'clock flight for Israel.

It was sad, of course, to be away from my wife and children for such an extended period of time; but the kids were in school, and it would have been too disruptive to their education to take them with me. As I've said, my family understood the necessity of travel in an actor's life. They knew I had to go where the work was, and they were very supportive of me.

The next morning, I found myself in Tel Aviv. Israel is a sunny desert country, and the warm, enthusiastic welcome I received from her people matched her climate—no doubt in part because we were doing a film honoring a great stateswoman and the country's birth. I'd visited there before and felt very comfortable, and as always was impressed by the extremely rich sense of history—especially in the beautiful city of Jerusalem, where each building showed the marks left by different centuries and cultures.

However, I did encounter a major bump in the road during shooting: I discovered that Harve and Paramount had hired me over British director Alan Gibson's objections. He knew me only as Spock.

I learned this after a couple days into shooting, when I got into a private conversation with him about how I thought I might approach a particular scene.

"What difference does it make?" Gibson snapped. "You're not the right person for this role anyway!"

I was stunned, angry, hurt; Alan Gibson was a talented man, but did he really think this was an appropriate comment to make to an actor on the job? I said nothing, only put on my best Vulcan face and went for a long walk.

SPOCK: *I regret any difficulties our association has caused you.*

NIMOY: It's all right. I'll get over it. It's because of you that I have this opportunity in the first place.

SPOCK: *But I fail to understand his attitude. Why does he assume that your portrayal of me makes you incapable of other roles? Acting is, after all, your chosen craft.*

NIMOY: He's human, Spock.

SPOCK: *(nods) Ah. That explains much . . .*

So I vowed to myself to forget about it and do my very best work as Morris Meyerson.

After a week or so of production, I received the *Star Trek II* script. To be honest, I thought it had problems, and called Harve Bennett to tell him so. Specifically, Spock's death—which, like Janet Leigh's in *Psycho*, came as an early surprise in the script—was a well-written scene (and very similar in content to the one that wound up being filmed), but his function in the plot wasn't clear. Although he died saving the ship, his act of sacrifice wasn't integrated into the rest of the story; it was just simply "there."

Since I would soon have a break of several days in *Golda*'s shooting schedule, we agreed that I would come to Los Angeles to meet with Harve and Nicholas Meyer, who had come on board as the director.

So, it was back to L.A., and Harve's office on the Paramount lot. I walked inside, and we exchanged greetings and a little small talk—and then Nick Meyer and his cigar made their entrance.

A few words about Nick, who is certainly one of the most colorful and theatrical individuals I've ever met: In *Star Trek IV: The Voyage Home*, Nick gave a line to the character Gillian, where she says, "I have a photographic memory; I *see* words . . . " I believe that Nick was talking about himself when he wrote that. Nick has a photographic memory where words are concerned—he can recall words, phrases, entire passages of literature perfectly and rattle them off without hesitation. He has a dictionary for a mind. I remember one day I told him, "Nick, you're one dramatic guy!"

He immediately quipped, "I don't think I fit that template." He loves to tell stories, long ones, with a jaunty Groucho Marx sort of air, punctuated by that ever-present cigar of his. And he always makes me smile.

But that day, when he came into the office with cigar in tow and his theatrical mannerisms, I confess, I was nervous that this would be a tough meeting. I expected a big confrontation. Instead, Nick said, "I understand you have some reservations about the script."

"Yes," I said. "I think the Spock death scene is effective taken by itself, but it happens very abruptly, and doesn't really tie into the storyline. In other words, it serves no purpose in furthering the plot."

In perhaps the most refreshing moment I have ever had in my *Star Trek* experience, Nick said, "I agree with you. Spock's death shouldn't be in the script unless it serves a dramatic function. Look, I'm doing a rewrite right now and will be done in a few days. You'll be able to take it with you on the plane back to Israel."

I was delighted and totally disarmed. I'd never before had such a straightforward and positive reaction to any of my comments. We talked a bit about some other more minor comments I had, then our meeting concluded on a very positive note.

Most important, Nick was true to his word. I had the script in hand on my flight back to Israel—and, even better, the rewrite was excellent.

With my hopes buoyed, I returned to work on the *Golda* set, where I had the great good fortune to work with two exceptional actresses—Ingrid Bergman and Judy Davis. Their professionalism and talent were inspiring, even more so when one considers that Ingrid Bergman was very ill with breast cancer at the time. The surgery and subsequent treatment had left one of her arms so swollen that she had to sleep with it raised and wear long sleeves, edged with lace, to cover it all the way to the wrist. Yet she never complained, and never permitted it to affect her daily work; she died only a few months later. It was fitting that she won an Emmy for that final performance. (I was very touched to be nominated for a Supporting Actor Emmy myself for the Morris Meyerson role; and frankly, I can be pretty gracious about not winning, because it wound up going to Laurence Olivier instead.)

Bergman never gave off the sense that she was sick, but we all knew it. I couldn't help approaching her with a sense of compassion, and she in turn approached me with a great deal of warmth.

Tuesday, October 6, 1981, was my final day of work in Israel. We had a night shoot scheduled on the streets of Tel Aviv, for a scene that depicted the Israelis' celebration of the declaration of statehood. I was looking forward to my scene with Bergman, which offered some poignant moments: Morris Meyerson, now divorced from Golda, comes to offer her his congratulations on her accomplishments, and to exchange personal information about the well-being of their two children.

Now, normally, the scene would have suggested some tension, some faint hostility between these two people; after all, they'd been divorced and estranged for many years.

But Bergman was a gracious and brave gentlewoman, and we shared a sense of camaraderie. And so, when the cameras started rolling, I approached and instinctively reached for her hand. I believe she was pleasantly surprised by the gesture, but she immediately responded to it in kind, with unfeigned warmth, by reaching out to me. It was the case of one actor responding to another's choice and validating it. I took her outstretched hand and held it between both of mine, and we played the entire scene that way, walking and talking like two intimate, long-time friends.

That heartwarming moment was filmed against the backdrop of great national tension—because several hours before we began filming, Anwar Sadat, Egypt's president, had been assassinated. The conservatives in Egypt were angered by his rapprochement with Israel, and it had cost him his life.

Everyone was concerned about the possibility of more bloodshed, even an attack against Israel. Even so, we kept on shooting, and filmed through the night. At dawn I went to my hotel to shower and change, then headed for the airport—and, ultimately, China.

As the plane took off, I felt a twinge of guilt, as though I were leaving the country and the film company holding the bag in a bad situation—even though there was nothing I could do to help, now that my work there was finished.

Since Israel and China had no diplomatic relations, there were no flights between the two countries. I had to fly first to Rome—the wrong direction—before I could get on a plane bound for Beijing.

The trip was enormously long and tedious. We had one stop in Rome, and another in Bahrain, for fuel. There I stepped off the plane to find myself in a different world, where dark-eyed women covered their faces with veils and the men wore gleaming 24-karat gold.

A day and a half after leaving Tel Aviv, I arrived exhausted at the Beijing airport, where I was met by a smiling Vicenzo LaBella. Vicenzo was a charming, worldly, educated man who took enormous pride in his Vatican citizenship. His forte was history, as reflected by the miniseries he had chosen to produce. I remember that he was always smiling, always cheerful, despite the travail the *Marco Polo* company had faced in China and Mongolia—and there was more to come.

Vicenzo escorted me to a car driven by a pleasant but silent local, and on the ride to the hotel, filled me in a bit more on the production.

The crew was mostly Italian, with a few local Chinese thrown in, which gave the set an interesting linguistic mix. A number of truly world-class professionals were on the job: Cinematographer Pasqualino De Santis, and costumer Rafael Sabatini (who would win an Emmy for his designs), as well as a number of respected actors. Ying Ruoshen, a Chinese national, played Kubla Khan; his English was surprisingly good, and some years later he worked in a Chinese production of *Death of a Salesman*, under the supervision of the writer Arthur Miller. I was also delighted to learn that F. Murray Abraham, whom I'd met at the Guthrie Theatre while we were involved in different productions, was on the job. Some years later, Murray would win the Academy Award for his marvelous portrayal of the jealous musician Salieri in *Amadeus*. Murray is a dedicated, passionate actor, and I enjoyed being around the energy he exuded.

As we neared our destination, Vicenzo explained that the driver and car were assigned to me for the month of my stay. My driver would take me to and from work, and would be available for evenings if I needed him.

Soon we arrived at the Beijing Hotel—within shouting distance of the now infamous Tienanmen Square. I thanked Vicenzo and the driver, who, LaBella explained, would be waiting to take me to work at seven the next morning.

The weather was much colder than in Israel, and the hotel was a large, dreary hodgepodge of styles. Various sections of it had been

FROM THE COLLECTION OF LEONARD NIMOY

Tienanmen Square, October 1981

constructed at different times under different influences, including Russian and French. I checked into a very old, greasy, cockroach-infested room, whose charm was outmatched only by the surliness of the employees.

In the morning, I walked out of the hotel and down the front steps, where my driver waited, smiling and bowing slightly. He drove me to the studio through streets clogged with bicycle riders—who clearly felt that cars had no business being there. They steadfastly ignored the honking of car horns behind them, refusing to yield. I couldn't help marveling at the lack of casualties.

At the studio I was wonderfully costumed, in sumptuous silk robes edged with gold brocade, and a very skillfully applied beard and moustache. (I don't know why, but the hair they used itched fiercely and caused me a lot of misery for the next month!)

The character of Achmet the Turk was an interesting one, and about as far from Spock as you could get: He was a consummate bad guy, a Machiavellian manipulator and abuser of women. Achmet would typically call in one of the local Chinese merchants to say, "You know, we've been watching you, and believe that the quality of goods you offer are superior. We'd like you to supply the royal court . . . And, by the way, don't you have a young daughter?"

I enjoyed the character and the work went well. At the end of the day, I cleaned up and walked out to my car, where my faithful driver ushered me into the back seat, then sat down behind the wheel.

And there we stayed, I in the back seat and he with his hands on the wheel, still in the parking lot.

After a full minute, he turned to me and smiled.

It was my first real brush with the language barrier in Beijing, but I got his message: He was making no assumptions. The car wasn't going anywhere until *I* gave instructions.

And I spoke no Chinese, while he spoke not a word of English.

But I tried anyway. "To the hotel, please. Beijing Hotel," I said, desperately hoping that he at least knew the word *hotel*.

He didn't.

He just kept smiling with his hands on the wheel, so finally, in desperation, I got back out of the car and hunted down an Italian crew member who spoke English (many of them didn't, which made life even more interesting). The crew member in turn tracked down a Chinese crew member who spoke Italian—and in a wonderful display of linguistic interaction, told the Italian crew member, who then told me, that the magic words were *"Beijing Fundyen."*

Repeating them all the way, I hurried back to the car, climbed in, and tried them out on the driver, praying this time that my pronunciation wasn't too mangled.

His smile widened with relief—as did mine when he turned the key in the ignition, then drove me back to the hotel.

It wasn't the only interesting Chinese-Italian-English experience I had while there. Later on, in one scene outside Achmet's bed chamber, one Chinese actor had a small part in which he had to rush up shouting, "My lord Achmet! My lord Achmet!"

Of course, he spoke no English—and the director, Giuliano Montaldo, didn't exactly have a firm grasp of the language, either. But he valiantly coached the young man on the pronunciation of his lines.

So when the actor was finally prepared and came running onto the set, breathlessly yelling, "My-a lord-a Achmet-a!" with the most *Italian* Chinese accent I've ever heard, it was all I could do to keep from cracking up.

The film company meals were excellent. The Italian crew had rebelled against the Chinese food some weeks earlier and a great chef had been imported from Italy, complete with a mobile kitchen. Bless those pasta lovers! The food at the hotel was good if you like Chinese cuisine, which I do, but the waiters were something else again. Their favorite expression was *mayo*—which in essence means, "Forget it. You're not going to get it." (A fairer translation would probably be something like, "We're out of it.")

The good-humored crew had learned to add "hold the mayo" to whatever they ordered. "I'll take the chicken *kung pao*—hold the mayo!" It certainly didn't increase our chances of getting what we wanted, but the laughter at the table made us feel better. "The customer is always right" is *not* the way it works in Beijing; the waiters seemed determined to teach us patience. But some customers didn't take to the lesson very well—we watched a fistfight between a customer and his server! Of course, the Communist policy called for the hotel to keep a book wherein customers could record their complaints. In theory, these complaints were to be read aloud at Party meetings, and the offenders dealt with—but the book was never in sight, and whenever requested, was mysteriously "lost."

Beijing itself was difficult, awesome, ancient, tacky, severe, frustrating, and educational. It was a city struggling with the first pressures of Westernization—and in a few years, those pressures would erupt in the demonstration and massacre at Tienanmen Square. Quite honestly, I wasn't surprised when it happened; while I was there, I could felt the social friction building between two very disparate groups: the Communist hardliners, and the admirers of Western-style democracy. Many of the people, especially the young, embraced the new freedom and capitalism—while the old guard of the Communist regime resisted.

The conflict between these two groups was evident everywhere. For example, the *Beijing Fundyen*, where I stayed, was run by a conservative Communist cadre, which embraced the old-fashioned Communist values of rudeness toward customers and terrible service. But just down the street was another hotel run by a liberal cadre, which was much more welcoming toward Westerners, and had more European-style food and service. When I was in desperate need of relief from my hotel's attitude toward its clients, I'd walk down the street to this other hotel. The same concept applied to every single shop. I could walk into a store and tell instantly from the clerk's attitude toward me whether the establishment was run by a conservative or liberal cadre. And it was very clear that these two groups deeply resented each other.

But I met many Chinese who were very enthusiastic about meeting a Westerner, especially an American. In fact, one friendly young local recognized me on the street as belonging to the *Marco Polo* group, and invited me to his home, to meet his family. He was so interested in learning more about the West that he had taught himself very passable English from watching *one* fifteen-minute propaganda-laden lesson on TV a week. (I tuned into a couple, just for fun; they always featured stories about evil capitalistic bosses taking mercenary advantage of the poor workers.) I was torn. As eager as I was for the opportunity to meet a Chinese family in their home and learn more about their fascinating culture, I decided against going—because I knew that, once I left the country, the young man and his relatives would no doubt have been taken in for questioning.

But I felt free to wander Beijing's streets, because China had never been exposed to *Star Trek* and had never heard of Spock or Leonard Nimoy. If I was stared at by the locals, it was because they were curious about Westerners. I enjoyed the anonymity, including the ability to wander into any restaurant or shop I chose without having to make security arrangements.

In fact, one day I saw a long line of locals outside a restaurant—a good endorsement of the food, I figured, so I stepped into the line and shuffled along with the quiet crowd. Inside, I discovered there was one—and only one—dish being ladled out from a huge pot. So, taking my lead from those ahead of me in line, I picked up a bowl and offered it to the server, who filled it full of meat dumplings for the grand sum of about twenty cents. I wandered with it over to a large family-style table, where a pair of parents made room for me among their kids. It was great!

Being in Beijing was as close as I've ever come to being on another planet, except on film; like everyone else there, I soon grew hungry for contact from the outside world. I couldn't listen to the radio, because it was all in Chinese, and television was almost as bad. The occasional news broadcast (in Chinese, of course) offered us only a few images, and although the *People's Daily* newspaper was published in English, it was so filled with silly propaganda that it was only good for a chuckle. The only daily English language newspaper that was worthwhile was the Asian edition of the *Wall Street Journal*, so I took to reading it.

Through it I learned about the forces back in Hollywood that would soon affect me. Word had leaked out about Spock's death in the new *Star Trek* movie, and some fans were being extremely vocal about their disapproval. A group of them had bought an ad in one of the film industry trade papers, and that shot was heard round the world . . .

At least, it made it all the way to Beijing, because one morning I picked up my copy of the *Journal* and read the front page headline:

FANS PROCLAIM PARAMOUNT WILL LOSE 18 MILLION IF SPOCK DIES!

The article went on to explain how the fans in question had justified the figure: They assumed a certain number would refuse to see the film at all, another number would see it only once instead of the typical three or four times, and yet another number would fail to buy the video or other merchandise.

I loved it! The tentacles of the Vulcan's proposed demise were reaching halfway round the globe. I had the best laugh of my entire China stay.

SPOCK: *(stiffly) I fail to understand why the issue of my death strikes you as humorous.*

NIMOY: I don't think it's funny, Spock—I wasn't laughing about that. It's just all this other stuff . . . (chuckles)

SPOCK: *I find your attitude flippant, at best.*

NIMOY: Sorry. But you are just a fictional character.

SPOCK: *We've had this discussion previously.*

NIMOY: You're right.

The last week in October, the weather in Beijing turned bitterly cold. The wind whipped in from the Mongolian desert, carrying a supply of dust to mingle with the city air, which was already polluted by copious wood and coal burning by homes and factories. I was glad when, on Friday night, I shot my final scene and took off Achmet's itchy moustache and beard for the last time.

On Saturday morning, my ever cheerful driver took me to the airport. Although we weren't that good at communicating with each other, his manner had always been so kindly that—although it was forbidden—I slipped him some small gifts. After much smiling, bowing, and repeated handshaking on both our parts, he left, and I was alone in the vast, cold Beijing airport. Actually, *cold* is an understatement—the temperature inside was no more than 40 degrees, cold enough to see my breath.

I made my way to the gate area, and to my amazement discovered a first-class waiting lounge. A first-class lounge in this supposedly classless society? I entered gratefully because it was on the east side, and the shaft of sunlight filtering through the windows brought welcome warmth. I was alone and sitting quietly when a cleaning man entered and, at the sight of me, began yelling, waving a broom in one hand and a dustpan in the other.

•

"First class!" he shouted, in barely understandable English, motioning for me to leave. "First class!"

I nodded. "Yes, I know, I have a first-class ticket."

"First class! First class!"

I realized attempting to communicate by the spoken word was useless; I pulled out my ticket. Without even looking at it, he gave a grunt like a bear who'd lost a territorial fight and left.

The culture shock of re-entering the Western world took hold when I deplaned for a change of flights in Tokyo. The airport seemed wonderfully warm and cozy, yet posted on the walls in a dozen different languages was the polite apology:

DUE TO FUEL CONSERVATION POLICIES, WE ARE REQUIRED TO MAINTAIN
THE TEMPERATURE OF THIS BUILDING AT A MAXIMUM OF 68 DEGREES.
PLEASE FORGIVE THE DISCOMFORT.

Because I was flying west, I actually landed in Los Angeles on the afternoon of the same day I'd left Beijing—even though I'd spent more than twenty-four hours in the air. When I landed in Los Angeles, a studio driver took me directly to Paramount, where filming on *Star Trek II: The Wrath of Khan* was already underway. I had makeup and wardrobe sessions, then a brief "welcome back" meeting with Harve and Nick.

From there I made my weary way home, where I would spend the weekend trying to step out of Morris Meyerson and Achmet's skins, and back into the psyche of a death-bound (or so I thought) Vulcan . . .

TWELVE

REMEMBER

WILL I THINK OF YOU?

Only
    When I die

    And realize
    That I am born again

    For dying is

        A beginning

        And I
                have died
                       thousands of times

                Sometimes
                Several times a day

I am learning
That from each death
    Comes a new vision
Of life

    A new sense of the miracle
    Of being and creation

For fear
    Is worse than dying

Fear prevents discovery
    And destroys the creative flow
    Of God-man's soul

And when I let my old self
    Hardened and rigid
             Die

I am re-born
    Vital, open and fresh

And this discovery
    This victory over the
                Fear of death
                    Came

When I thought I was dead
  And found you

So
Each time
I rise
Out of the ashes
Of my fear
I will gratefully

              Think of you

               —Will I Think of You?
                 Leonard Nimoy

How would you like to have a great death scene?

WHEN I FIRST WROTE THOSE WORDS about dying in the last chapter, I realized they set in motion a story line that would take three movies to complete and—greatest of ironies—would have an enormously rejuvenating effect on my life.

At the same time that I experienced some unease, even fear, about the notion of killing off Spock, I also felt a great deal of enthusiasm about working on *Star Trek II: The Wrath of Khan* (which translates into fanspeak as *TWOK*).

For one thing, there was a vastly improved story that was much truer to the feeling of The Original Series (fanspeak: TOS). For another, the moment I first walked onto the set, I noticed that, where *ST:TMP* had been a study in cool shades of gray, *TWOK* immediately established itself in warmer, more welcoming colors. *ST:TMP* had been influenced by Stanley Kubrick's *2001: A Space Odyssey*, attempting to capture the sense of space's mysterious silence, its cold, uninviting vastness. But *The Wrath of Khan*, even down to its much-debated title, was about heat. (Originally, Nick Meyer's script was entitled *The Undiscovered Country*, from the *Hamlet* quote: "But that dread of something after death, the undiscovered country from whose bourn no traveler returns, puzzles the will, and makes us rather bear those ills we have than fly to others that we know not of . . . "

However, powers beyond him changed it to *The Vengeance of Khan*, then to *Wrath* when it was decided that *Vengeance* was just too close to the upcoming George Lucas film, *Revenge of the Jedi*—which wound up ultimately being changed to *Return of the Jedi*.

Did the name switch affect the movie's success? I doubt it. Someone has wisely said that a great title is one attached to a hit. I distinctly remember disliking the title *Star Trek* when I first heard it!)

Even the new uniforms were warmer—both literally and metaphorically. Instead of *ST:TMP*'s neutral monochrome palette, *TWOK*'s costumes were brighter, more colorful—burgundy and white—and of heavier fabric, so that on hot days, we all sweated. And they had a curious idiosyncrasy: Whenever we sat down, the jackets hiked up, giving the feeling that the collar was riding up around our necks. So we actors all developed the habit of taking hold of the bottom and pulling down whenever we stood up. This quirk would later have a significant effect in my final scene in the film.

And although *TWOK* dealt with aging and death, it did so with exuberance, meaning and warmth, and the promise of new life. The Genesis device featured in the film—a device capable of turning uninhabitable planets into ones lush and verdant, capable of sustaining life—turned out to be a visual metaphor for the film's theme, and for Spock's death and rebirth.

With the effervescent Nick Meyer

Harve Bennett had already decided that special effects would take a back seat to the story and characters this time out. And, unlike *ST:TMP*, which made no mention of the fact that a few years had passed since the *Enterprise* crew warped out of spacedock together, *The Wrath of Khan* attacked the issue of aging head-on. In the film, Kirk deals with his reaction to his fiftieth birthday. Family, too, was an issue, and new characters were introduced: Spock's Vulcan-Romulan protege, Saavik (portrayed by newcomer Kirstie Alley) and Kirk's son, David Marcus (played by the late Merritt Buttrick).

The aging issue was further brought to the fore by showing the seasoned crew taking a group of raw cadets on what was supposed to be a training mission. Harve and Nick came up with a brilliant idea to open the film: A no-win battle simulation, which looks to the uninformed audience like the real thing. The *Enterprise* appears to be under attack, and during the battle Spock is wounded

Harve Bennett and Gene Roddenberry confer

during an explosion and convincingly dies. Yet, once the *Enterprise* seems to be fatally crippled and all is lost, it's revealed that this was all just a training scenario—a test of a cadet's skills.

It was a great way to get past the "Spock dying" issue that had stirred up so much controversy among the fans, and allow the audience to relax and enjoy the rest of the film, thinking that the Vulcan had been spared after all. (In fact, after the simulation, Kirk greets Spock in the corridor with, "Aren't you dead?")

TWOK also featured a larger-than-life villain: The vengeance-obsessed Khan, who has vowed to get even with Kirk for long ago stranding him on an inhospitable planet. When Harve Bennett first sat himself down to watch all seventy-nine original *Star Trek* episodes, the one that jumped out at him was "Space Seed," which had featured guest-star Ricardo Montalban as the genetically engi-neered "superman" Khan, intent on seizing power. The last scene in the episode has Kirk and Spock musing about what will become of the "seed" the captain has "planted" by marooning Khan. *TWOK* answers that question.

To our great good luck, Ricardo Montalban agreed to reprise the role, and did so with marvelous theatricality and power, creating a high standard against which we all tested ourselves. From his won-derful first appearance as Khan, to the gradual peeling away of his control to reveal the depth of his obsession, to his final demented Captain Ahab ramblings, he held stage whenever called upon. When the film was released, the response to Khan was over-whelmingly positive: The audience clearly found him the *Star Trek* villain they most loved to hate! (An interesting sidebar: As Khan, Montalban wore a costume that showed off his chest, which was so impressively developed that many viewers speculated it might be a false breastplate. I'm here to tell you: It most definitely wasn't! Those were Montalban's enviable pecs.)

We were also fortunate enough to have Merritt Buttrick and Kirstie Alley cast in the film. Merritt was a promising young actor who took his work very seriously—and he had been given a very difficult task in the role of Kirk's son, David. The introduction of a long-lost relative is a tricky device, which is sometimes less than successful. However, I believe Merritt's final scene with Kirk is an

•

"almost"; their interaction was quite moving, and the father-son relationship, given some more attention in later films, might have been successful. But the opportunity never arose: The character of David would take a sharp and tragic turn in *Star Trek III*, and Merritt Buttrick's life would sadly imitate art soon after.

Ricardo Montalban as Khan

•

Kirstie Alley had been cast as the young half-Vulcan, Saavik, and her performance—or, perhaps more correctly, presence—was simply amazing. As she was fond of saying, she was "fresh off the turnip truck" and had done virtually no acting; certainly, she had never worked in front of a camera. Yet she delivered her lines like a seasoned pro. I never got to know Kirstie very well, which was definitely my loss. And unfortunately, a communication breakdown (which I'll address later) made this her first and last visit with us.

Saavik (Kirstie Alley) with her mentor in STII: TWOK

I was pleased to be working with such wonderfully talented guest actors, and heartened to be working with the *Star Trek* regulars again. I certainly felt more at home on this *Star Trek* set than I had on *ST:TMP*'s, and was gratified that, when I came to work on Monday morning after a weekend's rest, my first scene was one with Bill Shatner.

There we were, two old Starfleet buddies chewing the fat. Whatever first-day jitters or misgivings I might have had faded; we were immediately back into our comfortable chemistry. When I look at the film now, I'm warmed by what comes off the screen in the easy camaraderie between Bill, De Kelley, and myself. Bill as Kirk in this film is mellowing—actually dangerously so—and melancholy about aging, which he plays very well.

And, as I've said before—specifically, on the day of the unveiling of De Kelley's star on the Hollywood Walk of Fame—De is a rock on which much of *Star Trek* stands. In the early scenes with Bill in TWOK, De's ease and comfort shine in an honest, simple delivery that reminds me of the "Quiet Great Ones" like Henry Fonda and Gary Cooper. The moment in Captain Kirk's apartment where he tells the morose Kirk, "Get back your command before you really do grow old!" is at once crystal clear and powerful.

And there was the added value that Jimmy Doohan, Nichelle Nichols, and George Takei always brought to *Star Trek*. Walter Koenig as Chekov also did a fine job, along with Paul Winfield, in the scenes where they are forced by Khan's torture to betray Kirk.

Speaking of those scenes, I'd like to think I saved Walter a little embarrassment. You see, in the film, Khan tortures Chekov by getting this truly nasty-looking "Ceti eel" to crawl into his ear, and do God-knows-what to poor Chekov's brain. So after Chekov is rescued and the eel extracted, he reports for duty on the *Enterprise* bridge, saying: "Could you use another hand, Admiral?"

For his rehearsal entrance, the costume department decided his ear should be bandaged. So when Walter came out onto the bridge set, he wore a cone-shaped white object over his ear, with the apex pointed outward. A strip of white elastic around his forehead held the contraption in place.

It looked pretty silly, and when I looked at it more closely, I realized that it was just what it appreared to be—a falsie, a bra pad! I contained myself for a couple of rehearsals, figuring that Nick Meyer or *someone* would say something, but no one seemed to notice. Finally, the time came to shoot the scene, and I had to speak up.

Before the cameras rolled, I said "Nick, could I ask a question?"

The set grew still as Nick turned expectantly toward me.

"Why," I asked, "is Walter wearing a bra on his ear?"

Everyone turned to stare blankly at Walter and the falsie, as though finally seeing the ridiculous contraption for the first time— and then a roar of laughter swept over the set. Nick agreed that twenty-third-century medicine ought to be advanced enough to permit the doctors to spray on a skin graft from a pressurized container; ear brassieres were definitely *not* necessary.

Walter and his ear were both greatly relieved.

The shooting of *TWOK* moved along on schedule, and the days and weeks passed without extraordinary incident. In a way, it seemed almost routine—not unlike the atmosphere surrounding the making of the original episodes. The work was satisfying, the story line strong. As the plot advanced, the classic theme came ever more sharply into focus: How hatred and vengeance leave a path of destruction in an ever-widening circle. Many poignant scenes were shot, showing the effect of the wrath mentioned in the title, as property was destroyed and people died. In one heartrending scene, Scotty's young nephew, a cadet in whom he had taken so much joy and pride, lay dead in Scotty's arms; the arc of Jimmy Doohan's performance was simply perfect.

In his relentless onslaught against Kirk, Khan triggers the Genesis device; ironically, its powerful creative force, unleashed against already living things, will destroy everything in its path— and the battle-scarred *Enterprise* is too crippled to get out of the way.

Soon the time came for Spock's contribution. Up to that point, his function in the film had been perfunctory, limited to the occasional piece of advice. Now it was time for the Vulcan to earn his keep, at the moment Kirk calls the engine room to say, "Scotty, I need warp speed in three minutes, or we're all dead."

The response is bad news—and Spock steps into the breach. He realizes that the only way to save the ship is to handle radioactive material so lethal that no human could survive the exposure long enough to succeed in the task.

But perhaps a Vulcan might live just long enough to finish the deed . . .

The next few film minutes of *The Wrath of Khan* would yield one of *Star Trek*'s most poignant moments.

Months before, Spock's death had occurred much earlier in a previous draft of the script, before the halfway mark—in the *Psycho* version previously described. (Like Janet Leigh, the Vulcan was to have been dispatched swiftly, suddenly, near the beginning of the film.) Same radiation chamber, same sacrifice that saves the *Enteprise* from certain doom, but without any real tie-in to the rest of the *Khan* plot. But Harve and Nick decided—wisely, I think—that the film might not recover from the tragedy, so they moved the scene near the story's end. Coming where it does now in the film, Spock's death seems appropriate and fitting.

Shooting the scene was something else again.

The closer I came to the day Spock was scheduled to die, the more a sense of ominous foreboding settled over me. The effect caught me totally by surprise; I suppose I could argue that I took each day's work as it came—but when *the* day finally came, it rocked me.

When I walked onto the set that fateful morning and saw the radiation chamber which would be the instrument of Spock's death, I felt like a condemned man viewing the gas chamber for the first time. I wasn't the only one affected by the realization of what was about to happen to this beloved character; the mood on the set was decidedly somber and hushed, as if out of reverence for the (soon to be) dead.

But I knew the best way to get through this was to focus on the day's work. It began with Spock's descent down a ladder into the main control room into the *Enterprise*'s engineering section. A cursory glance gives the Vulcan the information he needs: Scotty is unconscious, and only extreme measures will save the ship and her crew. Without hesitation, Spock makes his decision and moves toward the radiation chamber. But on the way there, he is stopped by Dr. McCoy, who insists the Vulcan cannot enter the chamber, as it would mean certain death. Calmly, logically—yet with unmistakable affection—Spock distracts the doctor, then renders him unconscious with the Vulcan nerve pinch.

This much was in the script, and De and I rehearsed the scene until we were ready for the cameras. I admit, I didn't really want to be finished with this scene—because I knew which one would be coming next.

But before the cameras started rolling, Harve Bennett stepped onto the set. It was perfectly appropriate for him to do so, since he often watched the day's work—but today he had a very special mission.

"Remember . . ."

He called me aside and said, "Leonard, I was wondering whether we could add something to this scene. A thread we could pick up later as a story point in another film . . . "

Now, I should comment here that Harve had worked a great deal in episodic television, and that's the way his mind worked: He didn't focus only on the story being shot but also on what dramatic opportunities might be created or damaged by that story. And at that instant, he was the only one actually looking to *Star Trek*'s future—I was struggling to get through the present, and Nick was looking at today's work with an eye toward evoking a sense of finality.

At this point, my mind was quite numb. My brain distantly registered the fact that Harve might be throwing out a lifeline for Spock, but I wasn't in any condition to understand all the implications. I was focused on the work yet to come, and anxious to be done with it.

"I'm not sure," I said. "What exactly are you looking for?"

Harve thought a second. "Well . . . Could you do a mind meld on McCoy?"

"Yes. Yes, of course."

"And what might you say to him?" Harve prompted.

I searched my dazed brain for something vague enough to cover a lot of possibilities, yet specific enough to open a dramatic door. "How about, 'Remember'?"

"Perfect! Let's do that!"

And with Nick's acquiesence, that's the way it was done. (I should also remark here that Nick's agreement was slightly grudging, because he felt very strongly that Spock's demise should be final. Earlier, when confronted with Paramount's concerns that the audience might not accept the character's death, Nick argued that they *would* accept it if it were done well. Good artistic high ground for him to stand on, but early test audiences argued against him.)

At any rate, De and I shot the "Remember" scene, with the new addition: Spock distracts McCoy, then gently disables him with the nerve pinch. After he lowers the doctor to the ground, Spock removes his glove and presses his fingertips to the unconscious McCoy's face, saying softly, "Remember . . . "

As I said, I thought nothing about the implications of that scene;

I was only doing what was requested to the best of my ability, then moving on—with a growing sense of unease—toward Spock's final moments.

Here's how they went: With Scott and McCoy out of the way, Spock enters the chamber, removes the large round head of a pedestal-shaped contrivance, and—exposing himself to a lethal dose of radiation—makes the necessary repairs.

For me, entering the chamber brought a renewed sense of oppression, but it passed quickly. In fact, those moments of high intensity action went easily, because I could focus on the physical tasks at hand: Remove the head. Reach into the brilliant blaze of

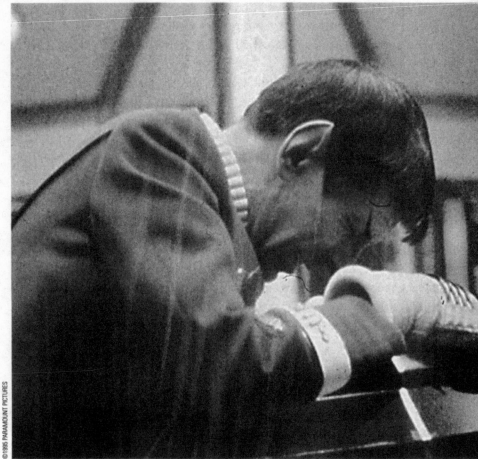

Inside the airless chamber

light and smoke created by dry ice. Make the repair. Replace the head.

It was all physical activity—and my only difficulty was physical as well. A surprise. After a short time in the chamber, I found I couldn't take a deep breath; it turned out the glass-walled chamber with its one revolving door was effectively airtight, and the hot camera lights quickly heated up what little remaining oxygen was there.

So the crew slid hoses underneath one of the set's glass walls and pumped in compressed air, but the pump made so much noise it had to be turned off whenever Bill or I delivered a line.

And the final scene had quite a bit of dialog—very well-written, touching dialog, I might add. Getting through it was more difficult, frankly, than trying to act without oxygen.

Rehearsal for that last encounter between Spock and his captain began with Kirk's entrance: The *Enterprise* is now safe. Summoned by an urgent call from McCoy, Kirk rushes off the bridge. Bill Shatner did a great slide down the engine room ladder, and was stopped by McCoy and Scotty as he tried to enter the radiation chamber.

"He'll die!" Kirk protests, and Scott delivers his hoarse, bitter, ago- nized line:

"He's dead already . . . "

We staged the rest of the scene. Realizing that any attempts to save his friend are futile, a grief-stricken Kirk moves to the glass wall and calls out to his Vulcan friend, who has collapsed. The sound of his voice rouses Spock, who struggles to his feet and meets his friend at the glass. En route, he staggers into the glass and recoils—causing us to realize the radiation has blinded him. As their final exchange progresses, Spock sinks weakly to the floor as his life ebbs away; Kirk follows, crouching down to remain close to his friend until the very last moment.

And then staging was over.

"Great!" Nick said. "That's the way it'll work. Let's turn it over to the crew for lighting while Leonard gets his radiation burn make- up."

It was silent in the makeup room as slowly, methodically, the burn makeup was applied to my face—or rather, to Spock's. What did the Vulcan think about what was about to happen? I'm sure he felt that sacrifice was simply the only logical course open to him—but Leonard Nimoy felt very differently. I watched the transformation in the mirror with a sense of impending doom, even grief at what was about to happen. I'd spent many years inside this character's skin, and I felt a great deal of respect, admiration—and yes, even fondness—for him.

And now I was condemning him to die.

Was there anything positive operating here? Of course. On the plus side, the script and scene were tightly constructed. There was an inevitable truth about the story; there was no easy way out. The characters were all solidly lined up to play their roles in the tragic structure. Simply put, it was damned good drama, and I knew it.

And yet, by the time I headed back to the set, I was an emotional wreck, in deep pain, and the deference everyone displayed toward me only added to my inner turmoil. The hushed stage crew parted in waves as I came walking through, and Bill, De, and Jimmy were somber; for once, Bill wasn't in a joking mood.

And then Nick Meyer made his grand entrance. Nick is a great Sherlock Holmes buff, as well as an opera lover, and once shooting wrapped that evening, he was heading directly from the studio to see a performance of *Carmen*. Thus he was dressed in his evening attire—as Holmes himself, complete with stalking hat and Inverness cape!

He was cheerful, looking forward to his evening out, and completely detached from the solemnity of what was about to happen. As if to emphasize that point, he called for an eight-foot ladder, then proceeded to climb to the top rung, from whence he intended to direct the scene—like a judge making calls at a tennis match.

To be honest, Nick's attitude rattled me. But I made my way through one final rehearsal, and forced myself to concentrate on my lines, on Spock's final act of saying good-bye to his captain and friend. That's what the scene was about for me—not about confronting mortality, or pain, or personal sacrifice—but about Spock's desire to not leave anything unsaid, while still maintaining his Vulcan dignity.

(In fact, years later when I saw the movie *Dances with Wolves*, I felt the exact same type of emotion when I viewed its final scene, where a young, strong Indian warrior bids good-bye to Kevin Costner's character. As Costner rides away, the Indian, poised on horseback atop an outcropping of rock, calls out: "Dances with Wolves! Do you hear me? I am Wind in the Hair! I am your friend. I will always be your friend . . . ")

Then it was time to start filming. First, however, Nick had decided that green Vulcan blood should be applied to Spock's hand. (Nick, I should mention, is very big on blood; his movies always feature copious amounts of it, as evidenced by the floating pools of violet Klingon blood in *Star Trek VI*.) It made medical sense, since a high dose of radiation damages cell structure, causing spontaneous bleeding. And it was certainly dramatic, since Spock was going to be pressing his hand to the glass—and leaving a bloody smear.

So once that last rehearsal was over, I came out of the chamber to have the blood applied to my hand. While that was being done, Bill came over to chat with me, and I was distracted; by the time I finally looked down at my hand, it was completely coated with green "blood." It was a simple misunderstanding, easily remedied— but I confess, the tension was just too much. I snapped, and lost my temper.

The blood seemed a completely unnecessary distraction—the radiation burns on Spock's face were sufficient to indicate the degree of his physical suffering, and performance would do the rest.

"Nick!" I yelled, waving my green palm at him. "Is *this* what you want? My *whole* hand dripping green blood? This is too much!!"

Nick scrambled down off the ladder, and saw to it that the makeup was toned down. Finally, we proceeded to the moments I'd so dreaded.

I stepped inside the chamber, took my position sitting on the floor at the far end . . . and the cameras started rolling.

"Action!" Nick called, and Kirk made his way slowly over to the glass and cried out: "Spock!"

Slowly, I pulled myself to my feet and stood erect; but before I moved toward Bill and the glass, I gave a slight downward tug on my jacket, which had, as usual, crept up on me. I was quite conscious of doing it, but hoped it would appear to be in character, because despite the physical agony, Spock would have wanted to make a proper and dignified appearance when presenting himself to his captain for the last time.

(Many weeks later, when I finally saw the film in a public theater, the audience let out a nervous laugh at the gesture, as if saying, "Look—see? He's okay after all. He's going to pull through this . . ." Not this time.)

Despite all my emotional travail preceding it, the scene played easily and well, and Bill Shatner gave a truly wonderful performance. My only problem turned out to be the lack of oxygen in the chamber. The toughest moments came after the final lines had been said, and Spock had obviously breathed his last. The camera drew back slowly from the Vulcan's image—and I mean *slowly*—as I held my breath. It seemed an eternity before Nick yelled "Cut!" and I could gasp for air. Naturally, we had to play the scene several times for the various angles—and each time, it grew harder and harder to hold my breath for the required amount of time.

Then—sooner than I realized—it was over. I stripped off the ears, the makeup, the uniform, until Spock gradually disappeared, leaving behind only Leonard Nimoy.

In some ways, it was just another day's work on a Hollywood soundstage, just another one of thousands of death scenes recorded on film. After all, I was an experienced actor; I'd "died" before in movies, usually as the "bad guy" getting his just desserts.

But never before had any character I'd played had such a profound impact on my psyche, my career, my life . . . and I had just conspired to bring about the end of our long, strange, and fascinating relationship. Never again the raised eyebrow; never again the delicious teasing of the irascible doctor, or the offering of logic to my impetuous friend and captain. Never again the mind meld, the neck pinch, or the Vulcan salute and blessing, "Live long and prosper." The weight of it finally struck me full force as I was driving home. I asked myself, "What have I done?"

NIMOY: Spock . . . ?
        (silence)
NIMOY: Spock . . . I'm sorry . . .
        (silence)

THIRTEEN

REBIRTH

or
What
I Really Want
to Do Is Direct

.

SPOCK: I was dead on the Genesis planet . . . yet you came back for me.
          Why?

NIMOY: Because the good of the one outweighed the good of the many . . .
          or the few.

SPOCK: I do not understand.

NIMOY: Because I missed you, Spock. Because I'm sorry I let you be killed
          off, okay?!

SPOCK: In that case . . . apology accepted.

IN STAR TREK II, we had entered into a dangerous abyss
with the idea that Spock would die. Harve, Nick and others had
decided to take the risk, to explore, to not be afraid. And it was
done, fearlessly—despite the dire predictions that fans would boy-
cott the film. (Did they in fact stay away in droves? Well, you be
the judge: Star Trek II: The Wrath of Khan pulled in the biggest opening weekend gross of any movie up to that time.) In fact, even those
fans who protested the loudest were pleased. Their attitude could
best be summed up as: "Oh. Well, we knew you were going to kill
him, but we didn't realize you were going to do it that way . . ."

As I wrote in the preceding chapter's quote from Will I Think of
You?, out of death comes a new vision of life . . . And out of the fear-
less decision to explore Spock's death came this enormous new
energy, which would extend to a third Star Trek film . . . and
beyond.

Several weeks after we finished shooting Wrath of Khan, I was
invited to a screening of the movie in the studio theater on the
Paramount lot. Typically, cast and crew, along with their immediate family and close friends, are invited. I watched the movie
unfold and thoroughly enjoyed myself, until suddenly the
Enterprise was facing utter destruction at the hands of the dastard-
ly Khan and the Genesis device. Once again, I heard the familiar
dialog repeated, as Kirk called Scotty and got the bad news that the
ship wasn't going anywhere.

And I saw Spock absorb this information, and make his decision.

By the time Spock got up to leave the bridge, tears began gathering in my eyes, because I knew better than anyone else what he was about to do.

Once again, I had an impulse to bolt, to run out of the theater, to hide; it had been difficult enough to perform in the upcoming scenes—but now I would have to watch. And now that I didn't have the distraction of focusing on the work itself, it was excruciating. All I could do was apologize silently to the Vulcan.

It was bad enough to watch Spock die—a character for whom I had the utmost admiration, respect, and . . . well, outright fondness—but I also knew that *I* was partly to blame. A co-conspirator in his death, if you will, and the guilt was awful. I was sincerely desperate to leave the theater, but years of experience with the public and the press held me there. The last thing I wanted was for someone to misunderstand, to think that I was somehow unhappy with the film or my role.

And like a grieving friend, the last thing I wanted to do at the moment was endlessly explain myself in public. So I stayed put and watched McCoy, Kirk, and Spock play out their final scenes together. I watched as the Vulcan gently pressed his fingertips to the unconscious doctor's forehead and murmured, "Remember." I watched, too, as Kirk and Spock pressed their hands together, separated by a wall of glass as the Vulcan said, "I have been, and always shall be, your friend."

By the time it was over, the tears were rolling down my cheeks.

There followed the funeral scene: A touching eulogy by Kirk, who said, "Of all the souls I have encountered in my travels, his was the most human." Spock's sleek black burial tube was loaded into the torpedo bay, then ejected into the starry void of space.

Then came a new piece of footage—one not called for by the original script, but filmed as an afterthought in response to the audience reaction at test screenings. (Harve and others at Paramount were concerned by the somber pall the original ending seemed to cast over the audience, and agreed that a more hopeful finish was called for.) The camera cuts to the surface of the Genesis planet, where it pans slowly over the mist and foliage of the surface to reveal . . . Spock's burial tube, lying intact and gleaming in the sunlight.

Now, I knew that the "Remember" mind meld with McCoy had left open a door of *some* kind for Spock . . .

But I'd been so involved in the work itself that I'd never really thought about just *how* open that door might be for me. I sat there for a moment in the darkness, staring with surprise at that burial tube—and then, just as it had when I'd seen *Star Wars* some five years earlier in New York, the realization struck me:

"I'm going to be getting a call from Paramount!"

The movie was a hit. Critics' and fans' reactions were positive, and the lines at the box office were long.

It didn't take long for the phone call to come; soon after, my agent Merritt and I were invited to come to Paramount for a meeting with Gary Nardino. Gary was the studio executive assigned to oversee the next film.

What the studio wanted was clear. We'd left some provocative story threads dangling at the end of *TWOK*: What, exactly, was McCoy going to "remember"? What about Spock's burial tube lying there on the Genesis planet? What effect would the Genesis device have on his body . . . ? And if it *does* have some kind of effect, does that mean we'll actually see Spock as we knew him, or someone—something—else?

What wasn't so clear was what *I* wanted. Money wasn't the major issue; my kids had finished college, and I owned my house free and clear. We'd been careful with what I'd earned, and I knew there'd be plenty of income from other sources. In short, I didn't need the money; what I wanted most was an interesting challenge.

But by the time Merritt and I arrived at Gary Nardino's office for our 9 A.M. meeting, I still wasn't certain what I wanted in return for my work on *Star Trek III*. Perhaps it was another stroke of good luck (for me, at least) that when we got to Gary's office, his secretary informed us he hadn't reported in yet, but had called from the car to let us know he'd be ten minutes late. And so she shepherded us to a couple of comfortable chairs and brought us some coffee, adding: "The trades are there, if you want something to read."

So Merritt and I sat down, and I began browsing through the most recent editions of *Variety* and *The Hollywood Reporter*, our two daily business trade papers.

There it was, on page one of *Variety*—a review of *Star Trek II: The Wrath of Khan*.

A very, very good review—glowing, one might say. And for some reason, as I read it, something that had been in the back of my mind for years suddenly clicked into place.

As far back as 1967, during the original *Star Trek*'s second season, Bill Shatner and I had both campaigned for an opportunity to direct an episode. We were met with a flat-out rejection. Thus far, both Robert Wise and Nick Meyer, neither of whom had the benefit of a long relationship with *Star Trek*, had been given the reins.

I suddenly remembered a line from Shakespeare's *Julius Caesar*, where Cassius says to Brutus, "Men at some time are masters of their fate."

Well, I determined at that moment to prove Old Will right. I turned to Merritt and said, "What would you think if I told them I wanted to direct this film?"

God bless him, he didn't even blink, but responded with admirable agently aplomb, "I think that's a great idea!"

"Then I will," I said. The words were barely out of my mouth when Gary Nardino arrived, with eerily appropriate timing, for our meeting.

Gary's a portly gentleman, businesslike, blunt and direct; along with him was a gentleman from Paramount Business Affairs. We made small talk for a minute or two, then Gary got right to the point with:

"So, Leonard—would you like to be involved in any way in the making of *Star Trek III*?"

Not, "Will you play Spock again?" but, "Will you be involved *in any way* . . ."

It was as though, with that gracious and knowing question, he had anticipated precisely what I was now going to propose; as though he were intentionally opening a door for me.

And I walked right through it.

"With all due respect to Robert Wise and Nicholas Meyer," I said, "I've had a much longer and more intimate experience with *Star Trek* than either of these two gentlemen. I believe I could bring something to a film that hasn't yet been found. I'd like to direct the picture."

Just like Merritt, Gary didn't even flinch. "As a matter of fact, Leonard, I've had that very same thought. We'll be in touch."

No protest, no list of reasons why I shouldn't direct. Just "Yes, that's a good thought, and we'll consider it and let you know."

And, before I knew it, the meeting was over. I walked out, swept

•

along by a rush of pure adrenaline. Could it really be as easy as that? Just ask, and it shall be given me? I was stunned; Merritt was exuberant. "You did great!" he crowed. "Just great!"

"Maybe," I said, "but do you really think it'll happen?"

"It'll happen," Merrit said, with enviable confidence.

Now, right here I have to stop in order to give credit to my old friend Harve Bennett. You see, until the success of *Star Trek IV*, Harve was the only person who had ever called me and said, "I'd like you to direct for me." He did so while he was producing a tele-vision series called *The Powers of Matthew Starr*, around the time of *The Wrath of Khan*. Something made Harve pick up the phone and call me to offer me that directing job, and his timing and instinct were perfect for my life and career. My experience directing the *Matthew Starr* episode gave me a sense of confidence and valida-tion, which I think gave me that extra bit of determination to ven-ture out into new territory and ask for *Star Trek III*.

Within two weeks, Michael Eisner, who possessed the power to say yea or nay, called to request a meeting. This time, I arrived at Gary Nardino's office alone, and together, we headed for Eisner's office, down a long corridor in the administration building. Since the 1940s, its walls have been covered with photographs of Paramount film stars—including me, in stills from the *Star Trek* pic-tures. There's even an old black-and-white photo from a 1951 film called *Rhubarb*, starring Ray Milland and Jan Sterling—and featur-ing a *very* young Leonard Nimoy.

As I walked past all those representatives of film history toward my own uncertain future, it suddenly occurred to me to ask, "Does Michael know what I'm coming for?"

"No," Gary answered.

His simple, matter-of-fact reply jolted me, and served as my first real taste of the political game in the upper hierarchies of filmdom. I realized then that Gary was being very shrewd: By making *me* make the proposal to Eisner directly, Gary could be kind and encouraging toward me—yet not take a stand either for or against me with Eisner, until he knew exactly how his boss felt about the issue.

Perhaps this was best for Nardino, but I was unnerved: I'd assumed Eisner had been briefed on my request. Now I was walk-ing in cold, and would have to start at the beginning.

So that's exactly what I did; when we were ushered into Michael's spacious office, I did my song and dance about directing, just as I'd done for Nardino. And as I talked, I realized the earlier meeting with Gary had been a useful rehearsal.

Michael's response?

You'd have thought he was my agent, not a studio executive.

"Great!" Michael thundered, with typical Eisnerish enthusiasm. "What a fantastic idea! Leonard Nimoy directs the return of Spock! I love it! The sales people will love it! Mancuso will love it!" (Frank Mancuso was, at that time, in charge of distribution.)

He was *so* enthusiastic, in fact, that I went totally slack-jawed. As an actor, I'd spent many difficult, tedious years building my career bit part by bit part, working my way up the rungs.

And you mean all I had to do to direct an important high-budget movie was *ask*?

Unbelievable. Yet here was Mike Eisner, asking me if I'd also like to write it!

I shook my head at that one. Harve Bennett had already

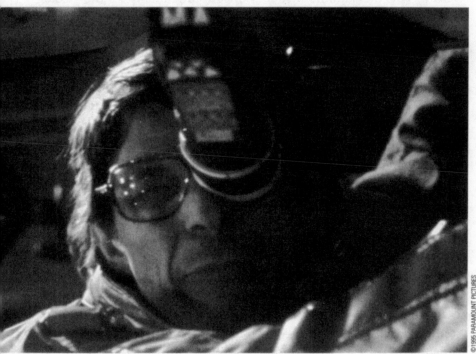

The director at work

expressed interest in writing the script, and I was quite comfortable to be working with him.

Then, once again, the meeting was over and I was floating out into the corridor on an adrenaline high. I couldn't quite believe that it had all happened—but I knew that I hadn't dreamed the words that had sprung from Mike Eisner's mouth. And so, dazed, I called my agent and briefed him, then met with Harve Bennett to let him know what had happened.

It all seemed too easy, too good to be true.

It was.

After Michael's enthusiasm, I expected to receive a call within a couple of days. But two days passed, then three; I was excited, ready to do business, so I had Merritt place a call to Paramount.

He never got through. The secretary politely took his message—but no one ever returned the call.

Another day passed. And another. I became concerned: Had Eisner thought about my idea and changed his mind, gotten cold feet? Or was this just a battle of nerves? I knew my position was strong; was this Paramount's way of softening me up on the price? (If it was, it was totally unnecessary; I would gladly have taken the Director's Guild scale for the directing job, and would accept the same fee as Bill Shatner for acting, which had been our policy since the first *Star Trek* film.)

Finally, after weeks had passed, I could wait no longer: I picked up the phone and called Mike Eisner. To my relief, he accepted my call immediately.

"Michael," I told him, "I don't understand what's going on here, after all the enthusiasm you showed at our meeting. Why aren't you returning Merritt's calls?"

He let go a deep sigh and said, "Look, I've got a big problem here, Leonard. I don't feel comfortable about putting you in charge of this very expensive and important movie. After all, you hate *Star Trek* so much—hate this character, Spock, so much—that you *insisted* we kill him off. You even made us put it in your contract for *The Wrath of Khan!*"

Once again, I was slack-jawed: The ghosts of *I Am Not Spock* had returned to haunt me again—this time in the form of the myth that *I* had been the one who wanted to kill the Vulcan.

When I recovered from the shock, I protested, "Michael, that simply isn't true! I don't hate Spock *or Star Trek*, and it wasn't my idea to kill the character off. And it certainly was never in my contract!"

"It *wasn't?*"

"Michael, a copy of my contract is right there where you are, in the administration building. Why don't you have someone look it up, so you can see for yourself?"

He was silent a moment, then said, "If you say it isn't there, then I believe you."

"It's not. Look, this is very important to me. I think we should meet again."

"How about tomorrow?" Michael asked, and by nine-thirty the following morning, I was back in his office. During an intense hour-long meeting, I explained the history of *I Am Not Spock* and the misperceptions it had created; I also assured him that I wanted to make a contribution to *Star Trek* and to revive Spock. He thanked me and promised I'd hear something soon.

This time, I did: within a day or two, my agent got a call from Paramount's Business Affairs department, and shortly after that, we'd negotiated ourselves a deal. I was to direct *Star Trek III: The Search for Spock* and also portray the back-from-the-dead Vulcan. Harve Bennett and I began talking about the script. And then there were more private conversations with my alter ego . . .

NIMOY: Welcome back, Spock.

SPOCK: *Thank you. I must admit that this entire process has been quite fascinating.*

NIMOY: How do you mean?

SPOCK: *Specifically, your personal behavior. It has been some time since I have seen you so single-minded, so goal-oriented. Clearly you value this directing assignment greatly.*

NIMOY: I do. I've always wanted to direct *Star Trek;* I guess I want to prove my value to it. To show I can make a contribution.

SPOCK: *I fail to follow your logic. You portray one of the most popular characters in science fiction—*

NIMOY: False modesty was never one of your weaknesses, was it, Spock?

SPOCK: *(stiffly) I was endeavoring to make a point. May I continue?*

NIMOY: Please.

SPOCK: *Since your portrayal of me is considered to be of paramount importance to the show—*

NIMOY: Pun intended, I assume.

SPOCK: *(ignoring him utterly) . . . I fail to see why you think you have not contributed.*

NIMOY: Maybe . . . maybe it's because I've always done so as *you*, Spock. I want to show that Leonard Nimoy *as himself* wants to make a contribution.

SPOCK: *Surely you are not jealous of me? As you are so fond of pointing out, I am merely a fictional character.*

NIMOY: It's not jealousy. It's that . . . if I give something beyond an actor's performance, maybe it'll put all those ugly rumors to rest about my rejecting *Star Trek*, about my wanting you dead. About my not wanting to appear in a second *Star Trek* TV series all those years ago . . .

SPOCK: *Ah, yes. The offer of the "parttime job," as you put it. Whose idea was that?*

NIMOY: It came from Himself. The "Creator."

SPOCK: *I see . . . As I have said before, I understand your search for validation and acceptance. But sometimes, it must come from other quarters than the one you seek. There is but one thing to be done: Plunge into the task at hand. You may indeed be approaching the final plain.*

NIMOY: "The final plain"?

SPOCK: *We can discuss it at a more appropriate time. For now, there is much work to be done.*

So I did as Spock wisely suggested: I plunged into *Star Trek III* with the enthusiasm of a hungry gourmet sitting down to a sumptuous nine-course feast. I planned to taste it all!

Harve and I began to meet regularly to discuss the storyline. We knew the basic ideas that would provide the framework: *Something* was bound to emerge from Spock's burial tube on the Genesis planet, and the Vulcan had told McCoy to "remember" something. All we had to do was figure out what those two things were—*and* set them in a dramatic adventure that would ultimately lead to the return of Spock. Early on, we decided that the Vulcan's resurrection should be accomplished near the film's end, in order to keep the suspense going.

Soon, the story ideas were hammered out: The planet enveloped by the Genesis "wave" is evolving rapidly—too rapidly, as we'll discover. Because of the danger to living creatures, the planet is declared off-limits—a fact that Kirk and crew will ignore, of course! To make things even more interesting, a life form is detected near Spock's burial tube, Dr. McCoy starts muttering about "logic" and trying out the Vulcan neck pinch on Federation officials, while the Klingons hear about the powerful Genesis device and decide to get their hands on it.

(An interesting sidebar here: Originally, Harve's outline featured the Romulans as the heavies. But I've always been more intrigued by the Klingons, so I suggested the switch, which Harve readily embraced. To this day, I wish I could have done a serious study of Klingon culture in one of our films; I think they're marvelous "dark side" adversaries. It was Bill Shatner who reminded me that Gene Coon, our valued line producer on the original series, gave us the gift of Klingons.)

In the meantime, Spock's father, Sarek, is hopping mad—in a controlled, logical way, of course—and confronts a grieving Kirk, demanding to know why the admiral has failed to return Spock's *katra*—his immortal spirit—to Vulcan.

The task left to Kirk and company becomes clear: Go to Genesis, get what's left of Spock, and bring it and McCoy back to Vulcan. (And hope like hell the Vulcans know what to do!)

Harve sat down to write the script (which he finished in an amazing six weeks) while I began to explore other areas—specifically the thousands of details, shapes, images, and colors that would set *Star Trek III*'s tone. Most important, I started considering its theme.

Clearly, the theme of *Star Trek II* centered around sacrifice, and the notion that "the good of the many outweighed the good of the few . . . or the one."

Was it possible that, this time, the good of the one might outweigh the good of the few, or the many?

The first time I saw a production of *Henry V*, I was struck by the call to camaraderie King Henry used in rallying his outnumbered troops for the battle against the large French force at Agincourt. "We few," he says, "we happy few, we band of brothers . . . for he that sheds his blood with me today shall be my brother."

This trumpet call to loyalty and friendship—loyalty to Kirk and friendship for Spock—would become the guiding theme of the film for me. What would our heroes risk in order to honor their commitment to their friend?

Because of this, we worked very consciously in *Star Trek III* (and would again in *Star Trek IV*) to define special moments for each member of the *Enterprise* bridge crew. Each one had a task to perform that would ultimately lead to Spock's return. In part, I think I was influenced by my experience in *Mission: Impossible*, where each character had a specific job to complete in any given adventure.

Kirk, of course, served as ringleader of the adventure, and De Kelley had some marvelous early moments in the film as a *katra*-crazed Dr. McCoy, who vacillates between Vulcan logic and his usual emotionalism. The good doctor winds up in a seedy bar (complete with intergalactic Muzak and waitresses with lacquered hair), spouting Spock/McCoy hybrid lines like: "What's the logic in offering me a ride home, you idiot?!" In addition, Scotty, Uhura, and Sulu would all have their moments in the film. While Chekov's abilities weren't specifically showcased in this movie, I hope we made it up to Walter with the wonderful Chekov scenes in *Star Trek IV*.

While Harve was working away on the script, it was also time for us to get to work on casting. We faced some challenges in that regard. We'd already decided that the character Saavik, Spock's half-Vulcan protégé, would return, as would Kirk's son, David. Merritt Buttrick was available to reprise his role as David, but we ran into a huge snag with Kirstie—which was unfortunate, because she had given a marvelous performance in *The Wrath of Khan*, and we were eager to have her back.

And she was just as eager to return. We contacted her while the script was still in the works, and the salary we discussed was reasonable. (We were relieved, because frankly, Paramount's Business Affairs had dropped the ball on her contract for *Wrath of Khan*. She'd been a total newcomer then, and Paramount had been within its rights to insert an option clause in her contract that required her to perform in a sequel for a predetermined price. But the company had neglected to do it—so Kirstie was now a free agent!) It looked like everything would work out, so when the script was ready, we sent it along for Kirstie and her agent to read.

Shortly thereafter, her agent called us back, and said, "Look, we didn't realize how large a role Saavik was going to have in this film. So we're withdrawing our earlier figure. Here's what we have to have now . . ."

And he quoted a price that was so far beyond our reach that it left me slack-jawed. I'm sure neither he nor Kirstie realized it, but the salary he wanted for her second *Star Trek* appearance was higher than what was being paid to De Kelley after seventeen years!

We couldn't agree to the price on either budgetary or ethical grounds, but Kirstie and her agent held firm. We had no choice but to search for a new Saavik, and Kirstie went on to a wonderful career, which included numerous movies and the series *Cheers*.

Robin Curtis as Saavik

•

Commander Kruge
(Christopher Lloyd)

©1995 PARAMOUNT PICTURES

Eventually, we discovered Robin Curtis, who delivered a lovely, sensitive performance as Saavik.

The other casting crisis we faced was that of the lead Klingon, Commander Kruge; in fact, Harve Bennett and I got into something of a tussle over it. We auditioned a lot of different actors for the role, but no one did it justice. And then, one day, I came upon a tape of Edward James Olmos (who would later go on to *Miami Vice*), and decided he'd be perfect as Kruge. Olmos had the intensity I was looking for, but Harve insisted that he didn't have the physical stature the role demanded. I kept trying to convince Harve that Olmos was the man for the job, and Harve kept steadfastly disagreeing; we were at a stalemate.

Until, that is, the day Christopher Lloyd expressed interest in the role. Lloyd was well known for his brilliant work as Reverend Jim on the series *Taxi*—and, in fact, some of the studio executives were concerned that, because of his connection to comedy, Lloyd wouldn't be taken seriously as a bad guy. But that presented no problem, because Lloyd is a fine actor and an absolute chameleon. (In fact, we remembered the powerful image of his contorted face that served as the closing frame of *One Flew Over the Cuckoo's Nest*.) Harve and I couldn't be dissuaded; when Lloyd indicated he wanted the role, we deemed ourselves lucky to get him. His portrayal of Kruge was a joy to watch; he literally smacked his lips as though savoring the role. It made me happier than ever to be working with Klingons!

Other casting of extraterrestrials proceeded fairly smoothly. A smaller Klingon role, that of Maltz, was filled by a then unknown actor named John Larroquette (who would go on to fame in *Night Court*). We also found the young actors to play Spock at various ages without much trouble (although one young man had to be fitted with colored contact lenses because of his unVulcanly blue eyes).

Soon I found myself faced with only one casting challenge left: The role of the Vulcan high priestess, T'Lar.

Now, ever since the episode "Amok Time," I'd kept in my memory the great performance by Celia Lovsky as T'Pau, the regal Vulcan matriarch. Unfortunately, Ms. Lovsky had passed away by this time—but my hope was to find someone of similarly magnificent bearing to play T'Lar.

Recently, I had seen a television production of *Medea* that featured Dame Judith Anderson in a secondary role, and had admired her powerful performance. She was now eighty-five years old, past the age to play Medea herself, but in her time she had been known as the greatest actress ever to fill the role.

I was determined to find her and cast her as T'Lar. I tracked down her agent and discovered she was living in Santa Barbara, little more than an hour's drive from Los Angeles. A phone conversation was arranged. I introduced myself carefully, only to learn that she had never heard of *Star Trek*!

Even so, I asked if I might come visit and bring her a script to read. She agreed, and on the following Saturday, I drove up to Santa Barbara, where we met for lunch. She turned out to be a charming woman with a delightful sense of humor—and, despite her "stature" as an actress, not even five feet tall. We hit it off immediately; I explained that we had a mutual friend in Elliott Silverstein, who had directed her in *A Man Called Horse*, while she related, with a twinkle in her eye, that her nephew was a devoted *Star Trek* fan who threatened to disown her if she refused the role! We had a great time swapping theater stories over lunch, and when it was over, I handed her the script and asked her to call me.

She did, several days later.

"Leonard?" she said. "I've had quite a trip!"

"Where did you go?" I asked, nervous; I had no clue what she was talking about.

She laughed. "I've read your script. It's delicious, and I'd love to be involved!"

•

With all casting obstacles surmounted, it was time to start the actual shooting—but we ran into a few new problems there, too.

Now, I'd rather naively thought that Bill and the rest of the cast would accept my taking the reins as director comfortably—that of course, they would understand that I had the best intentions for everyone. But I was out of touch with their concerns. They were uneasy because of the shift in dynamic, and they wondered, "Why is Leonard being given this job? Does he know what he's doing? What are his intentions toward me and my character? Is this an ego trip, a lark, or is he really serious about this job?"

Shortly before shooting was to begin, Bill Shatner asked for a meeting with Harve and me about the script. To say the encounter was tense is putting it mildly; Bill was accompanied by his attorney, and his first statement was, "I want nothing to do with this script."

Well, Harve and I decided the best way to handle it was to deal with Bill's objections one by one. We said, "Okay, let's go through this scene by scene, and you tell us the specific details that bother you."

So, for the next several hours, we did. And once Bill realized that any legitimate gripes he had would be listened to, and dealt with, he relaxed. (I'm still not certain whether he was intentionally overreacting, to test the waters, or whether he was sincerely that upset.) As for the other six of the Magnificent *Enterprise* Seven, they, too, had their reservations about this new director, but decided to keep silent and see what happened. (I was blissfully unaware of it during the shooting of the film, but I learned about it afterwards, when everyone con-

The marvelous Celia
Lovsky as T'Pau . . .

. . . and the magnificent Dame Judith Anderson as T'Lar

©1995 PARAMOUNT PICTURES

fessed in interviews: "Yeah, we were a little worried at the beginning; thank goodness, Leonard worked out okay!") Once the actual filming of *Star Trek III* began, the cast came to realize that I didn't view my role as director as a license to dictate. I was far more interested in collaborating with the actors, who had each spent years getting to know their characters. I also tried my best to prepare meticulously for each day's work, and I believe that fact, combined with my genuine affection for each of the *Star Trek* characters, helped any tension to gradually ease.

At long last, shooting got underway in August 1983—and things started getting *really* interesting. First, there is no work in my business more demanding or exhausting than directing. Up to that point, I'd directed a couple of *Night Gallery*s, an episode of *Mission: Impossible*, an episode of Harve Bennett's series *The Powers of Matthew Starr*, and one of *T. J. Hooker*. But this was my first major motion picture.

Let me explain a little bit about the director's responsibilities: He or she is the person responsible for making sure *everything* goes right. For example, in the case of *Star Trek III*, I typically had a certain number of scenes scheduled to be shot on each given day—and I had to be sure that the shooting of those scenes went smoothly, and that what was captured on film was good. In order to do that, I first had to make a *lot* of decisions: Exactly how will the scene be laid out? How will it be lit? Are there any special physical demands being made on the actors? Should stunt doubles be used? If we use doubles, at what precise instant will the camera cut to the principal actors? Will the effects department need to supply smoke and steam? Should there be sparks given off? If the character's clothing is burned, *how* burned should it be?

So in order to do the all-vital preparation, I'd walk through the scenes in advance with the various department heads (from lighting, makeup, camera, special effects, wardrobe, and so on) and we'd discuss everything and coordinate. In order to accomplish this, and my other responsibilities, I had to be on the studio lot no later than 7 A.M. every morning, and never left before dark.

But no matter how meticulously one prepares, it's a law of physics that *something* has to go awry at the last minute, requiring on-the-spot adjustments. If we were shooting outside, the weather would change, or some much-needed piece of equipment wouldn't show up on the set because somebody goofed. The real challenge was to be able to adapt to all the last-minute changes while still accomplishing the day's task—to film that scheduled scene, enough different ways and from enough different angles so that it can be cut into a montage that adds up to something exciting.

And, of course, the director is the one responsible for seeing that the actor's performance hits the mark. I had to keep my eyes open for an enormous number of details—and for that reason, I was (and still am) grateful when people brought my attention to problems. For the same reason, I also tried to maintain an atmosphere of collaboration on the set, so that people weren't afraid to speak openly about problems or ideas.

Now, despite Mike Eisner's outspoken enthusiasm about what a great marketing ploy it was to have me directing the return of Spock, to be candid, the folks at Paramount had some understandable anxiety about putting a novice in the director's chair. As much as I enjoyed working with Harve Bennett, a degree of tension existed between us, because Harve felt responsible for protecting both the studio and the film just in case I didn't know what I was doing. He played the role of the studio's vigilant watchdog, who observed my every move and took care lest something go awry in a remarkably expensive way—while *I* was the dog on the very short leash!

•

Everything I did was scrutinized microscopically. I remember the very first scene I directed on the film: It showed Bill looking out an observation window on the *Enterprise*. My intention was to keep the camera on Bill alone, and pull back slowly while Kirk does a wistful voice-over about the sense of sadness and loneliness aboard the ship. Very gradually, the camera would draw back and reveal only a few people left on the bridge.

However, this pull-back couldn't be physically accomplished in one shot. I had to design it so that the first shot would come to an end, and the next would show Bill moving. The shots had to be cut together—a common practice, but apparently there was a definite question in Harve's mind as to whether the two shots would cut smoothly. Unbeknownst to me, he immediately took the film and rushed it to the editor to see if my first day's efforts were successful.

I found out about it the next day, when Harve came on the set and mentioned to someone else (with fairly obvious relief), "Those shots cut like butter!" I had passed the first test.

Yet despite all the tensions and challenges I faced as director, I was never happier. The work was exhilarating and fulfilling. And with *Star Trek III*, I truly came to understand Joe Sargent's enthusiastic note to himself, all those years ago, when he wrote on the script: "And we're off!"

We were "off" very quickly in the early scenes of *Star Trek III*, where almost immediately a mystery surrounding Spock's death is established: McCoy is found in Spock's quarters in a strange mental condition, urging Kirk in the Vulcan's voice to "Remember . . ." Soon after, Kirk gets a surprise visit from Sarek, Spock's father—and learns that he must find Spock's body and take it and McCoy back to Vulcan. I was very pleased with the mind-meld scene between Kirk and Sarek, played wonderfully by both Bill Shatner and Mark Lenard. Composer James Horner's music with its distant, haunting woodwind sound added to the scene's sense of mystery.

One of the film's most exhilarating moments comes when Kirk, having been denied the *Enterprise* and warned against returning to Genesis, reports back to an expectant Sulu and Chekov.

SULU: The word, sir?
KIRK: The word is no. I am therefore going anyway!

That's our hero! Shortly thereafter, Kirk goes to spring McCoy from the hospital, where the doctor's undergoing psychiatric testing. Kirk explains that McCoy's mental condition is the result of Spock implanting his *katra* in the doctor's brain. The response brought one of the biggest (and fondest) laughs in the film.

McCOY: That green-blooded son of a bitch! It's his revenge for all those arguments he lost!

Now, in that particular scene, Kirk greeted McCoy with the line, "How many fingers am I holding up, Bones?" while raising his hand in the Vulcan salute. But Bill had the same problem as Celia Lovsky in "Amok Time"—he simply could *not* make his hand form the necessary shape. (Let's face it—Bill's just not Vulcan!) We finally had to help him out; we lined the sides of his rebellious fingers with double-sided tape, then *tied* them into position with a piece of fine monofilament fish line.

It was during McCoy's "great escape" from the hospital that the character of Sulu performed his "*Mission: Impossible*" task, without which Spock could never have been brought back from the dead. In order to help McCoy, Sulu distracts a humorless, towering monolith of a security guard, who at the beginning of the scene is slumped at his station.

SULU: Keeping you busy?
GUARD: (rising to his full, intimidating height) Don't get smart, Tiny.

After Kirk escorts McCoy out of his cell, the confused guard tries to stop them—but Sulu steps in and easily hurls the gargantuan guy over his shoulder. As the guard lies stunned and unable to move, Sulu calmly destroys the security console with a blast from a small weapon, then, on his way out, says over his shoulder: "*Don't* call me Tiny!"

George Takei was happy to see his character well used—but vehemently opposed to the use of the epithet "Tiny" in regard to Sulu. "Sulu *isn't* tiny," George insisted, "and the fans won't buy this scene for a second!" After much discussion, Harve Bennett finally convinced him to shoot the scene two ways—one with the "Tiny" reference, and one without. And whichever scene worked best would be the one used. (Harve, bless him, was running interference for me—I didn't learn about George's protests until much later.) George felt so certain that the "Tiny" scene wouldn't fly that he was shocked to see it in the finished film. But when he heard the thunderous cheer from the audience at the "Don't call me Tiny!" line, he realized that he'd been mistaken, and was gracious and good-natured enough to tell everyone so.

The next of the crew members with a mission was Uhura, who was manning a quiet spacedock transporter station. With her was a young ensign we all nicknamed "Mr. Adventure," because in his dialog, he makes it clear that, while Uhura's career might be winding down and she might be content stuck in "the hind end of space" where nothing ever happened, *he* was young and yearning for adventure and surprises.

And a surprise is just what he gets, when Kirk and crew unexpectedly appear at the station so that Uhura can illegally beam them over to the *Enterprise*. She then waves a phaser at the wide-eyed "Mr. Adventure" and forces him to lock himself in a closet.

Unfortunately, up to that time, Nichelle had rarely been given much dialog in a *Star Trek* script beyond the de rigueur "Hailing frequencies open, sir," especially with individuals other than the immediate crew. We felt it was long overdue to show her character really taking charge of a situation, in a way that made it obvious the scene's outcome rested in her hands. Nichelle was clearly aware that she

©1995 PARAMOUNT PICTURES

Larger than life: George Takei as Sulu, blasting the "don't get smart with me, Tiny" guard's console

A woman to be
reckoned with:
Nichelle Nichols,
in the wonderful
"Mr. Adventure" scene

©1995 PARAMOUNT PICTURES

had a special moment here, and it really shows in her performance. The audiences adored it!

They also loved Jimmy Doohan's performance as the wily Engineer Scott, who stole the "juice" out of the *Excelsior*'s transwarp drive, so that Starfleet's newest and finest starship would come to a sputtering stop when she tried to pursue the hijacked *Enterprise* and its merry band of outlaws.

Once our twenty-third-century "impossible mission" team has succeeded in stealing the *Enterprise* and warping toward the forbidden planet, Genesis, the film's ebullient mood darkens abruptly when Kirk's son, David, is killed by Commander Kruge and his men. (Actually, when Harve was first writing the script, he couldn't decide whether Saavik or David should die; as he puts it, "We were passing the knife over Saavik just like the Klingon in the film." Eventually, he decided that it was dramatically just for David to die—since it was David who used unstable protomatter in the Genesis device. In a way, David's murder was karmic retribution for fooling with Mother Nature.)

Kirk's reaction to the news of his son's death is a very powerful moment, and before we prepared to shoot the scene, I said, "Okay, will everyone please leave the set? I want to talk to Bill." I felt the scene was so important for the character of Kirk that it would be best for us to discuss it in a very private and relaxed atmosphere.

Obediently, the cast and crew—even Harve Bennett—filed out, leaving Bill and me alone on the bridge.

•

Now, let's face it—Bill and I have been known to disagree with each other upon occasion. And for some reason, at that particular moment, both of us suddenly got in a whimsical mood, despite the seriousness of the upcoming scene; maybe we were both looking to release a little tension before getting down to such somber business. Anyway, don't ask me how it began, or who started it. All I remember is, Bill got this sudden twinkle in his eye, and I *knew* what he was thinking.

And he obviously *knew* that I knew, because we shared a surreptitious wink with each other. Once everybody else was gone (but hanging around well within earshot), we paused for a moment—then Bill picked up his fist and slammed it down against the console.

"Dammit, Leonard!" he roared, in one of his less convincing performances. "I don't care *what* you think! Kirk would *never* do it that way!"

"Well, *my* way is the right way!" I shouted back, with as much un-Spockian fury as I could muster. "In case you haven't noticed, *I'm* the director! And *that's* the way you're going to do it!"

"Oh *yeah*? Well, we'll *see* about *that*, Mr. Director!" Bang! Down went his fist again on the console.

I started in with a little fist-slamming of my own. Crash! "Damn straight we will!"

At that point, neither one of us could keep it up any longer. Bill grinned, and I cracked up at that point, and we both had a good laugh before tackling the more serious stuff. It's a good thing the cameras weren't rolling, because our little performance didn't fool anyone. The cast and crew just ignored us mightily, so we settled down to work.

In the scene in question, Kirk is standing on the *Enterprise* bridge when he hears from Saavik that David has just been killed by the Klingons on the Genesis planet's surface. Kirk's line was, "You Klingon bastard! You've killed my son," and it could have been delivered a number of ways—with fury, machismo, grief . . .

Bill was very receptive to what I had to say—but in all honesty, I really couldn't give much advice, other than: "This is *your* decision; *you've* got to decide how far you want to go with this, how emotionally vulnerable Kirk is going to be at this moment, how much of the impervious hero's veneer you want to strip away. My feeling is that you can go pretty far—but it's up to you."

•

We started staging the scene, and Bill decided that Kirk's instinct upon hearing the terrible news would be to retreat, to withdraw, in an effort to get control of himself. I agreed, so we positioned Bill near the captain's chair, and he was going to step backwards toward it.

Well, Bill took it further than I expected, all right—he stumbled backwards and fell, as though the words "David is dead" had reached out and physically struck him. It was very moving, very touching, very powerful—and in a way, a little frightening, because we hoped that everyone else who saw the film would agree. All it takes is one little kid out in the audience to snicker at Kirk losing balance and falling on his own ship, and the moment is lost.

But Bill kept going—and I watched as Kirk rose from the floor, out of stunned despair and into anger with the words, "You Klingon bastard, you've killed my son . . . !"

It was so utterly convincing—I really thought he'd accidentally fallen—that afterwards, I rushed over to him and said, "Bill, are you all right?"

"Of course," he said. "Think we can use that?"

Bill and the director, in a typically violent confrontation on the set

His performance was so beautiful that the next day, after the Paramount executives had viewed it, an elated Jeff Katzenberg called me on the set.

"Leonard! Congratulations! I just saw that wonderful scene with Bill. Why have you been wasting your time acting all these years? You're a director!"

Thanks, Jeff—but I really think the call should have gone to Bill.

Speaking of Jeff Katzenberg, he and I had a little side wager going about how the audience would react to a particular scene. You see, in *The Search for Spock*, Spock's regenerated body ages rapidly, along with the Genesis planet. And as we learned in the episode "Amok Time," Vulcan males undergo a mating period, the *pon farr*, every seven years. Unless they're able to mate, they die.

So by the time teenage Spock hits his first *pon farr* on the Genesis planet, it's a pretty desperate situation. Luckily, Saavik is there and realizes what is happening to him. In perhaps the film's gentlest moment, she compassionately guides him through the beginning of the Vulcan mating ritual (by teaching him the Vulcan two-fingers-touching "embrace," used many years before by Mark Lenard and Jane Wyatt as Spock's parents in "Journey to Babel").

Whenever I watch this scene and see Saavik leading young Spock through the sedate Vulcan version of foreplay, I'm reminded of the play and film *Tea and Sympathy*. Instead of Saavik's voice, I can almost hear Deborah Kerr delivering the famous last line: "When you are older and speak of this—and you will—please be kind."

Harve Bennett and I were pleased with the scene when it was finished, but Jeff shook his head when he first saw it in the screening room.

"Leonard, Harve—you really ought to cut this. The audience is going to laugh."

"No, they won't, Jeff," I said.

"Want to bet?"

"Sure."

"Okay," Jeff said. "Bet you both a dollar you and Harve are wrong."

"Only a dollar?" I said. "Why not a hundred? A thousand?"

"Yeah," Harve added. "A million. If you're that confident, Jeff—"

"One dollar for each of you if I'm wrong. And one dollar *from* each of you if I'm right," Jeff repeated firmly. "Is our wager on or off?"

"You're on," Harve and I chorused.

I don't know where Harve keeps his dollar, but *mine* is hanging on my office wall. It's signed and framed, above a small brass plaque that reads:

I BET THE PON FARR SCENE GETS A LAUGH. JEFF KATZENBERG, APRIL '84.

Although *Star Trek III* revived Spock, it *did* kill off another very valued member of the crew: the *Enterprise* herself. The story leaked, of course, before the film's release—it's virtually impossible to keep anything a secret for long from *Star Trek* devotees. Once again, there was an outcry—nothing like the reaction to the news of Spock's death, but enough that we heard about it. But we had survived the Vulcan's demise, so we took news of the protest in stride. In fact, I was more than pleased with the scenes in the film surrounding the *Enterprise*'s destruction; the folks at Industrial Light and Magic provided us with spectacular images of the ship descending to her fiery death, and the scene where the crew stands on a Genesis mountaintop, watching her streak across the sky, was memorable.

KIRK:　My God, Bones—what have I done?
McCOY:　What you had to do.

The final days of shooting were the most challenging for me, because up to that point, the adult Spock hadn't appeared in the film. I soon developed a hearty respect for those who both act and direct in a film! At first, I tried coming in at my usual 7 A.M., getting the day's work started, then slipping off while other work was in progress to get my Spock makeup done.

What a mistake! In the middle of it, I'd be called away to check someone's wardrobe, or the lighting, or a special effect, tearing around the set with *one* Vulcan eyebrow in place, or *one* Vulcan ear. And when the time came around for Spock to appear on camera, I'd still be looking like a very strange Vulcan-human hybrid. I soon realized that the only way to get anything done was to have the makeup completely in place before I ever stepped onto the stage as the director.

And that meant coming in no later than (shudder) five in the morning, and staying put until the Vulcan makeup was finished. Quite honestly, I wasn't fond of it. (Though I'd have to do it even *more* often in the next *Star Trek* film.)

One of the first scenes featuring Spock had him lying unconscious on a bed in sick bay, with McCoy talking to him. Now, as a director, this presented some frustrating moments for me. As an actor, I knew I couldn't blow the scene by opening my eyes to watch how things were going—I couldn't actually see De Kelley's performance, I could only go by the sound of his voice, and by the cameraman's sense of whether the scene worked or not. So at the end of each take, I turned to De and said, "Well, how'd it go? Are you doing it right?"

Now, if it'd been someone else—a new actor, I would have been *really* nervous. Thank goodness it was De Kelley, a *Star Trek* veteran, who pretty damn well knows how to play a scene!

But De teased me mercilessly about directing with my eyes closed. "Just stop it, Leonard!" he'd say, grinning, the minute we finished a take.

"Stop what?"

"Don't think I can't see you peeking at me! You're trying to direct me by fluttering your damned eyelids!"

In some ways, the final scene of the movie was the most difficult to capture, because, as an actor, I had to focus on my dialog as Spock—and, as a director, on everything and everyone else at the same time.

The scene in question called for Spock to struggle through a conversation with Kirk, while trying to recapture bits of our relationship, as the other *Enterprise* crew members looked on with anticipation. The Vulcan's memory banks haven't kicked in yet, so he's full of questions: Who are you? Do I know you and these other people? Why did you come back for me? The final lines of the movie are full of hope that Spock would soon be himself again.

SPOCK: (with a flicker of repressed joy) Jim.
        Your name is . . . Jim.
KIRK: Yes, Spock! Yes.

The scene ends with the crew happily gathering around their Vulcan friend to welcome him back. As director, I encouraged them all to embrace Spock—if they could. Interestingly, while all their

·

239

faces clearly shone with joy, not one of them dared hug the Vulcan (although Nichelle Nichols did reach out warmly toward me, and De Kelley eased any tension by smilingly tapping his skull, as if to say, "Remember, my friend? You were a tenant here . . ."). I guess you just don't grab Spock!

Finally, shooting wrapped. We put the finishing touches on the film, and then it was time to prepare the main titles. Now, traditionally, on any *Star Trek* episode or film, William Shatner's name comes first, followed by mine, then De Kelley's. But in this case, it was time to break with tradition—because I realized that, if the audience saw my name in the opening titles, the mystery was over. It would be obvious that Spock as we know him was back.

I explained the problem to the Paramount executives, and they agreed—so, to this day, long after the mystery has been solved, my name doesn't appear in the film's opening credits (except as director). As I think back on it now, it sets me wondering: Was I making some unconscious gesture? Trying to say that, while Spock might have been in this film, Leonard Nimoy wasn't?

Three weeks before *Star Trek III: The Search for Spock* opened, Jeff Katzenberg invited me to a meeting in his office. The Paramount brass had all viewed the finished film, and when I saw his beaming face, I knew the response had been good.

"Leonard," he said, "congratulations! We know that *Star Trek III* is going to be a success—but there's something we want to tell you now, so that you know our decision has nothing to do with the box office: We want you to make another one for us. This time, the training wheels are off! Give us your vision of *Star Trek*!"

> SPOCK: *I am becoming concerned about your penchant for violence.*
> NIMOY: Me, Spock? But I consider myself a pacifist!
> SPOCK: *Might I point out your last film, which featured the destruction of the* Enterprise *and the deaths of the* Grissom *crew, David Marcus, Commander Kruge and assorted Klingons, not to mention the wounding of the security guard at Dr. McCoy's hospital room and the—*
> NIMOY: You made your point! I'll try to do better next time . . .

FOURTEEN

I, SPOCK

or
"The Final Plain"
on the Streets
of San Francisco

•

Here are some things I know:

I am Spock, son of Sarek of Vulcan and Amanda of Earth; I am a scientist, a recipient of the highest awards and degrees conferred by the Vulcan Science Academy. I spent my early years beneath my parents' watchful gaze . . . and the derisive stares of my young schoolmates, who ridiculed my mixed heritage. At times, I reacted emotionally to their taunts—which served only to increase their scorn, and provide support for their claim that I could never function as a true Vulcan.

As a result, I have persevered throughout my life to achieve a logical thought process, free from the contamination of emotion. This has caused my human mother some distress; but she understands, for she, too, has come to some accommodation on this issue. She has chosen to live among Vulcans, if not indeed to live as one; one might say she has found a way to live as they do without trying to be one of them.

I, on the other hand, take some pride in calling myself Vulcan.

These things I know, and more:

I left home and family under troubled circumstance to cast my lot as science officer, among a polyglot collection of various species from various worlds, brought together as an organization known as Starfleet, beneath the auspices of the United Federation of Planets. Over a period of years of service aboard the Enterprise—*first under Captain Pike, and subsequently under Captain Kirk—I have been involved in a number of challenging missions, one of which led to my death.*

I tell all this now as it has been told to me. Subsequent to my death, several of my fellow crew members risked their careers—and indeed, their lives—to go to the Genesis planet, because they had reason to believe there was some hope of rescuing me. This, in fact, they did.

It was a rash adventure on their part, utterly illogical and totally human.

I am grateful.

My friends returned my body to Vulcan, where the physical shell was reunited with its spiritual "essence," its katra, *by means of an ancient Vulcan ritual. I have since come to remember, through much prodding and discussion and research, who these people are. I have also been absorbing vast amounts of scientific and historical data so that I may usefully embark with my associates on another journey: to return to Earth to face trial for their actions in connection with my rescue.*

Having lost much of my experience memory, I have educated myself by rote. Yet for all the knowledge I have relearned, I realize there is much I do not yet know. There is an ancient adage that says: "He who does not know what he does not know is a fool to be shunned."

My mother insists I will discover that I have feelings. Is this a willful projection from her human heart? She offers me love; perhaps someday I will find a way to respond.

But for now, it is time to depart with my friends. I board the Klingon *Bird of Prey, the ship that will carry us to Earth. There is something of a dreamlike quality that pervades the atmosphere on this voyage—evocative of mirror images reflecting each other.*

It seems I have a doppelganger, *a ghostly counterpart.*

NIMOY: You'll come in through this door, Spock. Saavik has told Captain Kirk about the events surrounding his son's death. She'll wish you well on the voyage, and you'll respond with "Live long and prosper, Lieutenant." Then she'll leave, and you'll have a brief exchange with Kirk. You'll apologize for misplacing your uniform; he'll tell you to take your station, and then you'll leave. Now, during the whole piece, you're vaguely disoriented—trying to put together the pieces of the puzzle.

SPOCK: *Very well. And when shall I do this?*

NIMOY: You wait outside the door. I'll say "action." When Kirk and Saavik have finished their lines, the door will open. You'll come in and begin.

SPOCK: *Very well.*

•

The information I have received is evidently known as "direction."
It is clear, economical, to the point. Admiral Kirk, Saavik, and I per-
form our function—two, three, even four times, although I'm mystified
by the need for repetition, since I do precisely as instructed each time.

Finally, the "director" says, "Good! Now, let's move on." I have seen
him before. When my colleagues brought me to Vulcan for the fal tor
pan, *the refusion ceremony, I was unconscious—but after the proce-*
dure, when I confronted Kirk and the others, he was there. I was
dazed, scarcely aware of my surroundings...but I knew he was there:
"Nimoy, the director."

Now I am much more conscious of his presence. He is energetic,
decisive, seemingly well-prepared and qualified to do his work, and
yet...there is an urgency, a subtext, something unspoken that colors
his activity. I sense there is something hidden here; something per-
sonal at stake, as there was with me when I prepared for "The final
plain."

NIMOY: What is that, Spock? You've mentioned it twice
now, once when I began shooting *Star Trek III.*

SPOCK: *"The final plain" is a test: a summing up of talents*
acquired during a long period of diligent apprentice-
ship. An attempt, as well, at personal integration.

NIMOY: So it's a Vulcan practice?

SPOCK: *Yes, but it possesses universal application. The phrase*
is applicable whenever there is a trial, a test of an indi-
vidual's skills and total integration.

NIMOY: What is the test?

SPOCK: *There lies on Vulcan a stretch of flat, barren desert*
known as the "plain of thought," which has come to
symbolize ultimate accomplishment. At one end of the
plain stands a millennia-old fragment of wall. At the
other end, approximately one of your Earth kilometers
away, rests a tall, slender obelisk. During the heat of
the desert day, one starts at the wall and walks slowly
toward the obelisk. Every step, every movement of
every muscle, every stride must be measured, counted,
and mentally recorded. Even wind velocity and direc-
tion must be factored in.

NIMOY: And that's the task?

SPOCK: *Only half. When the walk is done, one waits for dark.*
And in the moonless black of Vulcan night, one returns

*to the fragment of wall. To do so requires a precisely
accurate replay of everything the brain recorded earlier—otherwise, the individual will wander aimlessly
through the darkness. It is more than a mere physical
"trick." It requires total integration of the individual's
mind, body . . . and spirit. Young Vulcans aspire to
this task; few have the opportunity, and when one
makes the attempt, all our people are aware and await
the results. If successful, the one who has accomplished
this task wins the right to wear the symbol of Kolinahr,
a great achievement.*

NIMOY: So it's more than just a physical trick.

SPOCK: *Precisely. When done, one is in unity, at home in one-
self.*

NIMOY: And you think I'm doing this, or something like it?

SPOCK: *Yes. An attempt at integration. Perhaps we both are.*

S POCK KNEW WHAT HE was talking about: With *Star Trek IV*, all my skills, physical and mental, were definitely put to the test. Yet when it was done, the sense of satisfaction was definitely worth any trials undergone. I'd wanted to give something back to Spock, and *Star Trek*—and with this film, I sensed I had a special opportunity.

But let's start at the beginning, when the story line for *Star Trek IV* was no more than a gleam in Harve Bennett's eye, and a twin-kle in mine.

Both Harve and I had decided it was time to lighten up. *Star Trek: The Motion Picture* (or, as some fans called it, the *Motionless* picture) had been a grim, gray exercise in special effects, while *Star Trek II* had featured the death of Spock and *Star Trek III* the death of Kirk's son, David, plus the destruction of the *Enterprise*. With the fourth film, it was time to bring to *Trek* some levity, some of what Harve calls "tap dancing"—the ability to bring a sense of glee, of pure joie de vivre, to even the most dramatic moment.

Certainly I was feeling pretty lighthearted myself at the time. After the success of *The Search for Spock*, I moved into a new and

·

rather grand suite of offices on the Paramount lot. I had good tables in the studio dining room, a terrific parking spot, and a spring in my step. It was clear the studio anticipated that the fourth movie would become a major event not just for *Star Trek*, but for Paramount.

I'd hardly settled into my seat at my new desk when the phone rang. Jeff Katzenberg was on the line.

"Leonard," he said, "I've got to talk to you about an idea. It could be either the best idea in the world—or the worst. You ready?"

"I'm ready."

"I had dinner last night with Eddie Murphy. We were talking about a lot of different things, and then I mentioned your next picture. Eddie's eyes lit up, and he said, 'Jeff, I'd kill to be in a *Star Trek* movie!' So I promised him I'd talk to you."

I paused for a moment to consider it. On the surface, it seemed like a terrific idea to combine two successful franchises—Eddie Murphy and *Star Trek*—in the hopes that it would draw Murphy fans who might not otherwise go to a *Trek* movie. But it meant an enormous investment of both money and talent in one film—and also more intense scrutiny from the critics. If it didn't work, it would hurt both Murphy and *Trek*. So I replied cautiously, "You're right. It's either the best or worst idea in the world."

"Well, will you meet with him to discuss it, Leonard?"

"Sure," I told Jeff, and he agreed to arrange it.

I should remind you all that in 1985 when this occurred, Eddie Murphy was a very, very hot Paramount star. This was shortly after he'd encountered enormous success in *48 Hours* and the first *Beverly Hills Cop* film. Since then, his career has cooled somewhat, but at the time, there were few actors with more star power. On the Paramount lot, Eddie was like that proverbial 800-pound gorilla: he could sleep anywhere he wanted to.

And, amusingly enough, he was an enormous *Star Trek* fan—with a capital "E." In fact, the story about his signing his studio contract has become legend. It goes like this:

At the time, Paramount courted Eddie when he was a bright, hungry young talent on *Saturday Night Live*. They felt he had potential as a movie star—an absolute dream goal for anyone in Murphy's position. So he struck a deal with Paramount, with the proviso that, when the contract was signed, he'd get a million-dollar bonus.

You'd think Eddie would have been chomping at the bit to sign on the dotted line, so he could collect his check, right?

Wrong. When, contract and check in hand, the studio execs arrived at the New York studio where Eddie was rehearsing, they had to wait. Why? Not because he was working. No, Eddie was glued to the tube, watching an episode of *Star Trek*, and refused to be distracted. The guys from Paramount had to sit and wait until the final credits were rolling to the brisk strains of Alexander Courage's end-of-show music. Only then would Eddie sign the contract and take his million dollars. The man had his priorities.

With all that in mind, on the appointed day, I drove with a Paramount rep to Eddie's place up in the Hollywood Hills. The house was vast, even palatial, but when an assistant let us in, I noticed there was hardly any furniture. (I suspect Eddie was renting at the time.) At any rate, we made our way through huge empty rooms, and found Eddie waiting for us in the dining room. This time he happened *not* to be watching *Star Trek*, so after a polite round of handshakes, we got right down to business.

"So," Eddie said. "What did Katzenberg tell you?"

It was a direct question, so I responded in kind. "He said you'd kill to be in a *Star Trek* movie!"

He flashed a grin. "That's right!"

We talked for a while. I told him that Harve and I were going to be discussing story ideas, and that we'd take his request very seriously. But I also told him, "Eddie, we like you, and you like us. You know if it's announced that you're in our movie, there'll be some sharp-shooting skeptics waiting to gun us all down if it doesn't work well. My feeling is that your part has to be terrific—or nonexistent, because we don't want to hurt your career, and I know you don't want to hurt ours."

"Then keep in touch," Eddie said. "Let me know how your story ideas are progressing."

I agreed, because that way, either side could get off the train if it wasn't tracking well.

Meanwhile, I was offered a role in an NBC miniseries production of *The Sun Also Rises*, which was being filmed in Paris and Segovia.

I accepted, knowing that during the two months I'd be in Europe, I'd have plenty of time to work on story ideas for the next *Star Trek* film. Until then, Harve and I agreed to tackle the film's basic concept.

So, before I left for Europe, I contacted three leading space scientists: Frank Drake at UC Santa Cruz, Paul Horowitz at Harvard, and Philip Morrison at MIT. I introduced myself over the phone, and explained that I was gathering information for a new *Star Trek* film. All three generously agreed to meet with me, with the result that I had some wonderfully stimulating discussions with them.

These three men have been on the cutting edge of extraterrestrial communication for many years; all have contributed to SETI, the Search for Extraterrestrial Intelligence. Frank Drake is the father of the Drake Equation, which demonstrates the probability of intelligent life on other planets, based on the number of planets that have life spans similar to Earth's and that orbit suns similar to our own. Paul Horowitz showed me the equipment he designed that hooks up to radio telescopes and greatly enhances the process of listening for signs of technologically advanced civilizations elsewhere in the universe. And Philip Morrison helped me understand the complications of communicating with other species: With lips and teeth and tongues that might be structurally different from our own, extraterrestrials would find the mere mechanical process of attempting to articulate our language difficult, if not impossible. Now, add the fact that their brains and thought processes might be markedly different, and you'll begin to get an idea of the problems they—and we—might face someday, when we first attempt a conversation.

The meetings gave me rich food for thought in terms of the next film. In the meantime, Harve had been doing some thinking—and viewing of *Star Trek* episodes—on his own. He sat down and made his own "top ten" list of all the episodes, and discovered that he and the series' fans shared the same tastes! Almost every episode he picked was among the best-selling videocassettes. One of his very favorites was Harlan Ellison's "City on the Edge of Forever." And so, when Harve and I got together to discuss *Star Trek IV*'s basic premise before I left for Europe, he said, "Leonard. We've got to do time travel."

•

I thought it was a great idea, and we both had already agreed that it was time to lighten up. With that much accomplished, I left for Europe. Harve and I would continue to work on story ideas during that time, and eventually, we'd meet and work together in Paris.

My work in Spain and France went easily, leaving plenty of time to begin building the story. Of course, there were certain threads to pick up from the previous film: For example, our crew was now on Vulcan, and considered outlaws by the Federation because they had violated a direct order not to go to Genesis. We also know that the *Enterprise* is destroyed, and the only ship available to them is the Klingon *Bird of Prey,* which had been commanded by Kruge in *Star Trek III.* It logically follows that the Klingon Empire would be angry at Kirk for causing the deaths of several of their men, then stealing their ship. And as for Spock—well, he's back on his home planet and on his feet, but his mind is like an empty computer bank, crying out for information.

So should our gallant crew go back to Earth to face the charges, or would they remain renegades for a while? I felt they would responsibly agree to go home—but could be caught in a time warp. And to give them the stronger hand, I decided that their going back in time should be intentional, rather than simply an accident.

Once that was established, Harve and I started thinking about what time period the *Enterprise* crew might visit. We tossed around all kinds of ideas: Ancient Rome, the American frontier, and the War for Independence. But the idea that pleased us most—and, we therefore hoped, our audience—was contemporary America.

Soon, Harve joined me in France; and in a Paris hotel room, we sketched out the concept Paramount requested. (Actually, I think if we had simply said, "We're going to lighten up," they would have been happy.) We let them know that the Magnificent Seven were going home—after a little side trip to present-day San Francisco (which is, after all, Starfleet Headquarters).

But the *real* riddle that remained was the ultimate question: Why? Obviously, our heroes were headed into the past to solve a problem. But what was that problem, and how would time travel solve it?

I should mention at this point that, around that time, I was reading *Biophilia,* a recently published book written by Harvard biologist Edmund Wilson. In his work, Wilson talks about the vast numbers of species becoming extinct, and predicted that by the 1990s, Earth would lose as many as 10,000 species per year. That's *one* species per *hour*! Most disturbingly, many of these lost species would never have been catalogued; we would never have the chance to know what they were or what function they performed in the cycle of nature. They would simply vanish without leaving behind a record of their existence.

The grim future painted by *Biophilia* haunted my thoughts. What key species were being lost at this very moment—and how might that loss affect civilization three hundred years hence? I felt certain that this was our theme—the sins of the fathers being visited upon the children. I felt I knew the basic "sin," but what had been lost, and what price would be paid?

For a time, I played with the notion that perhaps there was a widespread epidemic in the twenty-third century, a deadly illness whose cure had been destroyed centuries earlier along with the rain forests. But the depiction of thousands of sick and dying people seemed rather gruesome for our "lighthearted" film—and the thought of our brave crew taking a six-hundred-year round-trip just to bring back a snail darter wasn't all that thrilling!

Finally, after several weeks of mental thrashing about, I had a breakthrough. It came during a late-night conversation with a friend, Roy Danchik. We were talking about *Biophilia* and discussing endangered species when Roy mentioned the humpback whale. Humpbacks are true giants, weighing in at twenty tons each; yet they are gentle mammals possessed of a fascinating mystery: their song.

Male humpbacks emit a series of moans, cries, and clicks that add up to a continuous "song" of several minutes' length. These "songs" are passed intact from pack to pack through the world's oceans—and when a song is changed by *one* whale, it is changed by all.

How? No one knows. Nor do we know whether the song's function is sexual, territorial or navigational. It remains one of nature's most intriguing mysteries . . . and from such a mystery, a *Star Trek* story would be spun.

I had a restless night, thinking about the humpback's mysterious song. And early the next morning, I called Harve and said, "Let's talk."

The minute he stepped inside my office, I said, "Tell me if you think I'm crazy, or if you think we can physically pull this off: The *Enterprise* crew goes back to the twentieth century, because what is needed to solve the problem is a pair of humpback whales."

Well, he didn't say: "You're crazy." He didn't say much of anything for a moment, but I could see the wheels turning in that producer's mind of his. He *did* say, "Well, humpbacks aren't trainable, like killer whales are, and there've been too many killer whale movies anyway." But he also said, "The question is, does the necessary footage of whales exist, or would we have to create it? Let's do some research."

That's how we began. We hired an editor to go through hours of marine footage, and soon we had the answer.

It wasn't the one we wanted. We'd have to create most of the footage ourselves. In the meantime, there was yet another question: What was the problem in the twenty-third century, and how would whales solve it?

Let me digress again here to say that I've always been attracted to stories about communication. That's why "Devil in the Dark," with its message about the disastrous consequences of a lack of communication, remains one of my favorite *Star Trek* episodes. In fact, one of my favorite science fiction stories is "The Foghorn," by Ray Bradbury, which deals with a giant sea monster. The creature thinks its loneliness is over when it hears a distant cry much like its own—but its hopes are shattered when it discovers the sound is merely the foghorn from a lighthouse. In its rage, it destroys the sound's source.

That story came to mind when I was puzzling over the humpback question. And I thought, "We don't know the purpose of whale song. What if it had been intended as communication with an intelligence on another planet?"

And on the day the last humpback died, the songs would cease forever. This loss of signal might bring a visitor to Earth to search for a lost friend, just as you or I might go to a friend's house if we could no longer get him on the phone. At last, the concepts of the SETI program, and Morrison's concepts about nonlinear communication began to find their way into the story: The whale song is a language we don't understand, being received by another intelligence. But when the songs stop, a probe is sent to Earth to search the oceans. That search initiates violent rainstorms, literally threatening to drown the planet. Only the humpback's song can get this probe to relax and go back to where it came from.

At long last, Harve and I had our basic story; now it was time to start on a screenplay. Steve Meerson and Peter Krikes were hired and quickly set to work. We all agreed that the destination of the crew would be twentieth-century San Francisco, where they would set about searching for humpback whales.

But now it was time for another big question: What role would Eddie Murphy play in the story?

We struggled with it for weeks. At one time, his role was conceived as that of a college professor, at another, that of a con artist. The best idea we developed had Eddie as the "psychic-investigator" host of a late-night radio talk show dealing with *National Enquirer*-type questions: Is Elvis alive? Can psychics really predict the future? Are there aliens walking around on this planet?

Of course, in the script, there *were* aliens—or at least, one half-Vulcan—walking around! Eddie's character was to have a hunch that we were really spacemen, and he'd chase us all around during the story, trying to get evidence to prove himself right. Frankly, the character didn't work very well; he simply played the same note over and over. We finally decided it wasn't good for him or us, so Eddie moved on to other projects.

Steve and Peter worked very hard and

Pinching the punk rocker
(Kirk Thatcher) into oblivion

gave us several drafts, but it finally became clear we needed a fresh eye. Nick Meyer agreed to help us out, and when he came to talk to Harve and me about the project, I told him, "Look, Nick. We've got a chance to do something nice. In this story, nobody kills anybody. Not a single shot is fired in anger. The villains are circumstance, a lack of information, and a lack of education."

Nick took that to heart, and he and Harve divvied up work on the script. Nick has a wonderfully raffish sense of humor, so he agreed to write the middle portion of the script, which finds our heroes wandering through twentieth-century San Francisco. (Nick's contributions start with Spock's line: "Judging from the pollution content of the atmosphere, we have reached the late twentieth century.") Harve, on the other hand, wrote the opening and closing scenes, which included some rather military, structured scenes— his forte.

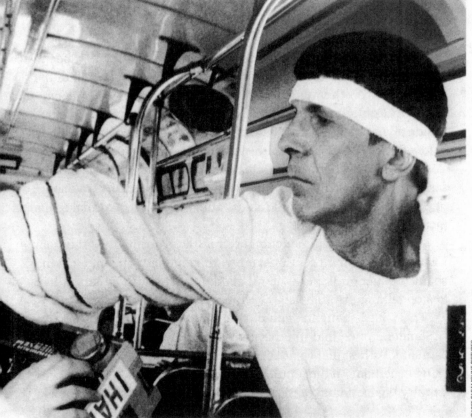

Beaming into "Golden Gate Park" (actually, L.A.'s Will Rogers State Park)

I contributed some personal Spock moments—such as Spock's interaction with the computer, and the infamous neck pinch of the punk rocker on the bus. (The scene sprang from my own experience, on Columbus Avenue in New York City. I was once stuck beside a young man with a blaring boombox, and I wanted nothing better than to pinch him and his music into oblivion!)

I have to say here that Harve and Nick turned in a fantastic script. In fact, Ned Tanen, who was the studio executive in charge of *Star Trek IV*'s production, told us after reading it, "I'd make this picture even if it wasn't *Star Trek*!"

Soon, work on preproduction began. It was during this time that I was walking up a flight of stairs with some crew people, talking about production issues, when I suddenly ran out of breath. I had to stop talking just to be able to finish climbing the steps.

"That's it!" I thought. "Time to quit smoking and get in shape."

Someone once told me that making a movie was like eating an elephant: At first glance, it seems impossible, but if you take a bite or two each day, it'll eventually be gone. *Star Trek IV*, I knew, was a pretty big elephant—certainly bigger than anything I'd ever tackled before, and logistically more complex than any of our previous films. (Where *Star Trek III* had been shot mostly on soundstages, *IV* would be filmed on locations from San Diego to San Francisco, hundreds of miles apart.) And unlike *The Search for Spock*, where my part as an actor was minuscule, this fourth film called for me to do a lot of acting.

I knew this would be the most physically demanding project I'd ever done. I was going to need all the stamina I could muster, so I enrolled in a program to quit smoking. Simultaneously, I started an exercise program at the Paramount gym. I still work out fairly regularly, and haven't smoked a single cigarette since that time. In fact, I have no doubt that *Star Trek IV* was instrumental in improving my health and extending my life.

The first "bite" of the elephant consisted of scouting for loca-

©1995 PARAMOUNT PICTURES

George and Gracie, the mechanical humpbacks, courtesy of ILM

tions—a time-consuming, tedious job. Along with our cinematographer, production designer, and a producer or two, I spent endless hours in airplanes, cars, and vans—most of it in northern California. We scouted Golden Gate Park in San Francisco as the landing site for the invisible *Bird of Prey,* which happened to be the actual spot where Kirk told Sulu to land.

Unfortunately, shortly before we were to film there, the area was inundated by heavy rains, which made the ground too muddy for

The happy—and logical—family: Spock with Vulcan father Sarek (Mark Lenard) and human mother Amanda (Jane Wyatt)

our equipment. We wound up switching to Will Rogers State Park in Los Angeles, which actually worked quite well.

We also scouted the Monterey Aquarium—and this time, had great success filming there. By intercutting the footage there with footage shot in a tank in Los Angeles, we were able to create the impression that our humpback whales actually existed in a large contained tank at an aquarium. Of course, there were never any humpbacks in the aquarium; the facility doesn't have a tank large enough to hold them.

The whale special effects were created by a number of very talented people, most notably visual effects supervisor Ken Ralston and art director Nilo Rodis from Industrial Light and Magic. I felt very secure in Nilo and Ken's hands, because they're simply the best in their field. They brought in a talented robotics expert, Walt Conti, to design our whale "puppets." I suspect that most people who saw Star Trek IV never realized that there was only two shots of a live whale in the film—one of a humpback breaching the ocean's surface, which was provided for us by Mark and Debbie Ferrari, and one of a humpback briefly surfacing during the hunting sequence, when the Russian ship is in pursuit of the whales. Every other shot of a whale was accomplished using either a mechanical miniature or a life-size reproduction of part of the whale's anatomy (such as the tail).

Interestingly enough, right as work was beginning on designing the whale's special effects, Humphrey the humpback whale swam into San Francisco Bay. (The joke around the set was that he'd come to audition for us!) Unfortunately, we failed to get anything on film that could be used in the movie, but our special effects did manage to get some useful reference footage, which helped them in designing the radio-controlled puppets. Many of the impressive, authentic-looking underwater sequences of the whales were actually shot with four-foot mechanical puppets at a nearby high school swimming pool.

While our talented whale wranglers were off working their special brand of magic, it was time for me and Harve to do some casting. Of course, we'd already decided that we wanted to bring back as many members of the Star Trek "family" as possible, so Robin Curtis was invited back to reprise her role as Saavik. We also included Grace Lee Whitney as Janice Rand, and Majel Barrett as Commander Chapel for their own special moments at Federation headquarters. And Spock's parents, Sarek and Amanda, were portrayed by Mark Lenard and Jane Wyatt.

The newcomer in this movie was the character of Gillian Taylor, the cetacean biologist who would ultimately assist the *Enterprise* crew in transporting the humpbacks back to the twenty-third century. Catherine Hicks, who gave a wonderful performance, was cast.

Cathy brought a wonderful fresh, wide-eyed innocence mixed with street-smart cynicism that worked very well for the role. When she first came to audition in my office, I decided that we ought to read through the scene where Gillian is in an Italian restaurant with Kirk, and demands to know *why* Kirk is so interested in these whales. While she's talking, Kirk (to his chagrin) gets a call on his

Catherine Hicks as Gillian Taylor, in the actual "I knew outer space was gonna come into this" scene

communicator from Scotty, who addresses him as "Admiral." So she basically says, "Let me guess. You're from outer space."

"No," says Kirk, "I'm from Iowa. I only *work* in outer space."

To which Gillian replies, "I *knew* it! I *knew* outer space was going to come into this!"

When Cathy Hicks read that line for me in my office, she read it as a believer, without any sarcasm. I'd expected that she'd deliver those lines with the attitude: "Okay, you guys are pulling the wool over my eyes!" It jolted me—in a pleasant way, because, interestingly enough, that was exactly how we would have intended Eddie Murphy's "psychic investigator" character to react—with belief. There was something very charming about her character's naivete.

Once I pointed out that Gillian was being cynical, Cathy immediately picked up on it, and her delivery was right on target. I was impressed, so some days later, I invited her to lunch with Bill Shatner and myself. We went to the Equestrian Center in Burbank, where Bill was working with his horses.

I wanted to be sure that the two of them hit it off, since so many of Gillian's scenes were with Kirk. Cathy charmed the horses—which of course charmed Bill. We had an enjoyable conversation over lunch, then as she and I were leaving, I cast a surreptitious glance over my shoulder at Bill to gauge his reaction. He gave me a little wink and nod, so I turned to Cathy and said, "Welcome to *Star Trek*."

We were very pleased with the choice, because Cathy attacked her role with a great deal of spunk and energy. She was very believable in her part—maybe a little *too* believable for fellow actor Scott De Venney, who portrayed her co-worker at the aquarium. They had a scene together where Gillian runs up to the whale tank and discovers that the whales have been transported out to the open sea earlier than scheduled, without her knowledge or approval—and Bob, Scott's character, was in on the scheme. In her anger, Gillian slaps him, then stomps off in a rage.

When we were staging the scene, Cathy turned to me and asked, "Well, how hard should I slap him?"

I said, "Show your anger. Make us believe it."

"Okay," she said, with a faint hint of that "be-careful-what-you-ask-for-because-you-may-get-it" tone in her voice. When the cameras started rolling, she hauled off and whacked Scott full force, right on the jaw. I mean, she hit him *hard!* The poor guy's eyes were visibly tearing, but I have to give him credit; he could have blown the scene, but he bit the bullet and hung in there as long as we kept shooting. Fortunately for him, Cathy'd done such a convincing job of smacking him the first time that we didn't have to do too many takes.

Once casting was done, shooting began on location in San Francisco, with the scenes where the *Enterprise* Seven wander out onto the streets. True, there were some "hired passersby" who were working for us, but the sidewalks were also full of regular pedestrians *not* under our control, which made the whole thing pretty exciting (and nerveracking, when you're the director praying someone walking by won't ruin the shot). The most amusing part about it was the fact that no one bothered us, despite the fact that the *Star Trek* actors' faces are well known. San Francisco is known for attracting colorful, eccentric people—and for the most part, the pedestrians treated us like run-of-the-mill weirdos and ignored us.

But the scene where Kirk steps out into traffic and is almost hit by a car had to be carefully choreographed (I wasn't *about* to let Bill Shatner step out into *real* traffic and get flattened, although I'm sure he would have been game), and wound up being pretty difficult to get. (The driver had to call Kirk a "dumb ass," and Bill was to respond with the line, "Double dumb ass on you!") We had about two dozen cars driven by our people, and it took a lot of careful timing to get them all through traffic and at the proper intersection at the proper instant that our actors crossed—with the proper car *almost* hitting Kirk. It was extremely tricky choreography—we kept failing to get the shot—and the frustrating part was, every time we had to reshoot, it took a minimum of twenty minutes to get our little caravan of drivers around the block and at the right intersection again.

We shot the scene again and again and again—and after about three hours of failing to get the shot, I started to worry, because word had gotten out that we were filming a *Star Trek* movie, and a crowd of onlookers had finally begun to gather. It soon became more and more difficult to keep gawkers out of the shot. I began to think we'd have to abandon the shoot . . . and then, after the umpteenth attempt, everything suddenly fell into place like magic. The cars all arrived at the intersection at just the right moment, we actors all stepped off the curb, and the "double dumb ass" stunt driver managed to look like he'd *almost* nailed Admiral Kirk without actually crippling Bill Shatner.

I breathed a deep sigh of directorial relief and we moved on, to the scene where our intrepid crew wanders over to a newspaper vending machine and takes a paper from the box. I'd puzzled over an appropriate headline for the newspaper (the *San Francisco Register*, to be exact)—one that would seem timely and appropriate to a contemporary audience, while still being vague enough so that, when the movie opened many months later in the theaters, the headline wouldn't seem dated.

I finally settled on NUCLEAR TALKS STALLED, because I figured that, no matter what happened politically in the following months and even years, *someone somewhere* would be negotiating with someone else about nuclear arms. The scenes that followed—Kirk going into an antique shop and selling his old-fashioned spectacles, then taking his hundred dollars and dividing it up among the crew— went easily enough. (By the way, that antique shop was authentic!)

While filming on the streets, we ran into both snags, when carefully planned scenes went awry—and happy accidents, when unexpected events turned out to work beautifully in our favor. Unfortunately, soon afterwards, we ran into one of those snags— with a scene that would have given George Takei's character Sulu a wonderful onscreen moment. While walking on the street, Sulu— who, we earlier established, had been born in San Francisco—is approached by a little Japanese boy on the street, who mistakes Sulu for his uncle. After a short conversation with the boy, Sulu realizes he's talking to his great-grandfather!

Because of economic considerations, the child actor chosen was from San Francisco; otherwise, we would have had to fly him up from Los Angeles, and pay to house him and his mother. Therefore, a San Francisco–based casting agency provided us with several videotapes of local children; Harve and I looked at the tapes, and both agreed on the most promising candidate.

But when the day arrived to shoot the scene, we simply could *not* get it done, despite all our careful preparation. The child arrived on the set and was so uncomfortable that he soon became too distraught to speak, to look at anyone, to do anything but cry. We did our very best to try to coax him to take his place with the other actors and deliver his lines, but he refused to budge. George tried valiantly to cheer him up, in both English and Japanese, and I even took a shot at it (in full Spock regalia)—but there was simply nothing we could do. The more we tried to get the little boy and his mother to relax, the more distraught they became—until finally, the end of the day's shooting had arrived, and *still* the little guy wouldn't get near anyone else, wouldn't do anything but cry. It was

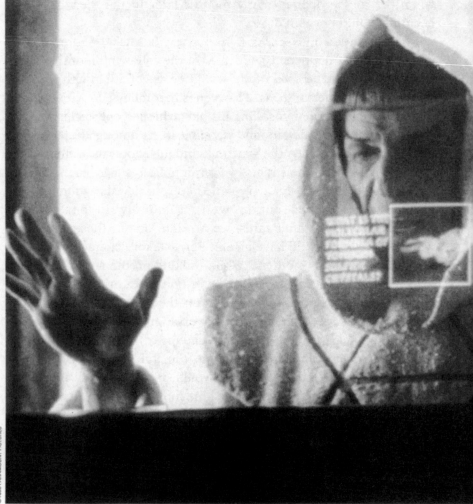

my very first experience with a situation where an actor simply could not be convinced to step onto the set to deliver his lines. We had to get ready to shoot other scenes the next day, so we were forced to move on. Naturally, I felt very badly for George, because I knew it meant a great deal to him, and it would have been a charming scene.

Perhaps my favorite "street scene" in *Star Trek IV* that we *were* able to film featured Walter Koenig as Chekov and Nichelle Nichols as Uhura. It was during the filming of this scene that one of those "happy accidents" occurred. I should set the stage by reminding you that, back in 1986, Russia was still the Soviet Union, and there was still very much a sense among Americans that the Russians were our main competitors in the nuclear arms race. Because of that, Harve and the writers and I had, a few weeks earlier, devised a scene where Chekov—in an attempt to procure some radioactive material necessary to power the Klingon *Bird of Prey*—asks people passing by where he can find some "nuclear wessels."

I decided to shoot that scene "candid camera" style, by laying back with the camera so that it wasn't very noticeable, and just filming the reactions of passersby to Nichelle and Walter's questions. The scene was very much improvised; there was no specific dialog, no script. I just told Nichelle, "Ask people where the naval base is." And I told Walter, "You ask them the same thing—but be sure to repeat the term 'nuclear wessels' loud and clear."

So we started the camera rolling, and Walter and Nichelle started asking. Some of the people that passed by were hired by us—but some weren't. In fact, there's a motorcycle cop in the scene who just keeps staring silently at Walter from behind his dark police glasses. He's not an actor, but a real San Francisco policeman who'd been assigned to help us with security and traffic control.

Nichelle and Walter did exactly what was needed, and everything was going great. Most pedestrians, including those who weren't in on the joke, just stared at them as though they were crazy, and walked past without a word. Then up walked this woman with long dark hair, whom none of us had ever seen before;

Interacting with the computer

she paused to listen to Walter, then said helpfully, "I think they're across the Bay, in Alameda." Her reaction was so ingenuous and perfect that we included the shot, and wound up negotiating a contract with her, so that we could pay her for talking. It was a wonderful accident, from our perspective as well as hers.

The only real unpleasantness involved a special-effects scene near the end of the movie, where the mysterious probe (designed by the brilliant Nilo Rodis) finally communicates with the humpbacks, who respond in "whalesong."

Let me backtrack a moment here. When I met with SETI scientist Philip Morrison, I asked him if he remembered the science fiction film *The Day the Earth Stood Still* (directed by Robert Wise, who'd also directed *ST:TMP*). Specifically, I referred to a scene that had made a great impression on me, in which an eminent Einstein-like scientist (Sam Jaffee) had, in his study, a large blackboard on

The "tell my mother I feel fine" scene, with Mark Lenard

which was written a long mathematical equation that filled the entire board. At the end of the equation was an equal sign, but no answer; the equation was unresolved. Now, when the alien character, played by Michael Rennie, walks into the scientist's office and sees the equation, he walks right over to it and fills in the answer.

Jaffee clearly realizes that he's in the presence of a superior intelligence; so, with a gleam in his eye and a smile on his face, he says to Rennie, "There are a lot of questions I'd like to ask you." His assumption is clearly that Rennie comes from a civilization that's ahead of ours, that has probably survived the turmoil that we're now going through.

I described the scene in detail to Morrison, then said, "If you found yourself in the presence of such an advanced alien, what would you ask?" I expected him to reply along the lines of "What's the cure for cancer?" "How did you survive the nuclear age?"

But Morrison did nothing of kind. In fact, his reply was fairly heated. "That's not the way it works! You're operating on the false assumption that other intelligent life-forms will travel on a similar evolutionary track with us, that they'll think in the same linear way we do, and communicate in a similar fashion.

"But that's not the case! For one thing, they'll have an entirely different sort of existence, a radically different form of culture, and probably won't share our sort of linear thought processes. Sam Jaffee's question probably would be meaningless to them—they'd never be able to understand it, even if you could translate it into their language!"

Morrison's response had a wonderful, profound effect on my thinking about these issues. (And upon the *Star Trek IV* script, in which Spock tells McCoy, "There are other forms of intelligence on Earth, Doctor. Only human arrogance would assume the [probe's] message must be meant for man.") Because of that, I felt very, very strongly that we should *not* anthropomorphize the probe. Therefore, when the whales and the probe communicate, I felt we should make no attempt to "translate" their conversation for our human audience by using subtitles. To do so would be to demean the mystery; I couldn't help thinking of how *2010* failed to succeed, because it attempted to explain the mystery and magic of *2001*.

Unfortunately, not everyone agreed with me—including Harve

Bennett. Because I felt so strongly on the subject, this led to friction between us, especially when Harve sent the studio heads a memo, suggesting some possible "dialog" between the probe and the whales. And, of course, there was always some degree of friction between us on this particular film, because, as Jeff Katzenberg put it, my "training wheels were off." I had more confidence after *Star Trek III*, and therefore was more inclined to hold fast to my own opinions. Also, there's the matter of Harve's television background: In TV, the producer has the final say, because directors are hired on a per-episode basis. But with feature films, it's quite the opposite; the director gets the last word, and the film is considered "his." So it was natural that we collide at some point. It was only after a great deal of insistence that I convinced Paramount *not* to use the subtitles, and to let the mystery of the probe remain precisely that.

But overall, the filming of *Star Trek IV* went well, and was a joyful—if exhausting—experience. As I mentioned before, in *Star Trek III*, I'd only acted in a very few scenes. But in *IV*, Spock appeared throughout the film.

During *Star Trek IV: The Voyage Home*, Spock's character underwent an interesting development. In the third film, the Vulcan's mind was essentially a clean slate; at the beginning of *The Voyage Home*, he is shown allowing his newly reacquired scientific knowledge to be tested by the computer. He's smoothly answering rapid-fire questions such as "What is the electronic configuration of gadolinium?" and "Adjust the sine wave of this magnetic envelope so that antineutrons can pass through it but antigravitons cannot," without a second's hesitation. He's memorized all the data he needs to be of use to his friends, but when the computer throws him a curve with the simple query, "How do you feel?" Spock cannot fathom the question.

His mother, Amanda, appears and explains to him that he is half-human; his feelings are bound to surface, even though he considers himself Vulcan. As the story progresses, Spock finally comes to the very human conclusion that the entire crew should risk rescuing the critically injured Chekov —a compassionate action based on the opposite of "The good of the many outweighs the good of the one."

At the film's end, when Spock is taking leave of his Vulcan-bound father, Sarek asks whether he would like to send a message to Amanda.

"Yes," replies Spock. "Tell my mother . . . I feel fine." And he takes his

©1995 PARAMOUNT PICTURES

I confess,
these guys crack me up

leave of his father with the Vulcan phrase, "Live long and prosper."
It marks for the character a moment of true integration of both of
his halves—Vulcan and human.

NIMOY: I understand, now—what you meant about "the
final plain."
SPOCK: *Ah. If I might indulge in figurative language: We seem
to have crossed the plain together.*
NIMOY: Well, you seem to have accomplished your goal of
integration, Spock. But . . . did I? Did I pass the
test?
SPOCK: *Time alone will judge.*

By the time shooting wrapped on *Star Trek IV*, everyone involved
in the production began to suspect that we had achieved something
special. Reviews and audience reaction validated our suspicions.
The Voyage Home went on to break box office records, earning over
$100 million in domestic release. In addition to the loyal *Star Trek*
audience, it drew large numbers of people who had not seen the
three previous films featuring the *Enterprise* crew. As of this writing, it remains the highest-grossing *Star Trek* film.

FIFTEEN

THREE MEN
AND
A
GOOD
MOTHER

.

SPOCK: *I do not understand: How did the public come to the conclusion that you lack a flair for comedy?*

NIMOY: Well, nothing personal, Spock, but—I think it came because of my association with you.

SPOCK: *Most illogical. You are, after all, human. And humans are noticeably afflicted with what is termed a "sense of humor."*

NIMOY: Well, what about you, Spock? You may be Vulcan, but *I* happen to think you're a pretty funny guy.

SPOCK: *(uncertain) Is this an attempt to insult me?*

NIMOY: Not at all. It's a compliment. To say you lacked a sense of humor— now, *that* would be an insult.

SPOCK: *Oh. (pause) Are you sure?*

WHEN THE FINISHED VERSION OF *Star Trek IV* was previewed by test audiences, I was very gratified to hear all the laughs coming in the right places—some very *big* laughs. But I soon came to an interesting realization: Most people were surprised by the humor in the film, because they didn't perceive me as a funny guy. Nor did they think *Star Trek* fans had a sense of humor. In fact, at a press screening of the film in New York, a critic for *Newsday* told me, "The fans aren't going to like this movie, because they prefer to be taken seriously. I don't think this humor will go down well."

And that statement surprised me. Because not only had we played some very funny scenes in the original series, but there'd been some lighthearted moments in the movies as well. I knew *Star Trek* fans had a terrific sense of humor, and their response to *Star Trek IV* confirmed it.

But from articles and reviews printed about the fourth film, I soon learned that the unsmiling Vulcan had thoroughly colored the public's perception of me. Everyone was startled to find that I could pull off comedy. Now, I'd done a number of comedies, particularly in the theater during the 1970s, and *I* saw myself as a funny guy. I may not be as fast with a pun as Bill Shatner, but I *do* enjoy a good laugh; remember, I'm a huge Abbott and Costello fan.

At any rate, Jeff Katzenberg—who, along with Michael Eisner, had moved from Paramount to Disney—was delighted with the humor in *The Voyage Home*. And therein lies our next tale.

I was enjoying the success of *Star Trek IV* (believe me, there's

A laugh a minute: Spock in Star Trek IV

nothing quite like the thrill I felt, stepping onto the Paramount lot the day after the movie opened to excellent reviews and box office receipts). And one glorious, euphoric Friday shortly thereafter, my agent, Phil Gersh, called.

"Leonard," he said, "Jeff Katzenberg called from Disney. You're going to be floated a script this weekend, along with three other directors. I think you ought to take a look at it."

"What's it about?"

"It's the remake of a French film, *Three Men and a Cradle*. Ever seen it?"

"No. Could you get me a video?"

Phil obliged, and that weekend, I had both the American script and the original French film, *Trois Hommes et un Couffin*, which had been written and directed by Coline Serreau. The film was wonderful, but severely Gallic in tone, with French attitudes and atmosphere.

But when I read the script, I was troubled, because it read like a "dubbing" script—a direct translation of the French, with very stilted English. The characters' attitudes toward life, work, love, and children were still extremely Gallic; they even had French names! An American audience wouldn't identify with the characters at all. Because of that, I felt strongly that new writers would need to be brought in.

Even so, I could see the project's potential, so I contacted Jeff Katzenberg, and got some clearer insight as to what was going on. It seemed that *Three Men* was already in preparation when the director, Coline Serreau, who'd also directed the French version, had abruptly left. A huge, expensive apartment set was already under construction in Toronto, and three actors had been hired— Tom Selleck, Ted Danson, and Steve Guttenberg—with pay-or-play start dates. (That meant that, if the film failed to commence shooting by a particular date, the actors would go on to other commitments, yet would still be paid.) So there'd been an enormous investment—and the starting date was only a few weeks away.

Jeff and I had a couple of conversations about the project, and I gave him some suggestions, which he apparently liked, because I soon got another phone call from my agent: Disney was ready to start making a deal. The other three directors—Colin Higgins, Mark

Rydell, and Arthur Hiller—had passed, for various reasons. Jeff could have looked into contacting other directors, but instead decided to give me the job.

The first thing I did was make it clear that I would take the job only if new writers were brought in, because the script had some major problems. Disney's response was: "All we ask is that you meet with these two writers and the producer, Robert Cort."

Despite my strong feelings about the script, I agreed to at least hear them out. The problem was that I was scheduled to be speaking in Odessa, Texas, for the next couple of days—and time was of the essence. So Robert Cort and the writers, Jim Cruickshank and James Orr, agreed to fly out to Texas and meet with me.

Around lunchtime at the Holiday Inn, they arrived. We went to one of the hotel conference rooms and called to order some food—and soon learned that the kitchen was closed. Room service finally agreed to send along a snack . . . and so, over a huge bowl of potato chips and gallons of cream cheese and onion dip, we discussed the fate of *Three Men and a Baby*.

Orr and Cruickshank were intelligent men with a strong agenda; Bob Cort was there, I think, to prevent fistfights from breaking out—but he needn't have worried. "Look," the writing team told me, "the script you've read in no way represents our talent or our concept of what this movie's about. We basically worked as scribes for Coline Serreau. She sat in the room while we worked and told us exactly what each character had to say. We weren't permitted to change the rhythm of a scene: If, in the French version, the character said A, B and C, then that's exactly the way we had to write it!"

It soon became clear that they understood the material, and they very much wanted the chance to present their version. It only made sense to let them, since they'd invested several months in the project.

"Okay," I said. "I'm willing to take a chance. Write your version of the script, and I'll be happy to read it."

So things were in motion. By the time I returned to Los Angeles, it was time to meet with the production personnel. I was very pleased to discover that the cameraman was Adam Greenberg, who'd worked on *A Woman Called Golda*. Adam's an enormously talented cinematographer who has gone on to a spectacular career with the *Terminator* movies, *Alien Nation,* and *Ghost*. They showed me a coffee-table-size model of the apartment set, and I agreed to fly to Toronto to look at the real thing.

I did so with quite a bit of trepidation; if the set hadn't worked for me, it would have been a gigantic problem, because we didn't have the time to overhaul it. Fortunately, the set was marvelous—it had great flow, great vistas, and a lot of different, really unusual areas. I was relieved, because most of the film took place in this one apartment, which could have caused a claustrophobic feel. And, although the apartment was in Toronto, it had a strong "New York" flavor; the windows looked out onto a painting of Central Park West, which was utterly convincing. In fact, when actress Celeste Holm (who played Ted Danson's mother) first walked onto the set, she said, "My God! This is the exact view from my Central Park West apartment! If I didn't know better, I'd swear I was home!"

The set was simply perfect, and one of the first indications that something enchanting and magical was about to take place. The next happy occurrence came only a few weeks later, with the arrival of Orr and Cruickshank's rewritten script—which resoundingly proved their case. They'd come up with fresh, wonderful concepts for each character, based on the idea that these three guys—Peter, Michael, and Jack—were Peter Pans who'd been totally irresponsible in their relationships with women. But all that changes when a little bundle of joy is abandoned on their doorstep! Peter, the Tom Selleck character, is an architect—still erecting toys—while Jack (Ted Danson) is playing make-believe as an actor. And Michael (Steve Guttenberg) is a comic strip artist, the creator of Johnny Cool, the tiger who's the "coolest cat in town." These three men are all playing: building, playacting, drawing. But they'd never grown up, never learned responsibility. (And when they do, they discover, to their amazement, that they *like* it!)

Within an amazingly short time, all of us—Robert Cort, Orr, and Cruickshank, and the three actors—were in Toronto, sitting around a table hashing out scenes. The writing team of the two Jims were busily cranking out new pages, which just kept getting better and better.

It was almost time to start shooting, but I still had one major concern with the script: the expository scenes that introduced us to our three main characters, Peter, Michael and Jack. Originally, it was established that the story began on Peter's birthday, and there were three individual scenes, each introducing one of the characters. For example, Peter (Selleck) was shown at the construction site where he worked as an architect, telling his co-workers he had to get home because his buddies were throwing a party for him. Jack (Danson) was shown leaving a theater after a rehearsal, saying, "I gotta get home, we're throwing a party for my roommate." And Michael (Guttenberg) was in a bakery shop, trying to pick up not only Peter's birthday cake, but the young woman behind the counter.

They were nicely written scenes, but not terribly interesting or innovative, and I kept racking my brain trying to think of something fresh, something other than the standard expository fare, to introduce these three guys.

While I was doing so, the apartment's unusual foyer came to mind: you see, the elevator opened onto a large "lobby" area, which the previous director, Coline Serreau, had draped with dark fabric featuring an Egyptian motif. It was very "old world" in feel—the kind of thing you'd find in an out-of-the-way bed and breakfast in France, but definitely *not* Central Park West. I'd had it removed, which left the foyer with these bare institutional-looking walls—which I knew wasn't right, either. So I was thinking about what to do with this foyer area at the same time that I was thinking about how to introduce these characters.

And suddenly, I realized that we could fix both these problems with *one* solution.

Now, just before I left for Toronto, my wife Susan and I had gone to an interesting exhibit at the Museum of Contemporary Art in Los Angeles. Featured there was an exhibit of conceptual artist Red Grooms's colorful wall murals. One in particular really impressed me—a bright, cartoonish interior of a subway car, populated with people.

Weeks later, in Toronto, it finally struck me; why not decorate the foyer walls with a mural, which not only made it unique and "New York" in feel, but also revealed a lot about these characters? So I talked to Peter Larkin, our production designer, about creating

a "wine, women, and song in New York" mural that featured cari-
catures of the three male leads.

Then I went to our writing team, and asked for a dozen very
brief, no-dialog vignettes showing the womanizing of our irresponsible trio. They came up with some great stuff: one scene showing
an accountant, her hair pinned in a tight bun, her glasses and MBA
commando suit all neatly in place, while Danson greets her at the
door, tax papers in hand. The very next scene shows the door opening the next morning—with the now decidedly disheveled accountant giving Danson (who's in his bathrobe) a passionate good-bye
kiss.

Each of our heroes in turn is shown in a similar situation; and
these "womanizing" shots were intercut with scenes which showed
how the Steve Guttenberg character, an artist, designed and then

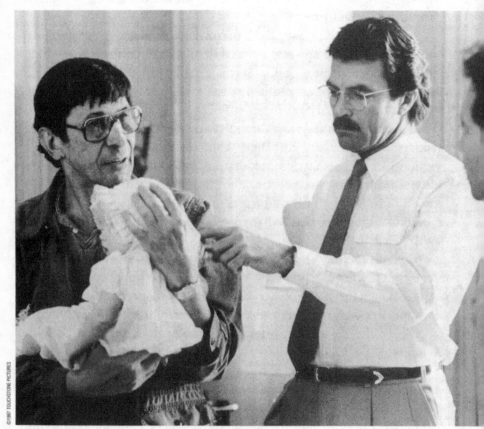

With the miraculous baby and her co-stars, Tom Selleck and Steve Guttenberg

completed the mural. To establish that the mural shows the lives of these three guys, the Tom Selleck character is shown posing so that Guttenberg can get his caricature just right.

The whole introductory sequence was cut together so that it took perhaps three minutes to establish these characters and what they did. In the meantime, the editor gave me a piece of music to use temporarily: "Boys Will Be Boys." The music turned out to be so perfect, theme-wise, for these little vignettes that we wound up keeping it (even though we'd hired Marvin Hamlisch to score the film for us).

Meanwhile, Robert Cort and I were working on casting for the "baby" of the title. Once again, things fell into place beautifully, almost magically. The baby herself was, in all respects, a small miracle.

Prior to my arrival on the project, Cort and the director had seen probably a couple hundred sets of twins. (Twins are routinely used to portray one child, because children can't work the long hours adult actors can. Also, if one twin's having a particularly cranky moment, it's easier to just bring in the other less cranky child.) They'd put together hours of videotape, which I watched when I got to Toronto. Through consensus, Cort and I narrowed it down to a half-dozen sets of twins. Finally, we asked for four pairs to be brought to Toronto with their parents.

And one particular pair of twins—actually, *one* specific beautiful and charming infant girl—was an absolute standout; her sister was a bit more reserved, and so worked mostly as our "back-up baby." In fact, this little girl was *wonderful* in terms of alertness, personality, and absolute predictability.

"When will she be hungry tomorrow?" we'd ask the mother, knowing that we had to shoot a scene about feeding the baby. "Two-fifteen," the mother would say, and bingo! Like clockwork, the little girl would happily take her bottle. "When will she fall asleep?" "Oh, about twenty minutes after you feed her." "And when will she be cranky?" "About five-thirty . . . "

So we'd schedule the sleeping scene to be shot after the feeding scene, and boom! At two thirty-five, the little girl would be sweetly asleep. It was simply amazing, and far easier than I ever thought it would be.

Even more amazing, the twins and their parents *lived in Toronto.* We could hardly believe our luck!

And we caught the girls just at the right time in their lives. They were five months old when we started filming, and about seven months old when we wrapped. (They'd spent almost a third of their short lives with us by that time.) You could see their personalities changing. As time went on, the one we used most became less and less entranced by the actors, and more interested in what was going on around her; she soon developed a passionate curiosity about the microphone. It got to the point that we had to start disguising the mike, and hiding it from her until the very last second, because she'd look up at it and follow it with her gaze instead of the actors. Toward the end of the project, I told myself, "If I had to shoot with this child one more week, I'd be in serious trouble!"

There were some marvelous scenes with the child, such as the scene where Tom Selleck and Steve Guttenberg struggle to give her a bath, and when the time comes to clean the part of the baby normally covered by the diaper, these two women chasers are completely unnerved. Neither of them wants to face the delicate task—at this point, they're handling the child as though she were a hot potato; they almost don't dare to touch her, much less her "private parts." To emphasize their reluctance, actor Steve Guttenberg came up with a truly inspired idea for his character: using a turkey baster to wash the off-limits area. Not only did it crack up everyone on the set, but the audiences roared!

There was also a wonderful scene featuring Peter (Tom Selleck) and his girlfriend, Rebecca (wonderfully played by Margaret Colin). Peter's been faithfully reading Dr. Spock (the pediatrician, *not* the Vulcan, *Mr.* Spock) and is worried because the book recommends feeding the child every two hours. Problem is—the baby's a slow eater, and it takes her two hours just to finish a bottle! "Should I wait two hours after she finishes?" Peter wonders. "Or should I be feeding her all the time?"

That dilemma actually came straight from real life. My daughter, Julie, was an extremely slow eater, and my wife and I were faithful Dr. Spock devotees. Julie could easily take two hours or more to finish a bottle; if we tried to get her to take it a little faster, we were rewarded with projectile vomiting. We worried about it for months!

(I'm happy to report that she *did* survive infancy, despite all our first-time-parental fears.)

At any rate, the making of *Three Men and a Baby* was a magical, serendipitous time where everything came together beautifully— the performances, the writing, the set design, the cinematography, all of it. I felt enormously fortunate to be involved with the project—except, perhaps, on the day we had to shoot perhaps *the* toughest scene I've ever had to choreograph before or since. (Even then, after it was done, I felt lucky again!)

It took place when we had returned to New York—specifically, to Central Park West—in order to film some exterior shots that take place in front of what was supposed to be the guys' apartment building.

The scene to be shot was this: Selleck and Guttenberg mistakenly hand the baby over to two men whom they think have come to pick the baby up. Seconds later, they discover that these two men are looking to pick up a very different "package"—filled with illegal drugs. And these two men have taken the baby because they believe the drugs are hidden on her as "powdered milk."

When Selleck finds the *real* package the men are looking for in the apartment, he runs down the stairs to give it to the men and stop them from taking the baby. On the bottom landing, he trips and falls—and the package bursts open, revealing a cache of heroin. He's shocked, but runs outside and tries to get the baby back. He and the drug dealer argue—and at this point, a policeman on horseback rides up and questions him.

Seems straightforward, right?

Not quite. When we shot the bit where Selleck falls and discovers the drugs, I also wanted action going on in the *background*, where the apartment lobby opened directly onto the street. While Tom Selleck stares wide-eyed at the packets of heroin scattered on the floor in the shot's foreground, in the *background* on the street beyond, we see the drug dealer trying to put the baby in the trunk of his car.

It took us dozens of painstaking shoots to get the timing right on that one—which wouldn't have been a big problem, except that we were supposed to be working quickly, because the sun kept moving in the sky (very annoying, if you're trying to capture something on film!), and we had to hurry before it went *behind* the apartment building and started casting shadows on everything.

Remember, this all took place on a bona fide New York street. So there's traffic passing by, and pedestrians, and clouds sailing overhead. And our "drug dealer" character has a car that is double-parked on a real New York street. We started shooting the scene, and immediately some swift-moving clouds came along and put the whole scene in shadow. We had to wait a bit until they moved off, and by that time, people driving by caught sight of Tom Selleck, and started screaming, "Hiya, Magnum!"

We had to wait for them to leave, and reshoot. After several takes, of course, we realized that the sun had finally moved behind the apartment building, and was casting shadows on the scene. So there we were, trying to decide whether to reshoot *everything*, so the light levels in the scenes would match—but we couldn't be sure they'd match perfectly, because the sun kept darting behind the clouds, then out again—then some more people were driving by, yelling at Tom Selleck, and we had this car double-parked, and the baby was starting to get a little cranky . . .

Then, to add that extra bit of excitement, we learned that the actor playing the mounted policeman had never been on a horse in his entire life. And the timing had to be just perfect; he had to maneuver the horse up to just the right place, then deliver his line, and keep the animal under control while waiting for Selleck and the drug dealer to deliver theirs.

The actor who played the cop worked valiantly to appear natural while controlling the horse, but it was tricky—it took take after take. I thought we'd *never* get those scenes done! Somehow, after hours spent out on the New York sidewalk, we did, and got film that matched well enough (though, if you watch that scene, you can definitely see the shadows encroaching).

But we had to cut the scene at the point where Selleck, having been asked to provide some ID, is followed up to his apartment by the cop. Originally, we were going to show him and the officer walking inside. But there was the small matter of the horse . . .

You see, our neophyte horseman did a decent job of dismounting the animal and tethering it to a post before following Selleck. But—like the sun and the clouds and the passersby—the horse had a mind of its own. As if to illustrate the principle that the best-laid plans of filmmakers are bound to go awry, it pulled itself free with a jerk of its head, and promptly headed *into* the apartment building and up the stairs after its "master."

It was hysterically funny—we were all roaring on the set—and the camera operators managed to capture it all on film. I was sorely tempted to use it, but it was unfortunately irrelevant to the movie, so I let it go.

Horses and clouds and sun notwithstanding, the experience of working on *Three Men and a Baby* was a joyful, magical one for me. And it worked quite a spell on American audiences, too; the film grossed more than $165 million in domestic release.

We shot the final scene at night, outside Lincoln Center in New York, and wrapped at around two o'clock in the morning. The next morning, I took a quick look at some processed footage, then my wife Susan and I boarded a plane which would take us to Paris and, ultimately, Russia.

Russia? you ask. Actually, in 1988, it was still called the Soviet Union. In order to celebrate the country's recent moratorium on whaling, the World Wildlife Fund had arranged some special screenings of *Star Trek IV: The Voyage Home*. And Harve Bennett and I had both been invited to attend. So it was that, the very day after I finished work on *Three Men and a Baby*, I found myself on a plane bound for Europe.

I'd been interested in returning to my parents' native land for many years, ever since the early 1970s, when I'd directed my first television show, "Death on a Barge," for *Night Gallery*. While we were shooting the episode, we had a couple of distinguished visitors: Secretary of State Henry Kissinger and Anatoly Dobrynin, the Soviet ambassador. Kissinger's young son, it turned out, was a *Star Trek* fan; while I signed an autograph for him, I mentioned my Russian heritage to Ambassador Dobrynin, and the fact that my parents had emigrated to the U.S. in the 1920s.

"Ah," he said. "Have they ever returned to the Soviet Union for a visit? And have you ever been?"

The answer to both questions was no.

"Then you should go, and bring them with you!"

To my surprise, my parents had no interest in returning to their native Russia. "What would we do there? There's no one left that we know. What would we go see, some old buildings?" Perhaps they had a point. Their village, Zaslav, was in the Ukraine, and during World War II had been occupied by the Germans; many of the locals, especially Jews, had been killed by the Nazi invaders. I also came to suspect that my parents might have reservations about returning to the U.S.S.R. because they both had left the country illegally—my mother in a hay wagon, as I said before, and my father by fleeing across the Polish border at night. But I couldn't help being curious about Russia.

So it was that, many years after "Death on a Barge," when Roger Payne from the World Wildlife Fund contacted me to ask whether I'd like to accompany him to Moscow for a screening of *Star Trek IV*, I leapt at the chance. I had only one proviso—that I be able to

My wife, Susan, and I with Boris Nimoy and family in the Ukraine, 1984

•

visit the village of Zaslav. He made some inquiries and came back with good news: The visit could be arranged!

Not long after, we learned that there were relatives living near Zaslav—to be specific, a Boris Srulevitch Nimoy. (The word *nimoy* or *nemoi* means mute in Russian. My parents and I have speculated that perhaps, several generations back, we had an actual mute in the family—or perhaps a person who simply pretended to be mute, in order to avoid being conscripted into the tsar's army. The length of service was usually twenty-five years, so you can understand why a lot of men feigned illness in order to avoid the draft!) Arrangements were made for us to visit him and his family.

Despite all my excitement, the visit to Russia was in some ways disappointing. For one thing, because of *Three Men and a Baby*, I was unable to arrive in time for the screening at the Russian version of the Academy of Motion Picture Arts and Sciences—the Domkino (literally, the "House of Cinema"). For another, while we arrived in time for the screening at the American Embassy in Moscow, there was a major problem with the sound system in the projection room. For some reason, we kept hearing an extraneous sound track from somewhere else. It got so bad that Harve Bennett went up to the American ambassador and said, "This is really disruptive, Ambassador; can't we do something?"

And the ambassador replied, with the sort of weary cynicism so prevalent in Moscow, "We deal with this sort of thing all the time. Trust me, there's nothing we can do."

In Russia, my parents' homeland, I felt very much an alien, an outsider. But this time, Spock didn't accompany me; like their Chinese neighbors, the Russian people had never been exposed to *Star Trek*, and had no idea who I was.

Such was the case for Boris Nimoy's family. They spoke no English at all, and I no Russian; we communicated a bit in Yiddish, but mostly relied on the services of a translator. They had never heard of me, or Spock, and were in fact suspicious of my motives in coming. All they'd been told was that an important person was coming to visit from the United States—but from their point of view, important people wore suits and ties, and here I was, casually dressed in a T-shirt! They didn't know what to make of me, and after our meeting was over, I learned that they were certain we were part of a government ploy designed to investigate them.

•

Still, seeing the town where my parents had spent their childhood days was extraordinary in every way. We visited with the Nimoys for three or four hours, during which time we tape-recorded some messages for my parents and took some photos.

Then it was all over, and we were completely exhausted. I'd just finished a grueling ten-week schedule on *Three Men*, and had flown directly from a late-night shoot to France. There, I'd spent one night before flying to Russia, where our days and nights were full of nonstop activity. My wife and I were looking forward to four days of vacation in Paris.

But the moment we arrived, we received some very bad news: My father was in the hospital, terminally ill. I immediately got on a plane and went to see him, grateful for the chance to share with him the pictures and taped greetings from his homeland. Sadly, he died a few days later.

At the time, I didn't realize how numbed and shocked I was by the loss. I somehow managed to deal with the necessary arrangements; and Bill Shatner was good enough to show up at my father's funeral service, which touched me greatly. I didn't get fully in touch with the loss until later, while filming the *Good Mother*. In the meantime, I continued rather stoically.

The situation calls to mind Amanda's line to Spock in *Star Trek IV*: "You're part human; you have emotions, and they will surface . . . "

Was I functioning in a Spocklike way? Probably. Would the emotions surface, as Amanda told Spock they would? Yes, but it took some time. In the meantime, I had distractions, work to do—for which I was grateful.

Not long after my father's death, *Three Men and a Baby* opened to phenomenal box office receipts and terrific reviews. The success was heartening, but also tinged with sadness. As I mentioned at the beginning of this chapter, most critics seemed amazed to find out that Leonard Nimoy actually had a sense of humor. The reviews typically read like the one in the *New York Times*, which in essence said, "Based on his past work, you wouldn't think Leonard Nimoy has the necessary sense of humor to make such a movie. Fortunately, he does!"

After the success of *Three Men*, Jeff Katzenberg called again. "Leonard, I've got an interesting project you might want to take a look at."

"What is it?"

"It's a drama based on a novel, *The Good Mother*. Pretty controversial stuff . . . "

"Sounds good. Send it along!"

"Okay, but I think you should know a little something about the circumstances. The producer's Arnold Glimcher, and he was hoping for a high-profile director, someone with a really solid rep for serious drama. We tried to get Streisand or Redford, but both of them passed, and right now the project's at a standstill. Eisner really wants to make it, but . . . "

"But?"

"Well, I'm sending it, Leonard, with the understanding that I can't necessarily promise it to you. *I* know you can do drama, but after *Star Trek IV* and *Three Men*, all everybody else knows is that you can do comedy. But if you like it, let me know, and I'll see what I can do . . . "

So there it was: Here I'd been reading all these reviews of *The Voyage Home* and *Three Men and a Baby* that said, "Gee, who would have thought Nimoy could do comedy?" Yet because of those two films' box office successes, I was already being labeled in Hollywood as a director who could *only* do comedy!

But Jeff sent me along the script, and I read it and the novel with great interest.

The Good Mother was written by Sue Miller, a novelist in Cambridge, Massachusetts. It dealt with the thorny issues of sexuality and child-rearing—specifically, how a young woman, Anna, is raised in a rigid, patriarchal family of Boston bluebloods and conforms all her life to their notion of "a good girl." She goes from being controlled by her rigid, iron-fisted grandfather to being controlled by her rigid, iron-fisted husband without a misstep—and, sadly, lives a life devoid of sexual passion. The only real love she knows is that for her six-year-old daughter, Molly, with whom she has a wonderful, strong relationship. She tries to do for Molly what was never done for her: teach the little girl not to be ashamed of her own body, or of sexual issues. Anna doesn't want her daughter to be raised with the sense of shame she was.

And then, sometime after Anna's divorce, she falls in love for the first time—with a freewheeling young sculptor, Leo Cutter. They have a very passionate, loving, honest relationship, and Anna lets

Leo know that she is trying to raise Molly in a very open, honest way. Therefore, when Molly discovers her mother and Leo nude together, the adults don't react with shame or embarrassment, but behave very naturally.

The three are very happy together, bound by honest love and caring—and then, one day, a minor incident occurs that will go on to destroy that happiness. Leo is in the shower when Molly comes in. He's careful not to display any embarrassment, knowing that that is what Anna would want; but then, Molly asks, very directly: "Is that your penis?"

"Yes," Leo allows.

"Can I touch it?"

Leo's taken aback, but struggles to hide his discomfort. "Sure," he says. Molly does so, satisfying her childish curiosity, and that's the end of the incident.

Until Molly tells her father. Enraged, the father immediately proceeds with a custody battle. Anna soon finds her attitudes about sex and her performance as a mother are dragged into a courtroom for microscopic scrutiny by the straitlaced judge. Very reluctantly, after much soul-searching and arguments, she submits to her lawyer's instructions, and tells the judge that what Leo did was "a mistake." She even agrees to give up seeing Leo, if that's what will permit her to keep custody of her daughter.

But the story is a true tragedy, in the Shakespearean sense: Despite her capitulation, Molly loses her daughter . . . and ultimately Leo, because she is simply too grief-stricken, too angry at the system, to continue the relationship.

I found the material powerful and thought-provoking, because it raised the sensitive issue of the juxtaposition of motherhood and sexuality. In our culture, there's still a very strong belief that motherhood and sex shouldn't be allowed to mix; it's the old "madonna/whore" concept, that a woman is either one or the other, but cannot be both.

I also liked the fact that there was no specific "villain" in the piece. No one set out to do anything terrible to Anna; the husband was sincere, the investigators were sincere, the judge was sincere... but they were all trapped within a social structure that ultimately leads to tragedy.

Excited, I contacted Jeff and let him know I was interested. He agreed to set up a meeting between me and the producer, who had already expressed reservations about hiring me.

But when I met Arnie Glimcher, we immediately hit it off on a personal level. "Arnie," I told him, "I realize you don't know enough about me to understand why I could successfully handle this material. All you know about me is *Star Trek IV* and *Three Men and a Baby*, so I don't blame you for having concerns. But you should know that I have a strong background in Odets and Chekhov, the literature that is the line that *The Good Mother* extends. I also happen to be from Boston, and know very well the environment in which Anna is tried and judged."

That seemed to put Arnie at ease, and we started discussing the approach to the material. We had a very strong meeting of the minds about the concept, and by the time we parted, we were fast friends. During the whole filming of *The Good Mother*, Arnie and I never wavered from that concept: that this film was a tragedy, in the purest Shakespearean sense, that there would be no pat, happy ending wherein Anna stood up on the witness stand to give the judge a piece of her mind, then walked off victorious with her lover and child.

But many actresses wanted that pat, happy ending, that moment where Anna overcomes her upbringing and the whole repressed, patriarchal system. But Diane Keaton had a strong grasp of the material, and an appreciation of what we were trying to do; we were very pleased to cast her as Anna.

And pleased, also, to cast Liam Neeson as Leo. Some prominent actors rejected the role because they worried about the effect playing such a character—who let a little girl touch his penis—might have on their careers (even though the script made it clear Leo never did anything wrong). But Liam never flinched from the work. His performance was so beautiful and sensitive that everyone loved it, even those critics who scorned the film.

Jason Robards was my definite first choice for the role of Anna's attorney. Let me mention here that the lawyer is not entirely sympathetic when he first appears in the story; he's a legal wheeler and dealer, a pragmatist who tells Anna up front that she can't win the case and keep her daughter if she tells the truth and insists she and

Liam Neeson as Leo Cutter

©1988 TOUCHSTONE PICTURES

Leo have done nothing wrong. She has to tell the judge that they both "made a mistake" in their handling of the child, or else Molly will be taken away.

(This scenario is solidly based in fact. To be sure we were on the right track in terms of how the legal system would view the situation, I discussed the story with an officer in the Boston Police Department. I explained to him that Anna and Leo were seen as making two "mistakes" with Molly—first, that Leo let Molly touch his genitals, and second, that Anna and Leo made love while the girl was asleep in bed with them. My question to him was: Was it believable that the judicial system in Boston would consider these sufficient grounds to take the child away from the mother?

"Absolutely," the police officer said. "She would lose her child."

"Because of the penis-touching incident?"

"No," he said. "That's iffy. But the minute she admits they made love while the little girl was in bed with them, it's all over."

"But the child was asleep—"

"Doesn't matter," he said. It was a good dose of New England parochialism, and I knew we were on the right track.)

But back to the subject of Anna's attorney. He realizes that her chances of keeping Molly are slim, and her admission to an investigator that she and Leo made love while Molly was asleep in their bed pretty much seals her fate. He urges her in essence to throw herself on the mercy of the court and confess that she had made mistakes, that otherwise she had always been a "good mother," and that she'd give up Leo forever if she could keep her daughter.

I knew Jason Robards would be perfect for the part. We'd known each other for some years, having met when we were both on a television talk show in Chicago. I was performing in *Four Poster*, and Jason was starring in *Moon for the Misbegotten* with Colleen Dewhurst. We had a pleasant chat after the show, and he invited me to come and see his play. My schedule was pretty full, so I said, "I'll try . . . " To which he passionately replied, "Please come. The piece is worthy, and we need you!"

How could I refuse? I went to see his play, and spent some time with him afterwards.

So in the case of *The Good Mother*, I sent Jason a script, via his agent, and offered him the role of Anna's attorney. For some time,

Jason Robards and Diane Keaton

I didn't hear back, and when I finally called his agent, I was told: "Jason can't do it. He's got some scheduling problems . . . "

"What are they?" I asked. "Maybe we can work them out."

"Well, actually . . . he's also not too keen on playing this character."

But at this point, I was determined. I called Jason myself.

"Leonard!" he said. "Good to hear from you again. Look, I know you sent me that script, but I really can't help you. The schedule would just be impossible . . . "

"Jason, we'd really like to have you. What if we worked out the schedule, and any other concerns you might have? Would you take the role?"

There was a long pause at the other end of the line. "Well . . . frankly, Leonard, this attorney character is a real asshole."

"Jason, I've got two things to say to you. First, *he* doesn't believe he's an asshole. He's a good old boy. Insensitive, maybe, to Anna's beliefs, but he's politically shrewd. He knows the realities of the legal system and he's trying his very best to help her keep her child."

Another long pause. "Okay, you've got a point there. Now, what's the second thing you have to say?"

"Please come. The piece is worthy, and we need you."

He laughed aloud, and I knew I had him! He was perfect in the role, and we gave his character a very important final moment: After he gives Anna the bad news that she's lost her child and she's fled his office in despair, he bows his head and slumps forward in a moment of deep regret. It was, in essence, a gesture that serves as the character's redemption.

Other wonderful actors joined the project—Charles Kimbrough (now a regular on *Murphy Brown*) and Tracy Griffith, Melanie's half-sister. Elmer Bernstein composed a lovely score, and we were fortunate enough to land David Watkin, a world-class cinematographer from *Out of Africa* and *Chariots of Fire*.

I was thrilled to be directing the film. At the same time, making this picture tore me apart emotionally, because it dealt with profound loss. I would wake in the night, weeping. It was extremely painful for me, perhaps in part because only a few months after my father's passing, my mother also fell ill and died.

Until *The Good Mother*, work had been solace for me, a means of escaping the deep sense of personal loss. But Anna's tragic loss of her child awakened the repressed grief I felt over the loss of my parents; making the film was cathartic for me. As the shooting of *The Good Mother* progressed, I found myself so deeply involved in the characters' problems, so absorbed by the particular scene we were filming that day, that I almost couldn't see ahead to what was inevitably going to happen. On one level, I knew the tragic ending—that Anna would lose both the loves of her life—but when it finally came time to film those scenes, the depth of emotion I felt took me by surprise.

Diane Keaton gave an absolutely stunning performance as Anna. I remember clearly the day we filmed a scene with her for which she truly deserved the Academy Award. It was a very powerful moment in which Anna is interviewed by a court-appointed psychiatrist about her parenting methods and the incident between Molly and Leo. At first she is reluctant to open up, but once she begins to, her heartfelt love and grief for both her child and Leo shine through with breathtaking clarity.

We'd given ourselves a day to shoot this interview scene. I asked the cameraman to put two cameras on Diane Keaton, one for the larger shots, and one for tighter close-ups. (Let me explain something about camera work; it's a lot easier to simply light a set for the wide shots and shoot those, then go back and redo the scene again with different lighting for close-ups. Lighting that looks good for *both* types of shots requires a lot of painstaking setup, and camera people would much rather not do it.)

So of course, when I told the cameraman to give us two cameras, which required the much tougher type of lighting, he asked, "Why?"

"Because," I replied, "the psychiatrist is going to ask Diane Keaton a few very difficult questions. Her character's tense 'mask' is going to be slowly stripped away while she delivers several pages of intense, emotional dialog. I want both cameras to be ready to capture both types of shots, so she doesn't have to go through this again and again. The fewer times she has to do it, the better."

"Okay," he said, and got right to work on it without further questions, because he understood what an enormous effort it would be for an actor to have to do such a difficult, draining scene—then go back and immediately do it once more.

He did the lighting, and everything was ready—or so I thought. For this scene, and other sensitive, emotional moments, we were using Agfa film in the cameras, because it gives a much softer effect; for the harsh "realis-tic" scenes, such as those in the courtroom, we used Kodak film for its crisper, "grittier" look.

So it was time for Diane Keaton to come and give her performance as Anna, speaking in halting, tearful tones about her desperate love for her daughter and for Leo.

Let me be honest here: As we watched her, it grew so still on the set that I could hear my own breathing. She gave such a clear, beautiful, heartbreaking performance that all of us had tears streaming down our faces by the time she was done.

"Cut and print," I said. "That's beautiful! Let's all take a break." And I walked out onto the street for a breath of air, and to recover from the intense emotion evoked by her magnificent performance. It was only eleven o'clock in the morning, Diane had given us a perfect take the first time around, we were ahead of schedule for the day, and I was absolutely thrilled with what had already been accomplished. I clearly remember thinking to myself, *"That* is the scene that will win Diane Keaton an Oscar!"

And just as I was dwelling on these happy thoughts outside on the sidewalk, I turned to see two members of the film crew running

toward me, with absolutely grief-stricken expressions. All I could think was that someone had collapsed and died right there on the set.

"Leonard," one of them gasped, "there's a problem! A terrible problem!"

"What?!"

"The two cameras—one of them had Agfa, like you wanted. But the other one was loaded with Kodak!"

I groaned. Kodak and Agfa films could *not* be cut together. It meant that we couldn't use Diane's terrific performance. We'd have to shoot the whole thing again!

"Run fast," I told them. "Go to a florist's and buy at least a hundred dollars' worth of flowers, because I've got to go tell Diane the bad news, and I'm *not* going empty-handed."

So it was that, when I knocked on the door to Diane's trailer, where she was

Directing Diane Keaton in The Good Mother

decompressing, I was laden down with roses. Diane was a trouper; she sighed and said philosophically, "Well, these are the kinds of things that happen when you make movies."

"Please, take all the time you need to prepare," I told her. "Whenever you feel ready, just let us know." You'd better believe that, when I went back to the set, we all made *sure* both cameras were loaded with Agfa film!

Within half an hour, Diane was back on the set, and gave us a second brilliant performance, which appears in the film.

By the time filming on *The Good Mother* wrapped, I felt the same way I had at the end of shooting *Three Men and a Baby*: that I had been blessed to work with a group of people who had all contributed their best to create something magical.

I'm not sure exactly what sort of response I expected to the film—some controversy, certainly, because of the subject matter. I only know that I was as proud of *The Good Mother* as any work I've ever done.

And the initial response seemed to validate that pride. After an early screening of the film in New York, I remember walking out of the theater onto the sidewalk, accompanied by Liam Neeson, Mike Ovitz, and Arnie Glimcher. About thirty or forty people, who had also attended the screening, had gathered there, and when we walked out, they applauded us—and kept applauding as we got into our waiting car and rode off! I was overwhelmed, and thought, "Boy, this could be even more of a rocket ride than *Three Men*!"

It was a rocket ride, all right—straight down. But I wouldn't learn about the full spectrum of response to *The Good Mother* until after shooting began on *Star Trek V*—and that's another story.

SIXTEEN

THE FINAL FRONTIER

— And Beyond

IN OCTOBER 1988, I read my first review of *The Good Mother*. We were a couple of days into shooting *Star Trek V*, and I was sitting in my trailer on the *Star Trek* set in full Spock regalia, ears included. I was still very hopeful after the incredible audience reaction at the New York screening, where the crowd had applauded us on the sidewalk outside the theater. The rocket was still headed straight up at that point, and showed no signs of slowing—especially after I read the review, which said: "With this film, Nimoy is elevated into the top echelon of filmmakers."

Wow! I literally floated out of my trailer on a cloud of euphoria . . . which, all too soon, would be replaced by disappointment. The rocket ride got very rough, then started plummeting back toward Earth.

Audience reaction to *The Good Mother* was uneven, to put it mildly. We'd known the film would generate some controversy; in fact, we were hoping for it, because it would help publicize the film. But I wasn't prepared for the extreme range in reactions. Critics gave it either the highest or the lowest rating; there was no in-between, and viewing audiences responded the same way. No one rated it "good" or "fair"—it was either "excellent" or "poor." Some were outspokenly excited by its tough, mature content; others were infuriated, and in essence said, "There's no place for this movie! Get it out of here!" Box office receipts were disappointing, and the film soon disappeared from theaters.

One provocative and lengthy letter, which was printed in the *Los Angeles Times*, called *The Good Mother* "wrongheaded and mean-spirited." The writer was angry because she felt we were saying that Diane Keaton's character, Anna, had "gotten what she deserved" by losing her child—when, in fact, we were saying just the opposite! She basically felt that "films are supposed to tell us the way life ought to turn out." (During this same period, a film professor at Columbia University told me that *The Good Mother* was the most underrated movie of all time!)

I suppose we could have made a more commercial film by having the character rise up in the third act and tell the judge and lawyers they were all dumb bastards and should have been ashamed of themselves—and they'd all have a change of heart and give her custody of Molly. But that wasn't what the story was about, anymore than *Oedipus Rex* is about a guy regaining his eyesight!

At any rate, this drama of viewer and critic reaction to *The Good Mother* was played out during the time we were shooting *Star Trek V: The Final Frontier*—which, as I said, is a whole other story in itself.

This fifth *Star Trek* project had something of a long and troubled history. Bill Shatner and I had first discussed it a couple years earlier, during the filming of *The Voyage Home*, when Bill expressed his desire to direct the next film. I was very much in favor of Bill doing his own movie. In fact, during the screening party for *IV*, at a Beverly Hills restaurant, I told him, "You know, you should start immediately on *Star Trek V*, while excitement is still high. Don't waste any time."

Bill agreed, and I immediately introduced him to Frank Mancuso (then head of Paramount). Bill pitched his story idea to Frank, and they had their first discussion about film number five that very night. Eventually, Bill contacted Harve Bennett and convinced him to come aboard as producer.

Soon after, I became involved in protracted contract negotiations with Paramount over *Star Trek V*. Then along came *Three Men and a Baby*, and *The Good Mother, and* a Writers Guild strike. The combination of those three things, plus difficulties in coming to an agreement with Paramount, worked to stall the project.

By that time, Bill was like one of his own horses, chomping at the bit to get on with the race. But, to be honest, I had a major problem with his proposed story line from the very beginning. The premise? Under the sway of a self-styled religious zealot, the *Enterprise* crew goes warping across the galaxy in search of God.

Early on, I let Bill know that I felt the story had problems. "Bill," I said, "there's no way you can go in search of God and find Him.

The audience won't buy it. And if you don't find Him, there's no story. Besides, everyone's going to compare this to *The God Thing*." (*The God Thing* was Gene Roddenberry's first proposed script for *Star Trek: The Motion Picture*; it was overwhelmingly rejected by Paramount execs because of the story line.)

But Bill was overflowing with typical steamroller-style enthusiasm, and would hear no dissent. "It's gonna work, Leonard, trust me. I know how to make it happen."

"Fine, Bill. I just have two things to say. First: This movie will get made. There's too much of a pro–*Star Trek* dynamic to stop it, no matter what. Second: Knowing that, your main concern should be, 'Is this movie one that I'll be proud to say I made?' You need to be sure you start out with a strong story, because all too soon, you're going to be caught up in a myriad of details, and by then, it'll be too late to make any major story changes. You'll be worrying about

As Spock with Sybok (Laurence Luckinbill)

thousands of questions like, 'How many times should this character fire the phaser? What does God look like, sound like? Who'll play Him? What kind of clothes does He wear?' You know, all of those things can be taken care of by anyone. But only *you* can decide whether the basic story line is working or not."

"Yes, yes, yes, I believe in it, Leonard. It's going to work. Just trust me."

Bill was adamant about sticking to his story line—though, eventually, Harve and the studio balked at the notion that the *Enterprise* crew really *does* find both God and the devil. After much resistance, Bill was finally persuaded that it would be more believable to filmgoers if "God" turned out to be an alien masquerading as The Big Guy.

Once the Writers Guild strike was settled after a year's delay, Harve Bennett and David Loughery (a young man whose writing credits included *Flashback* and *Dreamscape*) finally set to work on the script. (Bill had attempted to get Nick Meyer, but Nick was working on another project and was unavailable.)

I first read their draft of *Star Trek V: The Final Frontier* while I was finishing work on *The Good Mother*, and to say I was disappointed is putting it mildly. The draft I read had Spock and McCoy (and the entire *Enterprise* crew) betraying Kirk, and joining forces with a religious madman, Sybok—who just happened to be the Vulcan's long-lost brother. In addition, there was another fundamental problem: Spock served no function, no purpose in the script. I feel very

"Admiral" Harve Bennett

strongly that in drama, a character must be in the story for a *reason*, must in some way serve to advance the plot (much as our "impossible mission" *Enterprise* team each played a role in *Star Trek III* by getting our heroes onto their ship and back to the Genesis planet, to save Spock). Otherwise, the character has no business being in the story and should be cut.

I immediately sat down with Bill, and said, "Let's talk about Spock. I've got some problems here. For one thing, my character has no function in the script."

"How does he further the plot?"

Bill said, "Don't worry about it. We'll think of something . . . "

We had two or three conversations like this, and nothing was resolved. Finally I tried to be as specific as I could: "Bill, I won't let this conversation come to an end until I'm sure you've heard me

clearly. I have major problems with the character as he's written here. You must listen: Unless this is addressed, I cannot perform for you."

"Oh. Well, what should we do?"

We finally came to something of an agreement, although both De Kelley and I still had major problems with the notion of McCoy and Spock betraying Kirk. That problem, too, was resolved—somewhat—when I explained to Bill, "There's nothing that will make Spock follow Sybok. You can write it, but I can't play it, and the audience won't accept it."

Nor was I pleased about a flashback scene in which Spock's "pain" is revealed: he witnesses his own birth, and his father's obviously disapproving remark about his infant son: "So human . . . " But *Star Trek IV* had specifically highlighted Spock's coming to

terms with both his human and Vulcan sides. It seemed clear to me that, with that film, the character had resolved any internal conflicts in that regard.

I voiced all my concerns, and the script was rewritten. Rather than have Spock overtly betray Kirk, instead the Vulcan cannot bring himself to obey Kirk's order to fire a phaser at his half-brother, who then seizes the weapon and "takes over" the *Enterprise*. Was I happy with it? No. But it was at least playable. However, while my objections were registered on Spock's "birth" scene, it stayed put.

Even with numerous rewrites, the script and story remained weak. I believe this was the cause of *Star Trek V*'s woes at the box office.

It certainly had nothing to do with

Spock confronts his long-lost half-brother while Kirk and others look on

Bill's abilities as a director, because he shot the film as efficiently and cinematically as any of a number of talented directors might have. He got some very interesting footage, such as Sybok riding on horseback out of the mist. With us actors, he was personable, charming, well-prepared, and boundlessly enthusiastic. The problem was in the execution and design of the screenplay; what was on the page is what he shot. He was riding a bad script, and as I've said at other times and places, when you're riding a bad script, there's not much that can be done to salvage a film. (I can sympathize with him, because I'd soon have a similar experience with another Paramount film, *Funny About Love*.)

Bill also deserves credit for all his hard work and his extraordinary sense of responsibility. I can remember wandering into the motel coffee shop and finding him there one morning, talking with Ralph Winter, our executive producer. We were just finishing up filming the Yosemite scenes at the time, and Ralph was telling Bill that, before we left this location, Bill should make sure he had everything he needed in terms of filmed material—because once we left, it'd cost a lot more to go back and reshoot.

"It'd be wiser to just stay and go over schedule, if we need to," Ralph was saying.

I could see the look of both determination and queasiness on Bill's face. "Oh, no!" he said quickly, shaking his head. "No, we're absolutely finished here. Trust me, we've got all the film we need!"

I had to smile. I understand *exactly* how he felt: In the old days of the *Star Trek* series, they pulled the plug at *precisely* 6:18 P.M. every evening. (Remember, that's why we were so panicked trying to get that Spock scene done for "The Naked Time.") It didn't matter if an actor was in mid-sentence, delivering a line of dialog; at 6:19 P.M., boom! You were done for the day, and it was time to move on. Didn't matter if you didn't get the footage you needed—so we all learned to work quickly and efficiently, so the director and producer could get what was needed *before* 6:18.

I sat down at the table and put a hand on Bill's shoulder. "Listen carefully to what Ralph's saying," I said. "This *isn't* television. It's okay to stay if you need an extra day or two."

But Bill shook his head. He was determined to make a good film, and to bring it in on schedule. He didn't want to seem irresponsible. And he was absolutely right, anyway: He *had* gotten everything he needed. But I understood very well the sort of pressure he was under.

Script problems aside, working with Bill was great fun—if physically exhausting. Bill loves to film a lot of running and jumping—and in my case, hanging upside down! One sequence, which showed Kirk scaling the aptly christened El Capitan, required Spock to "fly" up and "float" in a pair of antigravity boots for a midair conversation with his captain. Distracted, Kirk loses his grip and hurtles downward—only to be rescued by the flying Vulcan.

In order to do that, I wore a special fiberglass "flying" suit, molded from my torso. A pipe actually connected the suit to the false "mountainside," but if shot from certain angles, the pipe was hidden and I seemed to be suspended in midair during Spock's conversation with his rock-climbing captain. That wasn't so bad, but

The mountain-climbing Kirk and his airborne first officer in Star Trek V: The Final Frontier

then Spock had to dive after Kirk when the captain falls. So to do *that*, my waist was hooked to a metal bar—and when the bar was flipped over, I went over, too, antigravity boots over pointed ears! Actually, I got rather used to hanging around the set upside down.

We did a "flying" sequence with those same boots, with Spock holding both McCoy and Kirk in the elevator shafts. The harnesses they made for us got pretty uncomfortable, so that we all started referring to the rig as "the house of pain."

Of course, there had to be horses in this film, because of Bill's passion for them. (No Dobermans or motorcycles, though.) We spent a half-hour engaged in a pretty amusing argument about how Spock ought to perform a neck-pinch on a horse.

"Have Spock struggle with it," Bill mused, as we both looked up at my potential victim—a snorting, high-spirited animal who eyed me with an unmistakable "just you try it" expression.

"What exactly do you mean, Bill?"

"You know, Leonard. Spock tries to find just that right spot—and fails—and keeps trying."

"You mean . . . while the animal's rearing up, trying to trample him?"

"Yes!" Bill's eyes lit up. "It'll look great on camera!"

I considered this for at least .001 seconds, then countered: "Actually, Vulcans possess in-depth knowledge of equestrian anatomy."

Bill frowned over at me. "Are you sure?"

"Absolutely."

Star Trek V wrapped filming in late December 1988. I went on to become involved in other projects—including directing *Funny About Love*, a comedy starring Gene Wilder and Christine Lahti. But one of the most meaningful projects for me personally came about by accident.

It happened in 1989, while I was researching another project that never came to fruition; in doing so, I spoke with some attorneys. As it turned out, one of the lawyers was doing some pro bono work for a gentleman by the name of Mel Mermelstein, and said: "You know, if you're really looking for a worthwhile project . . . "

And he proceeded to tell me a little about Mel.

Mel Mermelstein was born in Hungary. In 1944, when the

German army invaded, Mel and his family—his sister, brother, mother, and father—were rounded up along with other local Jews and sent to the concentration camp at Auschwitz-Birkenau. The day after Mel arrived, he watched his mother and sister (and a long line of women and children) enter the "women's showers"—the gas chamber. They never emerged.

He and his brother and father were forced into slave labor, and managed to survive for a time, despite the dismal rations, unspeakable filth, and consequent disease. (Malnutrition, overwork, lack of sanitation and close quarters caused frequent outbreaks of typhus.) But his father soon became ill; and when the elder Mermelstein was dying, he called his two sons to him and said: "Your mother and sister are gone, and I'll soon join them. But perhaps you two—or one of you—will survive. You must both swear to me that if you live, you will bear witness to the world of the crime that has occurred here, for all of us who cannot speak."

Mel and his brother made their father this last promise. Sadly, of all his family, only Mel survived, and was freed when Allied troops finally arrived to liberate the camps.

Mel emigrated to the United States, grew to manhood and built a good life for himself. He started his own business, became happily married to an American woman, and had children. But he never forgot his promise to his father, and so he took it upon himself to do exactly what his father asked—to serve as a witness to the world of the horrors that had transpired in the camps, to remind everyone of the heinous crimes human beings are capable of committing against each other. He started a Holocaust museum, filled with memorabilia from the camps, and those who had died there: photographs of victims, lists of names, pieces of clothing, bits of barbed wire painstakingly fashioned into Stars of David. And he lectured to schoolchildren about his own experience at Auschwitz.

Then, one day, he received a letter in the mail: an "invitation" from a group calling itself the Institute for Historical Review. They offered him $50,000 if he could prove, to the satisfaction of their "unbiased committee," that a single Jew had died in the concentration camps at the hands of the Germans. Their contention was that the Nazis had never murdered any Jews; the Jews that were rounded up had been "troublemakers," and those that died in the camps were victims of typhus, not gas chambers (which the Institute insisted had been "delousing" rooms).

Mermelstein was outraged, and took the letter first to the Anti-Defamation League, then the Simon Wiesenthal Center. He received the same advice from both places: The Institute was simply a cover organization for a neo-Nazi hate group, whose only interest was to drag Mermelstein into their sham "court" and ridicule him, then publicly announce their "findings"—that the Holocaust never happened.

But Mel felt he couldn't back down. He spoke with several attorneys, all of whom kept telling him that the letter from the Institute was "nonactionable"—there was nothing he could do legally to stop the Institute from spreading its hateful lies and making the same offer to other camp survivors.

Finally, he happened to meet with attorney Bill Cox—who agreed with everyone else that the letter was nonactionable, and that Mel shouldn't permit himself to be tricked into testifying in the Institute's phony "court."

However, after giving the matter further thought, Cox finally came up with an unorthodox but workable legal approach: The Institute's letter offering the $50,000 was in essence a letter of agreement—in other words, a contract. If Mel agreed to take them up on their offer, and received no reply *within thirty days*, then he could justifiably sue them for breach of contract. Once he managed to get the matter into a bona fide court of law, he could ask the court to legally recognize the fact of the Holocaust.

Mel agreed to follow Cox's strategy. He took the Institute up on their offer; they failed to respond within the thirty days, and Mermelstein then filed suit.

After much personal hardship—hour after hour of badgering by the Institute's lawyers, harassment of himself and his family (Nazi slogans were painted on his house, and a dead pig was thrown into his yard), even threats against his business, his family, and his own life—Mel persevered, and found a legal way to resoundingly honor his dying father's request.

At Mermelstein's request, the court took judicial notice of the fact of the Holocaust. It was the first time a U.S. court had ever done so.

Soon after my visit with the attorney who first told me the story, I went to visit Mel Mermelstein to discuss it further. I was so moved by what he had to say—and show, in the case of the memorial he had created for camp victims—that I contacted my longtime friend, Robert Radnitz. I was very interested in not only portraying Mel, but also in helping to bring the project to the screen.

Radnitz had produced *Sounder*, a landmark miniseries about the black experience in America. For some time, we had been interested in producing something together. I felt Bob had the background and reputation that might convince a network that Mel's story should reach a wider audience.

Bob agreed with me that the material was worthwhile, and we approached some networks with it. NBC responded very quickly and positively. Unfortunately, the first script was turned in after an uncomfortably long period of time, and proved to be unusable. We then hired writer Ronald Rubin, who gave us a sensitive, lovely

script for *Never Forget*. In a straightforward, honest way, without sensationalizing, he told a very touching story about a man who makes a stand. We were enormously pleased.

NBC, however, wasn't; the network put us in turnaround (in other words, they decided against continuing with the project). We took Ron Rubin's script to the Turner Network, who happily picked us up.

Casting the part of Mel was easy, of course; I'd already volunteered for the

As Mel Mermelstein in Never Forget

job. And Joe Sargent—whom I'd known for so many years, and who had directed some of the best *Star Trek* episodes—was always our first choice as director. We were thrilled to get him. I have to say here that Joe worked his usual magic again here, always finding the heart and core of each scene.

As for the woman who would play Jane, Mel's wife:—we had a very short list of actresses we were considering for the part. One of them was the very talented Blythe Danner, with whom I'd worked back in the seventies.

One day, before we'd had a chance to cast the role of Jane, my wife and I were traveling by plane when—lo and behold—in the seat across from us was Blythe! I realized Fate had presented me with a perfect opportunity, so I went over to say hello and tell her all about the project, *Never Forget*. She was immediately interested

Mermelstein in court with wife Jane (Blythe Danner)

because of the subject matter. Within hours after we all arrived in Los Angeles, I had a script to her, and she soon signed on.

Dabney Coleman then came aboard as attorney William Cox, and gave us a wonderful performance. Frankly, the entire assembled cast of that production was terrific—and we were also very pleased when Joe Sargent found a way to include Mel Mermelstein and his daughter, Edie, in cameo roles.

I must also give credit here to the people at the Simon Wiesenthal Center, and at the Anti-Defamation League. While researching *Never Forget*, we went to both groups. They freely admitted, "Yes, we told Mel not to pursue the matter with the Institute for Historical Review; we are happy for his success." They were extremely gracious about the matter, and offered their assistance.

With Dabney Coleman

Fortunately for us all, Mel couldn't walk away from the challenge. I'm grateful to him for his perseverance and integrity, and also for his willingness to share his story with us—and the world. If every project brought me the same sense of fulfillment that *Never Forget* did, I would truly be in paradise. For me, Mel's story goes beyond the Nazi/Jewish issue, beyond the horrors of Auschwitz; it addresses the fundamental issues of the human spirit. I am reminded of playwright Arthur Miller, who once said that all plays we deem worthy ask the fundamental question: How can humankind make of the outside world a home? What obstacles must we overcome, what must we personally achieve, in order to have a sense of belonging, of inner peace?

Surely Mel Mermelstein found his way through a great darkness into the light of spiritual contentment and personal dignity. The inspiration his story brought us all clearly showed in the production. *Never Forget* was nominated for a Cable Ace Award, and was heralded by the *New York Times* as "television that will long be remembered."

But I must add a dark, unsettling postscript to this story: The Institute for Historical Review suffered a setback after *Never Forget* aired, but they remain with us to this day, busily fostering falsehoods and hatred. Only a few days ago, I read that a woman working on their behalf recently published a "history" book about typhus outbreaks during World War II. Her premise is their oft-repeated lie that the millions who perished in the concentration camps were actually victims of typhus—not genocide. What disturbs me is that texts such as this one are slickly written and handsomely bound—and can often be found in university libraries. College students doing research on the Second World War can very well pick up such a publication and unwittingly believe it to be a "scholarly" work based on legitimate research.

SEVENTEEN

STAR TREK VI
AND
"UNIFICATION"

NIMOY: Spock, I can't help noticing that you've changed lately.

SPOCK: *Indeed? In what way?*

NIMOY: Well, frankly, you're more emotional.

SPOCK: *Not at all. I am simply choosing to display emotion at those moments where it seems most appropriate, and likely to assist in achieving my objective.*

NIMOY: In other words, you're emoting when it seems like the *logical* thing to do?

SPOCK: *Precisely.*

I N ORDER TO PROPERLY TELL the story of *Star Trek VI*, I have to begin by backtracking a little.

You see, at some point during the making of *The Voyage Home*, Harve Bennett had come up with a concept for another movie. Not a sequel this time, but a prequel to all of the *Star Trek* movies, and even the original TV episodes. The idea? A story involving Kirk, Spock, and McCoy during their Starfleet Academy days, with all of us being replaced by younger actors. I suppose the feeling was that this would give the "franchise" (as *Star Trek* is known on the Paramount lot) an infusion of new blood.

I knew little else about the project; Harve and I were both extremely busy at the time, trying to finish up *Star Trek IV*, and did-n't discuss it in detail. I did know, however, that Paramount had authorized him to write a script, which I would have been happy to comment on—but it never came to that.

It wasn't until after the release of *Star Trek V: The Final Frontier* that Harve mentioned his Academy project to me again; this time, it was to express his unhappiness over the fact that, after all the time he'd invested in it, Paramount had ultimately rejected the script. Our conversation was brief.

I heard nothing further about Harve and his project until a short time later, when Paramount exec Frank Mancuso invited me to lunch.

Once we were seated in the restaurant, Frank leaned across the table and said, "Leonard, I want to have another *Star Trek* movie out in the theaters in time for the twenty-fifth anniversary of the show—and I'd like you to be my partner, and make this movie for us."

My immediate response was, "What about Harve Bennett?" I knew that Harve had been working on a concept for the sixth movie, and even though the Academy script had been rejected, that didn't necessarily mean that Harve didn't have something else in the works. I didn't want to get in his way.

But Frank drew in a breath and said, "Harve's gone. It's over."

He was very, very definite about it; the Academy movie wasn't going to happen. And also very definite about his expansive offer: I could write, direct, executive-produce—in other words, be involved in whatever way I chose.

In all honesty, after the grueling pace required of me as an actor/director in the fourth film, I had no desire to direct another *Star Trek* feature. I also knew that we had very little time to get this picture out, so I said, "Time is short, Frank. Everything will have to fall into place perfectly."

"Well, we'll do whatever is necessary for that to happen."

I was intrigued—not by the thought of directing, of course, but by the thought of developing the story and of producing, of putting the movie together. "Let me give it some thought," I told him, "and I'll get back to you as soon as I can with a story idea."

That's the way we left it.

Now, as I've mentioned before, I've always been very interested in the Klingons and their culture, and it seemed to me that this movie presented us with a perfect opportunity to explore our favorite villains. I was mulling all this over, and thinking about the similarities between Federation/Klingon Empire relations and

U.S./Soviet Union relations—the "Cold War." Bear in mind that this was right as the Berlin Wall was coming down, and it was pretty clear that what Ronald Reagan called the "evil empire" was starting to crumble. (In fact, while we were filming *Star Trek VI*, the Soviet government collapsed.)

So three days later, I called Frank Mancuso and said, "Here's the idea: What if the Klingon Empire is in the same mess the Soviet Union is in right now? Their economy's collapsing, they're heavily invested in weaponry, there's dissent, and on top of it, they experience some sort of 'Chernobyl.' And they reach out to the Federation for détente and help . . . which is where the *Enterprise* comes in."

"Great!" he said. "I love it! Will there be a Gorbachev character?"

"By all means. I think we should get Nick Meyer to write it, and if he wants to direct, we ought to give it to him."

"What if Nick won't do it? Will you direct?"

"If Nick chooses not to direct, I'll do it myself—or we'll both agree on someone else. If you have no objections, I'll go ahead and contact Nick myself."

"That'll be fine. And Leonard . . . "

"Yes?"

"If at any point you feel this project isn't going the way you think it should, talk to me. We'll get things back on track."

"Thanks, Frank. I appreciate it."

As it turned out, Nick had just finished work on another film and was vacationing with his family on Cape Cod. I called him up and said, "We want to make another *Star Trek* movie. Can I come talk to you?"

"Sure! Come on out!"

So my wife and I flew to Boston and got on a little putt-putt plane out of Logan Airport, which in turn took us to Provincetown, where Nick's family has property. (I enjoyed the flight, as I love the area and took flying lessons there myself.)

At any rate, we landed in Provincetown, climbed out of this tiny airplane, and there was Nick waiting for us, grinning, cigar in hand (and, most of the time, mouth). He drove us back to his family place, and we all visited for a half-hour with his wife and kids. Then I with my sandals and Nick with his cigar took a little walk down the beach. We talked about lots of different things at first, but at last the conversation turned to *Star Trek*, and I said: "I want to do a movie about the Berlin Wall coming down in space."

"Perfect!" Nick said, and—to quote Joe Sargent again—we were off!

For two-and-a-half hours we paced up and down that stretch of beach, leaving disappearing footprints in the wet sand. I recapped for Nick what I'd told Mancuso: the plot-instigating "Chernobyl" in the Klingon Empire; the cash-poor, overarmed Klingons reaching out to the Federation for help; the Gorbachev Klingon character being assassinated.

We started hammering out plot details: Kirk would of course be the designated "diplomat," and I gave Nick the line, "Only Nixon could go to China," which wound up in the film. We talked about Kirk's anger at being chosen, since Klingons had murdered his son. And because of that history, Kirk would be convicted by the Klingons of the assassination—and McCoy should be involved too . . . They would be imprisoned on a Klingon prison world, during which time they and Spock, aboard the *Enterprise*, would separately begin to unravel the conspiracy that had led to the assassination and Kirk's wrongful arrest.

The conversation was lively, spirited, creatively exciting, and before we knew it, a few hours had passed. By then, we pretty well had the basic story line figured out—and we were pretty tired and hungry, too, so we headed back to the house, herded up the families, and all went out in search of clam dinners. It was a great day and a very special experience for me; I felt the same sense of gratitude I tried to express back in Chapter 1, when I talked about feeling lucky to be involved with *Star Trek*. That day, as I walked along the beach with Nick, I felt a great sense of satisfaction to be permitted to set creative waves in motion for *Star Trek VI*; after all, it really didn't seem all that long ago that I had been a struggling actor, driving a cab at nights trying to make ends meet, grateful to get even the smallest bit part. And here I was, being handed the reins of a major motion picture and told, "Whatever you want to do is fine with us!"

Of course, by the time we were finished eating our clams, we'd missed our return flight—but at this point, I was too content to care. My wife and I wound up taking a limo back to Boston.

And, as a result of that meeting with Nick, the script for *Star Trek VI: The Undiscovered Country* was set in motion.

Or so I thought.

Life is never without frustration, of course—especially where Hollywood studios and successful movie franchises like *Star Trek* are involved. I immediately let Frank Mancuso know that I had met with Nick, and he'd agreed to write the script and possibly direct. I had developed the story, and would go on to serve as executive producer for the film, with the producer's role filled by Ralph Winter and Steven-Charles Jaffe.

Simple, right? Unfortunately, in the interim, another studio executive—Teddy Zee—had decided to turn the project over to two other writers by the names of Konner and Rosenthal. (Why? To this day, I'm not sure. I suspect he was championing their cause, since he had been responsible for signing them to a studio contract.) While I assumed Nick was working away on the script, these two gentlemen were busily churning out a draft we never used. Meantime, Teddy Zee contacted Nick to ask him to help these two writers out, so Nick assumed *he* was out as writer, and that I knew about it! It cost us two very valuable months' time that could have been spent perfecting a workable script, and for that, I blame myself; the minute I began to suspect that something was awry, I should have done what Frank Mancuso asked, and told him about it.

Nick brought in a writing partner, Denny Martin Flinn, and the two of them worked at warp speed to produce a new script from scratch. (Interestingly, while the screenplay was being written, some right-wing Soviet reactionaries, angered by Gorbachev's reforms, came to his dacha and kidnaped him! It was indeed a case of life imitating art.)

When I read Nick and Denny's first draft, I had some concerns. The tone worked, and the plot worked, but the story never explored the Klingon culture the way I'd hoped it would. Basically, it was a political thriller that focused on the assassination, the mock trial, and the escape story. I was hoping for greater insight into the Klingons, which could help us understand why this warlike, honor-obsessed culture had come to be as it was. In fact, when Gene Roddenberry and I met to talk about the *Star Trek VI* script, Gene kept asking a very incisive question: "What can this story teach us about the Klingons that we don't already know? If it deals with them, we should learn something new about them." He had a valid point, which I agreed with.

So when I read Nick and Denny's first draft, I contacted Nick to discuss my hopes of getting to know the Klingons better. To be candid, we didn't see eye-to-eye about it, and became involved in a tussle that continued through the making of the film. Specifically, during the course of the story, both Kirk and McCoy are framed for the assassination of the Klingon "Gorbachev" (played by David Warner). They're taken into custody by the Klingons, and shipped off to a penal colony, Rura Penthe. I felt that, once our heroes were imprisoned, we had an opportunity to develop an inside story where Kirk and McCoy came into contact with another prisoner or

Chancellor Gorkon (David Warner) toasts "the undiscovered country"
at the Klingon/Starfleet banquet

prisoners—perhaps Klingons—who would lead them into some new insight about the Klingon mind, heart, and culture.

Nick disagreed—and ultimately, his story was what wound up on the screen: Instead of hooking up with a Klingon political prisoner, our guys instead run into a shape-shifter (played by Iman). Her character was simply a vehicle to help Kirk and Bones break out of prison—and then to betray them.

True, the plot device worked—but it bypassed what I saw as a rich opportunity to learn more about the Klingons. As it turned out, the finished film was a serviceable but simplistic *Manchurian Candidate* in outer space.

The mesmerizing confrontation between Spock and Valeris

All frustrations aside, there were some delightful moments in the movie. One of them included a wonderful scene, courtesy of Nick Meyer's inventive imagination: a diplomatic banquet aboard the *Enterprise*, where the Klingon "lions" sit down across the table from the Federation "lambs." It was a moment that threw the conflict between Klingon and human into sharp dramatic contrast (Kirk's son, after all, had been murdered by Klingons); and there was a wonderfully baroque feel, thanks to Shakespearean quotes, punk-Elizabethan/Klingon costumes, and the elegant presences of the actors who portrayed the Klingons: Christopher Plummer, David Warner, and Rosanna DeSoto.

Then there was the table setting, of course, complete with Romulan ale, shimmering futuristic goblets, shining silver, and a gruesomely stunning centerpiece of a slimy blue entree. Turned out it was perfectly edible chunks of lobster, doctored with food dye. Bill Shatner quickly dug into it, on a dare from Nick—while I, being fully immersed in my character, declined. Vulcans are, after all, vegetarians.

There were two very important moments for me—and Spock — in the film. The first centers around Spock's confrontation with his traitorous Vulcan protégé, Valeris. Let me pause here for an aside on the casting of this role. Originally, the political traitor in the story was to have been Saavik.

Given that, both Nick and I agreed that, if at all possible, we would like Kirstie Alley to reprise the role. However, she was currently playing Rebecca Howe on the enormously successful series, *Cheers*, and unfortunately, the price she now commanded was well beyond the realm of *Star Trek VI*'s budgetary possibility.

Once Kirstie proved unavailable, we began to reconsider the plot twist that the heretofore loyal Saavik had betrayed the Federation and engaged in a murder conspiracy. Would *Star Trek* audiences rebel at the notion that Saavik was a traitor? Or should we bring in a brand-new Vulcan character instead? We finally decided that the Saavik we knew wouldn't be capable of making this switch in loyalties. With that in mind, we continued our casting search for a yet-unchristened Vulcan female. We had a number of actresses read for the part, including the talented and good-looking Joan Severance, who was a strong contender.

Enter Kim Cattrall, a marvelous actress who is extremely serious about her craft. It just so happened that, during casting for *Star Trek II: The Wrath of Khan*, Nick Meyer's first choice for the role of Saavik just happened to have been Kim. And so, with a similar role available, Kim was called in for an audition.

The minute she delivered her first line, it was clear she had a grasp of the character. So it was that we welcomed her aboard. Kim shaved her sideburns (to better emphasize her Vulcan ears) and suggested part of her new character's name—Eris, for the Greek goddess of discord and chaos. A "Val" was tacked on, so that it sounded more appropriately alien, and thus the character Valeris was born.

Now, at the very beginning of *Star Trek VI*'s development, Nick Meyer described it to an interviewer as "a small story about Spock in love." It was a misleading statement which sparked a great deal of speculation by *Star Trek* fans; after all, in a recent episode of *Star Trek: The Next Generation* entitled "Sarek," Captain Jean Luc Picard casually mentions that he had met Ambassador Sarek once before, many years ago, "at his son's wedding." Wild rumors abounded: According to some, this sixth movie would culminate in Spock's marriage to the character played by Kim Cattrall.

Far from it, of course; the relationship of Spock and Valeris was played as a platonic one. (But it seemed that Nick's little comment did succeed in distracting fans from Valeris's role as a traitor.) Platonic, but very interesting, because here is Spock—a Vulcan who should be wise enough, experienced enough, not to be taken in by a young woman of questionable ethics—ethics that lead her to betray not only Spock, but the *Enterprise*, and indeed, the entire Federation.

Which brings us again to the first very important moment for Spock in the film. Actually, I should more rightly say, "moments," because there were two scenes in which I decided to take the character a bit further than I had before. The first was a scene in sickbay, where Valeris sneaks in, armed with a phaser, intending to kill one of her injured co-conspirators, so that he can't blab—and instead discovers Spock.

And Spock, in a brief but startling display of rage, slaps the weapon out of her hand. His anger is also visible in a bridge scene where he mind-melds with Valeris in order to draw critical information from her. These were what I call true "human/Vulcan" crossover performances, because both of Spock's sides were displayed.

It seemed to me to be a (pardon the term) logical progression of the character's development. In the first *Star Trek* film, Spock is utterly Vulcan, but over the course of the story, begins to see the need to accept both his human and Vulcan halves. In the second, Spock seems at peace with himself over this issue; and in the third film, of course, he's basically absent until the story's end. *Star Trek IV* picks up with the Vulcan trying to relearn all that he knew before his death, including acceptance of both sides of his heritage. Clearly, he has done so by the end of that movie, as he bids Sarek to "tell my mother I feel fine." *Star Trek V* seems to repeat the same ground, and so, by the sixth movie, it seemed time for Spock to come to grips with displaying emotion in appropriate situations. It could be argued that, at the moment he angrily slaps the phaser from Valeris's hand, that he suffers a loss of some of his Vulcan dignity—but knowing Spock as I do, I'm sure he felt it was worth it, in order to cut to the heart of the matter.

After we taped the dramatic scene in sickbay, I asked myself, "As keeper of this character—where does he go from here? If I ever play the Vulcan in the future, will I allow him to display this type of emotion again?"

At the time, the question seemed moot, because I felt strongly that this sixth movie was "it"—the ending. Why? I felt life was going to imitate art again: At the end of *Star Trek VI*, the crew has been called home to retire, and pass the torch on to a "new generation." Word on the Paramount lot was that there was plenty of momentum for a *Next Generation* movie.

And that brings me to what I feel was the most important scene for Spock (and for me) in the film. It so moved me that I mentioned it in Chapter 1: the scene where Spock—defeated and depressed after his realization that his protégé, Valeris, is a traitor—is lying quietly in his quarters, clearly indulging in a very human moment of melancholy. Kirk enters and makes an effort to cheer his friend and to rally him to action.

In reply, the Vulcan turns to Kirk and says softly, "Is it possible that we two, you and I, have grown so old and inflexible that we have outlived our usefulness?"

As I said earlier, it was a very poignant question for me as well as for Spock. For not only was the Vulcan on the verge of retirement, and meditating on the fact that, at long last, the *Enterprise*

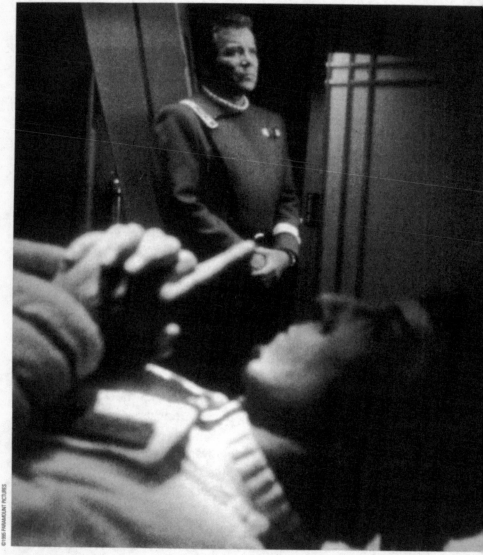

The decades-long mission finally comes to an end: Kirk and Spock in the Vulcan's quarters

crew's missions together were over—but I was well aware that this was most likely the last *Star Trek* film for both of us. And as I turned toward Bill and uttered those words, any sense of "mask" slipped away. I honestly felt myself merge with the character, Spock . . . and at the moment that the Vulcan spoke to his captain, Leonard Nimoy asked the same question of Bill Shatner. I recall looking at him and wondering: "Are you thinking what I'm thinking, Bill? That this really is the end of our 'mission' together . . . ?"

In my own mind, that will always be the moment of emotional closure for *Star Trek VI*—and indeed, all the stories involving the original *Enterprise* crew. For me and Spock, the original *Star Trek* ended at that very moment. True, there were other scenes to be shot, other plot machinations to wind down in order to properly finish the story of *The Undiscovered Country*, but at that moment, I felt we'd really come to the close.

To be frank, when shooting on *Star Trek VI* finally did wrap, I felt very much the same as I had when the original television series was cancelled—sad that it was over, yet also relieved, because I didn't want to see the quality of the films continue to decline.

But I wound up reprising the role of Spock much sooner than I ever dreamed I would.

During the making of *VI*, Frank Mancuso called me up one day, and said, "Leonard, I've got an interesting proposition for you. How would you feel about appearing as Spock in an episode of *The Next Generation?*"

It's time now for a flashback and a confession.

The flashback takes us to 1986, while I was involved in postproduction on *Star Trek IV: The Voyage Home.* I was busily editing mountains of footage when I got a call from Frank Mancuso.

"Leonard," he said, "could you carve out some time from your busy schedule to come to a meeting at my office tomorrow afternoon?"

I had no idea what the meeting was to be about, but when I arrived the next day in Frank's office, I found at least a half-dozen other people there. What were they all talking about?

A new television series based on *Star Trek*, with new actors, set at a time even further in the future than the original series's twenty-third century.

"Leonard," Frank asked, "will you consider being our executive producer?"

And now, the confession.

I thanked him and wished him well with the project, but explained it simply couldn't work. I felt the original *Star Trek*'s success was due to many factors: the themes, the characters, the chemistry between the actors, the timing (the future-embracing 1960s) . . . There was simply no way, I told him, that anyone could duplicate all those things and be successful with a second *Star Trek* show. And so I opted out.

While my argument sounded perfectly rational at the time, my ego was certainly involved. When I said to Mancuso and the assembled execs, "How can you hope to capture lightning in a bottle

Spock, in the aptly named Unification

again?" part of me was *really* saying, "How can you ever hope to do it without *us*?"

You know, crow isn't so bad. It tastes rather like chicken.

Star Trek: The Next Generation was developed without me, and not only went on to be a success, but a *whopping* success. They *did* recapture lightning in a bottle—and carved out their own unique niche. I congratulate them on their fine body of work.

So it was that, when Mancuso called me up during the shooting of *Star Trek VI*, I told him, "Sure, Frank. I'd be interested in appearing on *The Next Generation*." Spock, after all, is much longer-lived than a human; by the twenty-fourth century, he'd be in late middle age. And it seemed like a nice opportunity to tie the two *Trek*s together, to unite them with a common story thread. (Of course, it wouldn't be the first time such an effort had been made: De Kelley had appeared in a poignant cameo in the series' pilot, and Mark Lenard had given a beautiful performance in the episode "Sarek.") Why not have the episode refer to some events that would take place in the movie? We could do a "teaser" story that would air on *ST:TNG* (as *The Next Generation* is called by fans) and give the audience a hint of what happened in the "past" in the upcoming *Star Trek VI*.

The idea intrigued me, so I went to talk to the producers, Rick Berman and Michael Piller, about the idea and was well received. We decided on a basic concept that Spock would be involved in undercover work inside the Romulan Empire.

The script was written, and christened "Unification." While the title ostensibly referred to the political reunification of Vulcans with their distant cousins, the Romulans (and to the mind meld between Picard and Spock at the episode's end), it also seemed a fitting metaphor for the bridge that was being built between the original series and the new.

I liked the script, agreed to a very modest salary, and so the deal was done. When the time came, I reported for work on the *ST:TNG* set. Now, I'd met all the cast before, at a party I gave at my home when we kicked off production for *Star Trek VI*, so I knew them, liked them, and felt comfortable around them. I enjoyed the sense of camaraderie on the set, although I have to admit, there was a little bit of an "Uh-oh! Big Daddy's here! We'd better behave!" feeling among the crew, which amused me at the same time that it made me a little self-conscious.

I thought the story was wonderful, especially the final scene in which Captain Picard (who had mind-melded with Spock's father in the episode "Sarek") offers Spock the unique opportunity to contact the part of Sarek's mind that still lingers with Picard. I found it to be an extremely moving, dramatic moment.

©1995 PARAMOUNT PICTURES

And, at that precise instant that Spock—who never had the opportunity to join his thoughts with his late father's—touches Picard's mind and senses Sarek's presence, I decided to take the character a little further into the territory he'd begun to explore in *Star Trek VI*. A clear ripple of grief passes over the Vulcan's expression.

My scenes were mostly with Patrick Stewart and Brent Spiner, two exceptional actors whom I sincerely admire. Their acting is clean, clear, intelligent, and witty, and they're both extremely likable people. Patrick is in some ways rather like his character, Picard—absolutely charming, yet authoritative in speech and manner. And Brent is equally delightful, although there's a wispy, exotic aspect to his personality. (Sometime later, I worked with Brent on a production of *War of the Worlds* for National Public Radio that also featured Armin Shimerman, with John De Lancie directing. One of the reasons I took the job was because of the *Star Trek* people involved.)

After "Unification" was filmed, but before it aired, I had a number of speaking engagements at *Star Trek* conventions around the country. For many years, I'd often been asked at such events whether Spock would ever appear on *ST:TNG*; and, after the deed was done, I appeared onstage at a *Trek* convention and was asked the same question again by a young lady in the audience:

"Would you ever appear on *The Next Generation* if you were invited?"

I favored her with a smug smile and said, "Funny you should ask. You see, I *have* been invited . . . and, in the very near future, Spock will make an appearance on the show."

Now, I'm used to being warmly received at such conventions—used to the loud applause and the cheering that persists for a moment or two after I step onto the stage. I expected a very positive response to my statement—and foolishly thought I was prepared for it.

But there was no way I could have been pre-

Picard (Patrick Stewart) graciously consents to let Spock mind meld with his late father, Sarek, as Data looks on

The Vulcan meets someone openly envious of Spock's human side (Brent Spiner as Data)

pared for the thunderous blast of sound that emanated from the audience. Let's face it: I've gotten quite a bit of applause at these conventions—but I had *never* before heard anything so explosive from an audience. They cheered, they stomped, they whistled . . . and they kept *on* cheering, stomping, and whistling until I was emotionally overwhelmed.

The response of that first audience—and the second, and the third, and the fourth, with whom I shared the "Unification" news—made me realize that I'd tapped into an extraordinary "family issue." Apparently there were two camps in *Star Trek* fandom: the die-hard loyalists, and those who embraced the new show, and who may or may not have felt a bit of unease about their "defection." "Unification" did away with any friction between these groups, and brought them together for the first time. It was as though a breach had been healed: There were no longer two *Star Trek*s, or two groups of fans—only one. The episode had accomplished what its title proclaimed; Spock had bridged the gap. (Perhaps it's pertinent to mention here that, according to fan lore, the name "Spock" means "Uniter" in the Vulcan language.)

And how did the show (actually, *two* shows, as it was made into a two-parter) fare with the television audience?

Quite simply, "Unification" was the highest-rated episode of *ST:TNG* before or since.

NIMOY: So, Spock . . . How did you feel about the success of "Unification"?

SPOCK: *I beg your pardon?*

NIMOY: Er . . . I mean, how did you feel about meeting the crew of the *Enterprise-D*—Captain Picard and Data—some eighty years after your last mission aboard the *Enterprise-A*?

SPOCK: *Oh. I found them to be fascinating and worthy individuals. But . . . to be candid, meeting them did remind me of one distinct disadvantage to being Vulcan.*

NIMOY: Disadvantage?! Spock, you *have* changed—I can hardly believe you'd admit such a thing! So what is it?

SPOCK: *Being long-lived. I miss my human friends . . .*

EIGHTEEN

LIVE LONG
AND
PROSPER

.

SPOCK: Our association has been most unusual and fascinating. I have . . .
          enjoyed it. Live long and prosper, Leonard.
NIMOY: I think I've already done the former, Spock. And — in no small part
          thanks to you — I've certainly done the latter.

A S I SAID BEFORE, when we finished filming on *Star Trek VI*, I felt a sense of closure — a sense that the sixth film would indeed be the Vulcan's final appearance on the large screen. Certainly, *The Undiscovered Country*'s final scene was a "passing of the torch" from the original *Star Trek* to the new.

As things turned out, my premonition ultimately proved correct . . . for Spock, at least.

But shortly after the release of the sixth movie, I received another phone call from Paramount: A seventh film was being planned, one entitled *Star Trek: Generations*. It featured Captain Kirk's death, and the characters of Spock and Dr. McCoy had been included. Would I be willing to read the script, then discuss it with the producer, Rick Berman?

Of course.

But when I received the script, I had a number of concerns. For one thing, Spock's role was no more than a cameo, a walk-on; he served no function at all in the story. He was simply there for his marquee value.

So when I went to meet with Berman, I relayed that concern, along with others.

He listened to them all, then said, "All these suggestions of yours will require too many revisions of the script. We just don't have the time to make them."

He might have answered, "Well, let's talk to the writers about your concerns, and see if we can find a workable solution for us all." But he didn't. I took that as a message that it was time for me to excuse myself, and so I did.

Later, I spoke with my dear old friend De Kelley on the subject. De had also met with Berman, and his response was one that echoed my own sentiments:

"I had a better exit in *Star Trek VI*," De had said. "Why should I muddy it up?" He also had told Rick, "If Leonard isn't going to be involved, then I won't be, either."

So it was that I let it go. Was I sorry? On one level, no; I felt it was important that Spock have an onscreen departure befitting the dignity of the character. He could not have done so with *Star Trek: Generations*, and for that reason, I have no regrets in turning the project down.

But I wish those still actively involved with *Star Trek* long life and prosperity. On the day *Generations* began filming, I sent director David Carson a note, which said, "Sorry I can't join you, but I wish you all the best. Bon voyage, Leonard Nimoy."

These days, I'm involved in other projects. As I write these words, I've just finished performing for Showtime's new *Outer Limits*, in a remake of the classic Eando Binder tale "I, Robot." In the 1960s, I had a secondary role in the original "I, Robot" episode; this time, I'm playing the attorney who defends the robot accused of murder, and my son, Adam, is directing.

I also just finished directing the first episode of *Deadly Games*, a new television series that has been picked up by United Paramount Network, for which I also serve as a consultant. *Deadly Games* can best be described as a science fiction/action comedy: It features a reluctantly divorced young physicist, Gus (played by James Calvert), who attempts to create antimatter in his lab. He also creates a computer game, complete with villains (including the nefarious Sebastian Jackal, played by Christopher Lloyd) drawn from his own past — his meddling mother-in-law, a school bully, and his ex-wife's lawyer, among others. One day, a fusion experiment goes awry, and suddenly his game comes to life . . .

My plate is very full right now, even without *Star Trek*. If invited, would I ever go back?

Well, as far as I'm concerned, Spock is still under deep cover in Romulan space, working toward the reunification of the passionate, warlike Romulans with their cool, logic-loving Vulcan brothers. Knowing Spock's stubbornness — or as he'd probably prefer to put it, his persistence — some very interesting events are bound to result. And, if the right opportunity came along, he and I wouldn't mind picking up that story thread . . .

Do I miss Spock?

No, because he's a part of me. Not a day passes that I don't hear that cool, rational voice commenting on some irrational aspect of the human condition.

And if I'm not listening to Spock's voice, then I'm listening to the voices of those who know the Vulcan and consider him an old friend. On a recent visit to New York, I had the opportunity to speak with several people who warmly shared with me their gratitude toward *Star Trek* and Spock. It always amazes and touches me to discover how deeply the series affected so many people's lives — people who chose careers in science, astronomy, space exploration, all because of one television show called *Star Trek*.

During that New York trip, my wife and I were window shopping when I became rather uncomfortably aware that I was being stared at. I turned to see a well-dressed, obviously successful gentleman in his thirties standing beside us; he smiled sheepishly and said, very politely, "I'm terribly sorry to disturb you. I hope you don't mind: I just want to look at you."

I had to smile back. You see, I knew he was looking at me . . . but seeing Spock. I've gotten accustomed to that — and to the fact that Vulcans are renowned for their longevity. I'm only human, and I have no doubt Spock will outlive me by many years.

I can only hope that, once in a while, when people look at Spock's visage, they might sometimes think of me.

But it doesn't matter; because, as far as I'm concerned, we two are twins, joined at the hip. The image brings to mind an incident that happened many years ago.

It took place in 1974, to be exact; I was traveling and stopped in a little market in Hickory, North Carolina, to pick up some items. The lady who waited on me recognized me at once, and was extremely charming; during the course of my shopping, she insisted on introducing me to the other workers in the store.

Now, as often happens, she introduced me by quizzing the others: "John, do you know who this is?"

Most of the people recognized me, but there were one or two who stared at me curiously, and had to admit, with a bit of embarrassment, that they had no clue who I was.

That certainly wasn't the case for one woman, who enthusiastically replied, "Why, of *course* I know him! My son watches him on TV all the time!" And she reached out to shake my hand. "You're Leonard Spock!"

•

INDEX

Entries in **boldface** refer to illustrations.